Housekeeping Management

Housekeeping Management

MATT A. CASADO

John Wiley & Sons, Inc.

New York • Chichester • Weinheim • Brisbane • Singapore • Toronto

This book is printed on acid-free paper. ∞

Copyright © 2000 by John Wiley & Sons, Inc. All rights reserved.

Published simultaneously in Canada.

This publication is designed to provide accurate and authoritative information in
regard to the subject matter covered. It is sold with the understanding that the
publisher is not engaged in rendering professional services. If professional advice
or other expert assistance is required, the services of a competent professional person should be sought.

Library of Congress Cataloging-in-Publication Data:

Casado, Matt A., 1937–
     Housekeeping management / Matt A. Casado.
        p.   cm.
     Includes index.
     ISBN 0-471-25189-5 (cloth : alk. paper)
     1. Hotel housekeeping—Management.   I. Title.
TX928.C37   1999
647.94′068′2—dc21   99-22278

Printed in the United States of America.
20 19 18 17

To my wife Mary,
and to Cristina, Martin, and Carmen

Contents

Preface

This book has been written on the premise that the position of executive housekeeper in loding operations is one that requires proficiency in the areas of management and administration, as well as a thorough knowledge of professional and technical skills. The hospitality industry continues to emphasize downsizing practices that demand leaner management structures and fewer organizational and operational layers. As a result, recruiters for lodging companies view potential executive housekeepers as first-line managers capable of directing a housekeeping department by themselves, without the direct intervention of the property's upper management. For this reason, students of baccalaureate, associate degree, and technical hospitality programs who wish to become lodging professionals, must be instructed in the particular skills that this new era demands.

This book presents the three types of expertise required to become an ideal executive housekeeper: management of resources, administration of assets, and knowledge of housekeeping technical operations. Part One is geared toward preparing future executive housekeepers as department heads, covering management concepts and responsibilities as they apply to the housekeeping department. Part Two deals with housekeeping structural planning for large properties, including an effective model for staffing the department by teams. Part Three provides discussion of the technical skills needed for running the housekeeping department, including descriptions of material, inventory techniques, linen and laundry room management, and the function of cleaning. Part Four covers aspects of personnel administration, including employee motivation, worker satisfaction, and cultural diversity issues. Part Five focuses on productivity and cost control, risk management, and environmental issues related to the housekeeping department.

A unique feature of this book is the application of its theoretical content through presentation of practical case studies in each chapter. I devised these applied examples from experience gained throughout my extensive career as hotel rooms division director and general manager, and as a hospitality educator. The book can also be used as a professional resource for lodging industry practitioners.

An *Instructor's Manual* (ISBN 0-471-35669-7) with text questions accompanies this textbook. The *Manual* includes a discussion of each chapter's content, chapter outlines, key terms, discussion questions, outside resources, and minicases. In addition, there are multiple choice and true/false questions for each chapter, as well as transparency masters of selected tables and illustrations.

Matt A. Casado, Ed.D., C.H.A., C.H.E.

Part 1

Introduction to Housekeeping Management

Management of Lodging Operations

The Westin Peachtree Plaza, Atlanta, Georgia. Courtesy of Westin Hotels & Resorts.

CHAPTER OBJECTIVES

- ▶ Discuss the history of the lodging industry.
- ▶ Describe the classification of lodging establishments.
- ▶ Define the management structure of lodging operations.
- ▶ Explain the elements of the rooms division.
- ▶ State the importance of the housekeeping department.
- ▶ Discuss the interaction of the housekeeping department with other property units.

 ## OVERVIEW

This chapter explains the origins of lodging operations and describes the development of the lodging industry in the United States. The industry encompasses several types of establishments whose goal is to attract the different segments of the hospitality market.

Lodging establishments can be classified by size and type of service, ranging from the small, humble bed-and-breakfast inn to the colossal megahotels and resorts that offer luxurious accommodations and services. These lodging properties can be independently owned, franchised, or run by management companies. Students in hotel and restaurant management programs must be aware of the advantages and disadvantages of working for small companies as well as for multi-unit corporations.

The structure of lodging operations is also explained in this chapter, together with a description of the position of the housekeeping department in the organizational chart of large hotels. The chapter ends with a discussion of the importance of interaction between housekeeping and the property's operational and support units.

 ## HISTORY AND STRUCTURE OF LODGING OPERATIONS

Lodging operations are an intrinsic part of the hospitality trade and perhaps the most important of the segments into which this industry is divided. To *lodge* means to furnish guests with room or quarters, generally on a temporary basis. This broad definition implies that the lodging industry is quite diverse, for the renting of living space can range from a simple room in a boarding house to a spacious suite in a luxury hotel or a bungalow in a lavish resort.

Since the beginning of recorded time, people have traveled and therefore have been in need of lodging. For instance, the excavated ruins of Pompeii in Italy include houses of rest and solace where, as long ago as 79 A.D., wayfarers and seamen of the time were able to relax and be entertained for a fee. Lodging facilities that were used for economic purposes were built along transportation routes where traveling parties found it convenient to make rest stops en route to their destinations. In Marco Polo's time, rest areas were strategically placed at a distance of a day's ride by caravan. Polo was able to travel from Venice to the Mongol Empire of Kublai Khan in Central Asia by making scheduled stops along the way, where food and safe shelter were available.

Chaucer's *Canterbury Tales*, written around 1390 in England, contains lively descriptions of inn-keeping practices of the time. In *Don Quixote*, many of Cervantes' ideals are put into practice at an inn in La Mancha, Spain. What we know today as **inns** had their origin in England some centuries ago, the term meaning "a public house that provides lodging for travelers and others." These taverns with rooms for rent were usually located along highways to provide a convenient overnight stay for those traveling by coach. The introduction of railways in the nineteenth century created the need for a large number of these hostelries along the numerous lines that crisscrossed the country. Today, the term inn implies a small hotel, although properties called "inns" often contain a large number of rooms; for example the Holiday Inn Crowne Plaza in New Orleans has 439 guestrooms.

The term **hotel** derives from the French *hostel.* The modern French word hôtel suggests "a more or less commodious establishment with up-to-date appointments," though this was not necessarily true one hundred years ago. Today, the term hotel defines a lodging establishment offering accommodation, food and beverage, and amenities to guests. The New Orleans' Windsor Court Hotel, which consumers have rated as one of the best hotels in the United States, advertises meeting facilities, outdoor pool, health club, ballrooms, concierge services, five-diamond dining room, chamber music, and 24-hour suite service. Nightly rates at the Windsor Court range from $320 for regular guestrooms to $990 for two-bedroom suites.

The first **spas** were operated in Europe and consisted of resorts located by mineral springs, which were believed to have curative powers. Today, spas offer a wide array of health-related services ranging from curative massage and mud baths to weight-loss programs.

The Lodging Industry in America

The first American inns were similar to England's inns of the 1700s. In old colonial times, many of the American inns bore such names as "King's," "Queen's," and "Red Lion," but the revolt of the colonies produced a change, and these "royal" names gave way to those in harmony with the spirit of the time. A portrait of George Washington replaced that of George III on the swinging signs, as these once quiet taverns became the meeting places of patriots. Inns were often the backdrop for historic events that took place during and immediately following the Revolution. George Washington was a guest of the City Tavern, Philadelphia (1775), and the Bunch of Grapes

Tavern, Boston, where he enjoyed "an elegant dinner provided at the public expense, while joy and gratitude sat on every countenance and smiled in every eye." He stayed at a tavern in East Chester when he was ill, and it was in the assembly room of Fraunces Tavern that Washington bade farewell to the faithful men who, with him, had achieved the liberty of the States. The East Chester Tavern later played a part in U.S. history once again, when President John Adams made it a temporary "seat of government" by staying there during the yellow fever epidemic at the capital.

In 1794, the seventy-three room City Hotel was built in New York City. The National hotel was opened in Washington in 1827, and at once became the home of eminent public men. The Tremont House, which opened in Boston in 1829, was the grandest hotel in the land, boasting a lobby where guests could register instead of doing so at the bar. It was even claimed to be the largest and most elegant hotel in the world at the time, and certainly there was nothing equal to it in England. In 1833, the United States Hotel opened in New York, followed by the Louisville Hotel in 1834 and the Galt House at Louisville in 1835. In 1836, New York opened its rival to the Tremont of Boston, the Astor House, which was built of massive granite. In 1841, the Planters' house, St. Louis—known as the "largest hotel west of the mountains"—was opened. Charles Dickens stopped there in 1842, and even spoke favorably of it in his American Notes. In 1859, the Fifth Avenue Hotel, New York, was completed, and its claim to fame was the first passenger elevator.

At the turn of the century there were an estimated 43,500 hotels in the United States, which provided employment to over 3 million persons.

At this time, hotels in America were either first-class or quite rudimentary, and for this reason, the need for modern, hospitable, inexpensive commercial hotels became imperative. Ellsworth Statler, justifiably regarded as the father of commercial hotels, pioneered a new concept in lodging establishments. His **Statler Hotels**, built in Buffalo, Boston, Cleveland, and New York, at the turn of the century, offered the traveler a series of conveniences and services not previously available. Amenities such as light switches, private baths, full-length mirrors, and free morning newspapers were instantly appreciated by guests, who from then on expected to find them wherever they traveled. There was a boom in the hotel industry during the 1920s and a large number of hotels were erected around the country. After a severe slump that took place during the Great Depression, the lodging industry entered an era of extreme intensity. The fact that many people had to travel during World War II and the prosperous post-war years accelerated the need for yet more hotels. Additional newer hotels and motor inns were built, including several chains of establishments still in business today. Hilton, Sheraton, and Marriott Hotels, and Wilson's Holiday Inns soon appeared nationwide..

In the 1950s, **motels**, which for some time had been catering only to the motoring public, began to gain in popularity. Motels, which offered convenient access by automobile, lower prices than those charged by hotels, and basic but sufficient services, became a favorite form of accommodation, especially to families traveling long distances by automobile.

Air travel, and the fact that people had increasingly substantial disposable incomes, allowed large numbers of travelers to take vacations in distant places during the 1960s and 1970s. This prompted the appearance of **resort** hotels near natural attractions, sporting locations, or in places with balmy, tropical weather. Present-day resorts offer a full range of services aimed at providing guests with every necessity—and luxury—even in remote locations. The Phoenician Resort in Scottsdale, Arizona offers guestrooms sheathed in Italian marble, with Berber carpet and rattan furniture. Guests staying at the Phoenician have a choice of four restaurants, tiered pools with waterfalls, and golf courses and tennis courts amidst 130 acres of desert, garden, and mountain.

The end of the Cold War and the constant advances of technology continue to create new opportunities for business and leisure. As globalization advances, an increasing number of people from all parts of the world are traveling for business and leisure purposes, which further increases the demand for lodging facilities. American hospitality corporations are acquiring properties on every continent, specifically South America, Eastern Europe, and South East Asia. The old Soviet Union countries and the rest of Asia are sure to follow.

The future of the hospitality industry could not be brighter. Travel and tourism, of which lodging is an integral component, is the country's second largest employer. Domestic and international travelers inject billions of dollars in the U.S. economy every year and this bonanza is very likely to continue growing due to the increasing number of Americans traveling for business and leisure purposes and to the booming international travel market.

Types of Lodging Establishments

Besides hotels, motels and resorts the lodging industry today offers a variety of establishments aimed at fulfilling the needs of the current market. The most common are:

Bed and Breakfast Inns
Time-Share Condominiums
Cruise Ships
Institutional Lodging Establishments
Casinos

Bed-and-breakfast inns are usually small, privately owned establishments located in suburban and rural locations. They are often uniquely appointed converted private homes that cater to travelers seeking a homey, personal environment. **Time-share condominiums** are apartments, villas, or bungalows usually built near popular vacation spots (such as ski resorts, beaches, or Disney World, for example) that are sold to individual owners who use them or rent them out to transient guests. Time-share owners also have the option of trading with other owners of units located in different parts of the country or the world.

Cruise ships can be described as floating luxury hotels/ resorts that provide most of the same services and amenities as properties located on land. Having become quite popular in the vacation and convention markets, cruise ships are one of the fastest growing segments of the hospitality industry.

Institutional lodging is provided by housing facilities that are integral parts of institutional organizations, such as hospitals, retirement homes, universities, and colleges. In some cases this type of lodging requires limited services, such as weekly cleaning or catered meals, which are provided by contracting companies.

With the adoption of gaming by a large number of Native American tribes, **casinos** have grown in popularity in many states of the United States. Casinos are generally first-class hotels that provide elaborate facilities for gambling, ranging from the ubiquitous slot machine to the sophisticated baccarat or roulette tables. These highly profitable establishments often offer luxurious lodging and lavish entertainment at low cost to attract potential customers.

Lodging properties can be **independently owned**, owned by a **multi-unit chain, franchised,** or managed by a **management company**. Properties that are independently owned are not affiliated with any multiple-property entity and are usually managed by their owners. This type of property still represents the largest segment of the lodging industry. A typical independently owned establishment is small in size and is located in a relatively small community. There are advantages and disadvantages to independent operation: on the positive side, independent lodging establishments can provide guests with unique, personalized service while saving royalty and management fees that otherwise would have to be paid to franchisors and/or management companies. On the negative side, such properties may not have name recognition to travelers, they lack collective advertising power, and they are unable to benefit from a national/international reservation system. Often, independently owned and managed properties join reservation referral systems and marketing associations, such as Best Western International, Leading Hotels and Resorts, or Utell International.

Chain properties operate under the direct control of the chain's headquarters. Establishments belonging to the same chain display the same logo and offer identical services by category. For instance, a Hilton four-star hotel must provide similar service and amenities whether it is located in Florida or in Oregon. This assures guests of consistency in price, room layout, menus, sports facilities, and so on. There exist a large number of chains in the world, such as Ritz-Carlton and Loews in the United States, Four Seasons in Canada, and Grupo Sol Melia in Spain.

An effective way for owners of lodging properties to take advantage of the marketing and central reservation power of chain systems is to contract the right to conduct business displaying the logo of the chain by franchising. However, once the franchise is granted, the franchisee must comply with the corporation's requirements regarding service and amenities to be provided to guests.

When hotel owners lack the operative expertise necessary to manage their properties efficiently, they may choose to contract with a management company. In this case, the owner signs a contract delegating the property's operations to such a company in exchange for either paying a basic fee or allowing the management company to retain an agreed-upon percentage of the revenue or income, or a combination of the two.

Classification by Size

Lodging facilities can also be categorized by size. An arbitrary classification can be:

Small: up to 75 rooms
Medium: from 75 to 200 rooms
Large: from 200 to 500 rooms
Very large: more than 500 rooms

The size of a property can be used to estimate the amount of work required of the housekeeping department on a daily basis to maintain the property. For instance, while a 100-room property can be serviced with a relatively small number of housekeeping employees, the Sheraton Hotel & Towers in New York City, with 1,750 rooms, will require over one hundred section housekeepers to service the guestrooms at 100 percent occupancy. Add to that the supervisors, housepersons, janitors, linen room attendants, laundry personnel, and other support personnel, and the number of employees in the housekeeping department of a large hotel such as this can be astounding. This will be covered in greater detail in Chapter Three.

Classification by Type of Service

Lodging properties can also be categorized by service. **Economy** or budget properties focus on meeting the basic needs of the traveling public—that is, clean, comfortable rooms that are not expensive. The market segments typically attracted to economy properties are guests traveling with children, bus tours, and budget-minded retirees. Many of these properties do not offer food and beverage services except for breakfast, although they all feature TV and some have a swimming pool, whirlpool, and tennis courts.

   Mid-market properties offer all the amenities expected in a "home-away-from-home setting." Restaurants, coffee shops, bars, luggage service, meeting rooms, health club, and room service are generally offered in such properties. The quality of bed linen, towels, room furniture, lobby décor, and customer service must be good or very good. Travelers who frequent properties of this type are businesspeople, individual tourists, conventioneers, and guests wishing to receive a guaranteed level of excellent service. Often, mid-market properties feature suites that consist of a bedroom, adjacent living room, and a kitchenette with refrigerator. Suites are very appealing to families with children or to two couples traveling together.

Luxury properties offer world-class service, which includes any type of convenience that would be expected by any traveler in any country in the world. Committed to the ultimate in hospitality, luxury properties may feature extravagant amenities like Godiva or other imported chocolates, specialty toiletry items, slippers, silk robes, and special services like executive floors, concierge, foreign language translators, nanny, and private secretary. The American Automobile Association (AAA) is the most common rater of lodging establishments in the United States. As a service to its members, this organization provides travel guides that are updated annually describing the properties and evaluating their services. The ratings are determined by field inspectors who base their decisions on thorough evaluations of the properties' design, décor, fittings, comfort, and of their levels of service, cleanliness and upkeep. In general, AAA awards three diamonds to economy establishments while mid-market properties are assigned four diamonds. Invariably, luxury hotels and resorts receive a rating of five diamonds. In some countries, an official branch of the government performs the classification of lodging properties to ensure that the quality of their lodging establishments is consistent. Outside the United States, stars are usually used, instead of diamonds, to designate the ratings.

Importance of the Housekeeping Department

A characteristic common to all lodging establishments, regardless of size and category, is the need for housekeeping services, which can range from very sophisticated to a simple matter of "refreshing" rooms once a week. For instance, a luxury hotel, casino, or resort usually requires that the rooms be impeccably clean, that the bed linen is changed every time the bed is used, and that turndown service is provided daily. On the other hand, the service for a university residence room might consist in just providing the tenant with a fresh set of sheets every Monday morning. Mid-range service hotels generally require that guestrooms are thoroughly cleaned daily, that bed and bathroom linen is changed every day, and that

24-hour housekeeping service is provided seven days a week. In any case, because housekeeping services must always be provided, the management of the housekeeping department in every lodging establishment is of critical importance to the success of the property.

It is essential that future graduates of hospitality programs understand the options that the industry offers regarding house-keeping management positions. Graduates wishing to achieve the position of executive housekeeper in a relatively short period of time should keep in mind that a small or medium-sized property does generally offer the best option for candidates to reach their goal. In large or very large establishments, where housekeeping operations are quite complex, it will take longer for candidates to become managers of the department. In any case, the position of executive housekeeper will always be a challenging and rewarding one as well as an adequate springboard from which to work toward the goal of becoming the property's general manager.

When looking for their first job, hospitality graduates should understand the difference between working for properties that are independently or chain-owned, franchised, or run by management companies. An independently owned establishment might not offer substantial opportunities for advancement, as the owners do not usually have any other properties. In this case, the waiting period for reaching an executive position can be a long one. On the other hand, chains offer limitless job opportunities, as these corporations generally expand nationally and internationally by building new places or merging with other companies. If a management company manages a large number of properties, the possibilities for advancing could be as large as those offered by chains. However, it is not unusual for these companies to be rather small, in which case not many openings will occur regularly. Often, independent operators own franchised properties. In this case working for a "Marriott" or "Sheraton" hotel doesn't mean that you will be working for these corporations, as the owners have merely contracted with the chains the right to display their commercial names.

 ## THE ROOMS DIVISION

Lodging is an integral part of the **hospitality industry**. Hospitality involves the reception of guests and the provision of services to them with liberality and kindness. The task of providing hospitality and services to guests in a friendly and efficient manner falls mainly on the property's **rooms division**.

The overall success of an operation depends on the profitability of the rooms division, which generally accounts for a large share of a hotel's sales while generating a gross profit percentage from 70 to 80 percent of the revenue. Besides providing lodging, and professional services such as check in, luggage handling, and room upkeep, rooms division personnel must provide the "home-away-from-home" feeling so cherished by travelers who are temporarily separated from their families. Offering tastefully decorated guestrooms and public areas and impeccable cleanliness in a subdued, relaxing atmosphere is also of the utmost importance.

Large properties are divided into operational units called divisions. Two of these divisions—Rooms, and Food and Beverage—are **revenue-generating centers**, while the others are considered to be **support centers**. The executive in charge of the rooms division is the **Rooms Division Director**, who in some properties may be called resident manager, executive manager, or senior assistant manager. Figure 1.1 shows the breakdown of divisions in a large

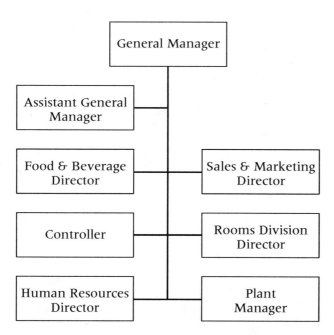

FIGURE 1.1 Sample Division Chart of Large Property

property. The rooms division director reports directly to the property's general manager. As a member of the **executive committee**, the rooms division director takes an active part in policy-making decisions related to operations. Other members of this committee generally include: the Food and Beverage Director, in charge of the food and beverage division; the Sales Director, who deals with sales, marketing, and public relations; the Controller or chief financial officer; the Human Resources Director, in charge of personnel matters; and the Plant Manager, responsible for the engineering and maintenance needs of the property.

Figure 1.2 shows the rooms division divided into departments. Of these, the **front office** and **housekeeping departments** are of critical importance to the property. The **Executive House-keeper** is the head of housekeeping and is therefore directly responsible for managing what is in most cases the largest department of the establishment. The position of executive housekeeper in the organizational chart is that of **department head**, equal in rank to the front office manager, the security manager, and the remaining managers in charge of departments in other divisions. In smaller properties, the division directors do not exist; instead, department heads manage the different units and report directly to the general manager.

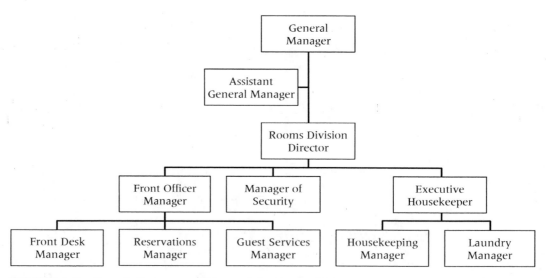

FIGURE 1.2   Sample Department Chart of the Rooms Division

INTERACTION BETWEEN HOUSEKEEPING AND OTHER DEPARTMENTS

The housekeeping department is an integral part of all the areas into which a lodging operation is divided. Although housekeeping's primary communication takes place with the front office and engineering departments, a strong relationship must exist with all the other units of the property as well. For instance, room service, a department in the food and beverage division that delivers food to guestrooms, must be in direct contact with housekeeping for the removal of trays and carts. The sales department, which often must have access to ready rooms to be shown to meeting planners or tour operator representatives, must communicate this need to the housekeeping department.

Communication with the Front Office

Guestrooms in lodging properties are sold by the front office. The front desk must know at every given moment what rooms have been cleaned and are available for occupancy. Housekeeping must provide the front desk with a listing of rooms that are ready for occupancy so guests can be checked in. If the communication between the two departments is poor or breaks down, delays in guest check-in will occur or people will be checked into rooms that are thought to be ready but that in fact are occupied or not ready. If this happens often, the property's reputation will suffer.

The cycle of communication begins early each day, when the front desk provides the housekeeping department with a written (or computer-generated) report called the **night clerk's room report**. The purpose of this report is to inform the housekeeping department very early in the morning of the status of all guestrooms in the property as it appears on the front desk records. Figure 1.3 shows a sample of this report. The nomenclature used varies from property to property, but the most commonly used definitions are:

SO = occupied (stay over)

OOO = out-of-order

V = vacant (on change)

C/O = guest has (or will) check out today

Night Clerk's Report

Date: _____   Prepared By: _____

Total Rooms Occupied: _____

Check Outs: _____

Stay Overs: _____

Out of Order: _____

Room	Status	Room	Status	Room	Status	Room	Status
1001	SO	2001	OOO	3001	SO	4001	V
1002	SO	2002	SO	3002	SO	4002	OOO
1003	C/O	2003	SO	3003	R	4003	SO
1004	V	2004	C/O-EA	3004	R	4004	R
1005	SO	2005	V	3005	C/O	4005	R

The report indicates that rooms 1001, 1002, 1005, 2002, 2003, 3001, 3002 and 4003 are occupied and staying over. Rooms 1003, 2004 and 3005 are checkouts. Rooms 2001 and 4002 are out of order. Rooms 1004, 2005 and 4001 are vacant and not ready. Rooms 3003, 3004, 4004 and 4005 are ready to be sold. There is a scheduled early arrival in room 2004.

FIGURE 1.3   Sample of Night Clerk's Report to Housekeeping

EA = early arrival today

R = ready room

The housekeeping employee in charge of opening the house transfers the information received from the front desk into forms to be distributed to the housekeeping supervisors who, in turn, will notify the room attendants before they begin to work in their respective sections. As guests check in and out of the hotel throughout the day, the front desk notifies housekeeping. As rooms are cleaned, housekeeping notifies the front desk that rooms are available for selling.

As soon as it is possible, an **A.M. guestroom check** is performed by housekeeping to ascertain whether the information provided in the night clerk's report was accurate. When discrepancies are found between the status of rooms received from the night clerk and the physical inspection of the rooms, the front desk is immediately notified. For instance, if the front desk reports that a certain room is vacant and housekeeping finds it occupied, a discrepancy exists and the front desk should be notified. There are several reasons why discrepancies may occur. The most common are:

▶ A guest switches from one room to another and the front desk neglects to change its records.
▶ An error is made by the night clerk when filling out the night clerk's report.
▶ A guest is given the wrong room key by mistake.
▶ The room is used by an unauthorized employee.
▶ The room is sold by the front desk without being recorded, and the money is pocketed by the clerk.
▶ A guest checks in or out between the time the report is made and the check is conducted.

The **P.M. room check** is conducted by the housekeeping department just before the end of the morning shift. This guestroom check consists of entering every room in the house at approximately the same time in order to generate a report showing the status of all guestrooms. The report is brought to the front desk and compared with the front desk records. As with the A.M. report, if discrepancies are found, they are immediately investigated and the records corrected. Besides reporting whether rooms are occupied, vacant, out of order, or ready, the report should provide the front desk with information that can help this department better control the guest records. The most common symbols used are:

B = slept out (guest did not use the room but baggage is still in the room)

NB = occupied, no baggage

DND = do-not-disturb sign on door

LO = lock out (room has been locked by management so that guest cannot re-enter)

As the evening progresses and the room attendants on the evening shift continue to clean rooms from late check-outs and day-rate occupancy, the front desk is notified of the rooms available for sale.

Other communications between the front office and the housekeeping department involve information about occupancy forecasts, the arrival of VIPs, the early check-in of groups, the closing of certain sections for deep-cleaning or repairs, delivery of guest laundry, lost and found items, special guest requests, and so on. The communication between the housekeeping department and the front desk is greatly improved when the property uses a computerized system. For instance, when a guest checks out, the front desk clerk enters the departure in the computer and it appears instantly in the housekeeping monitor. When housekeeping has rooms ready to be sold, the information is entered in the system and it too shows up quickly in the front desk terminal.

Communication with Maintenance

The relationship between housekeeping and the maintenance department must be as close as that with the front office. Every piece of equipment, fixtures, and furniture in the guestrooms, hallways, linen and laundry rooms, public areas, and employee locker rooms must be in perfect working order at all times. The number of items that may be in need of repairs in a single guestroom can be substantial: beds, chairs, desks, TVs, radios, lights, doors, toilets, faucets, walls, heating, air conditioning, and so on. It is therefore imperative that good communication between the two departments exists at all times. For instance, if a guestroom lock is broken, maintenance must be notified, the room must be put out of order, the work performed, the area cleaned, and the room put back in vacant-ready status.

There are two types of maintenance performed by the engineering department in hospitality properties. **Regular maintenance** is performed when an item is broken and needs to be repaired. In this case, a three-part **work order form** is filled out by a housekeeping employee who forwards two copies to engineering and keeps the duplicate filed until the work is completed. When work is completed, one of the copies is returned to housekeeping for comparison, the work is inspected, and the area cleaned. When a problem is urgent and engineering does not promptly address it, housekeeping generates a **second request** work order to remind that department that the work must be completed. If the repair needs to be done in order to be able to sell the room that day, an urgent request is sent to engineering so that the work is given priority over other nonessential jobs. Figure 1.4 is a standard form used

MAINTENANCE REQUEST

By _____ Date _____

Location _____

Problem _____

_____

_____

_____

_____

_____

_____

Assigned To_____

Date Compl. _____ Time Spent _____

Completed By_____

Remarks _____

_____

_____

_____

_____

_____

Original: Originator   Canary: Maintenance   Manilla: Maintenance

D105–106

FIGURE 1.4   Sample Maintenance Request Form

for requesting repair and maintenance services from the engineering department.

The orderly flow of information between housekeeping and engineering about items or areas in need of attention is of critical importance. As the housekeeping department staff is directly involved in cleaning most sections of the property, they are in the best position to find areas in need of maintenance or repair.

Preventive maintenance consists of inspecting guestrooms and other areas on a regular basis to identify repair and maintenance needs. In most hotels, the executive housekeeper and the chief engineer cooperate in combining room cleaning with preventive maintenance programs. This involves conducting a thorough maintenance inspection of all rooms in the property two or three times a year. Figure 1.5 is a sample maintenance checklist used to perform maintenance inspections. The form contains a list of every item that could be in need of repair. After the preventive maintenance inspection has been completed, a check mark will indicate that the standards of operation have been met, while an "x" mark will indicate that the item in question is in need of repair. Preventive maintenance programs are essential to assure that guests staying in the property find the rooms in perfect working order.

☑ Checked   ☒ Needs Repair

Room Number: _____

☐ Doors	☐ Lights	☐ Electrical
☐ A/C Unit	☐ Walls	☐ Ceiling
☐ Floor	☐ Furniture	☐ Windows
☐ Television	☐ Telephone	☐ Mirrors
☐ Drapes	☐ Closet	☐ Bed

Bathroom:

☐ Lights	☐ Paint	☐ Air Vent
☐ Tub	☐ Vanity	☐ Shower
☐ Caulking	☐ Drains	☐ Toilet

Remarks:

_____

_____

_____

_____

_____

FIGURE 1.5   Sample Maintenance Checklist

Communication with Human Resources

Communication between the housekeeping and human resources departments is necessary when considering personnel staffing. When an employee is needed in the housekeeping department, an **employee requisition** is filled out and sent to human resources to initiate the process. Figure 1.6 is a sample employee requisition that provides human resources with the necessary information for the job in question. After receiving the request, human resources advertises for the position, pre-screens the candidates, conducts the first interview, and checks references. The final candidates are then sent to housekeeping for a second interview and hiring selection.

Date: _____ Department: _____

Position: _____

New: _____ Replacement: _____ Number required: _____

Classification: _____
(Full-time, Part-time, Temporary, Pool)

Working hours: _____ Estimated no. of hours/week: _____

Desired starting date: _____

Starting rate of pay: _____ Base rate: _____

Specification (General description of duties): _____

_____

_____

_____

_____

_____

_____

Special Qualifications (Desired or required): _____

_____

_____

_____

_____

_____

_____

FIGURE 1.6   Sample Employee Requisition

Human resources is usually also involved in the orientation of new housekeeping employees, at which time the company's philosophy, compensation package, pay schedule, and rules and regulations are explained in detail to the new worker. This department also ensures that the new employee fills out all necessary forms related to legal residency, income tax, and personal information. Good communication with human resources will result in hiring the right employees to fill housekeeping vacancies.

Communication with Food and Beverage

Food and beverage is the second major revenue center in the property after the rooms division. The food and beverage division in large hotels comprises the property's kitchens, restaurants, coffee shops, cafeterias, bars, lounges, banquets, catering services, clubs, and room service. In large hotels, the housekeeping department should only be indirectly involved in the cleaning of food and beverage outlets. However, the communication between food and beverage and housekeeping is necessary in some specific areas.

There must be good cooperation regarding the pickup of room service material from guestroom areas. Housekeeping must see to it that hallways are free from trays and carts placed there by guests and section housekeepers; therefore, calls to room service must be regularly placed to remind this department to clear all areas. The laundry room must provide the food and beverage department with clean napery on a daily basis. This often means that the laundry manager must request that the soiled linen be delivered to the laundry room on time, properly sorted out, and free from food scraps and table debris. Furnishing clean uniforms to cooks, waiters, and bartenders is also usually the responsibility of the housekeeping department. As communication with food and beverage service personnel is traditionally difficult, efforts must be made to establish good relationships between departments.

Communication with Sales and Marketing

The primary goal of the sales and marketing division is to sell the products and services offered by the property. Given that cleanliness is one of the most important reasons for guests to choose a particular lodging property, the onus of providing this critical service falls on the housekeeping department. There must be good communication between sales and housekeeping if customer satisfaction is to be achieved. For instance, if sales and marketing has guaranteed late check-out to a large group of guests attending a convention without notifying housekeeping, some of the rooms might not be cleaned in time to be available for a tour group scheduled to check-in that same evening. If sales and marketing has promised that forty rooms will be available for early check-in to a company attending a conference at the property and housekeeping has not been notified, there might not be enough manpower that morning to clean the rooms on time.

Communication between sales and housekeeping is also necessary when specific rooms or suites must be available for inspection to meeting planners who are considering the property for a possible convention. If the rooms in question have not been impeccably cleaned, the company executive might well take their business elsewhere.

Communication with the Accounting Office

It is seldom acknowledged that communication between housekeeping and the accounting office is of great importance, yet there are several reasons why this is so. For instance, in large properties, the purchasing agent often reports to the controller; therefore, the executive housekeeper is communicating with the accounting office when placing orders for equipment and supplies for the department. Also, housekeeping must provide accounting with all information regarding wages and salaries—for instance, informing the office of pay increases, hours worked per week, overtime, bonuses awarded to workers, and so on. The executive housekeeper must also provide accounting with monthly inventory information in order to ascertain expenses of controllable goods and percentage costs.

 KEY TERMS

A.M. guestroom check	cruise ship
bed-and-breakfast	department head
casino	economy property

employee requisition	multi-unit chain
executive committee	night clerk's room report
executive housekeeper	P.M. guestroom check
franchise property	preventive maintenance
front office	regular maintenance
hospitality industry	resort
hotel	revenue-generating center
housekeeping department	rooms division
independently owned property	rooms division director
inn	second request
institutional lodging	spa
luxury property	Statler Hotels
maintenance checklist	support center
management company	time-share condominiums
mid-market property	work order form
motel	

DISCUSSION AND REVIEW QUESTIONS

1. What is the origin of the word inn? Is there a difference between the meaning of inn some centuries ago and the meaning of inn today?
2. How would you define the word hotel? Is there a difference between hotels and inns in today's market?
3. In which way were inns and taverns associated with the American Revolution?
4. Why is Ellsworth Statler considered the father of commercial hotels?
5. List the most common types of lodging properties in today's market.
6. How would you describe institutional lodging?
7. What is the difference between a franchised property and a property run by a management company?
8. What are the three categories in which lodging properties are generally classified by type of service?
9. Explain why the rooms division is considered a revenue center rather than a support center.
10. Indicate the purpose of the A.M. guestroom check report conducted by housekeeping.

11. Give two reasons why communication between the housekeeping and maintenance departments must be efficiently kept.

12. As an executive housekeeper, what department would you contact to solve a problem arising from unacceptable presorting of napery items?

MINICASES

Situation 1

As a student about to graduate from a hotel/restaurant management program, you receive three job offers from three different companies recruiting at your university. The first company offers you a position as assistant housekeeping manager paying $22,000 per year. The company is a partnership that owns five Holiday Inn–franchised properties. The second company is the Marriott Corporation, which owns a large number of hotels and resorts around the world. The position offered to you is that of housekeeping manager trainee at a salary of $19,500 per year. The third company would like to hire you as assistant executive housekeeper and is offering you a salary of $22,000 per year. This is a management company that runs 150 properties in 16 states. (a) Which job would you rather accept? (b) What are the reasons that you would provide in support of your decision?

Situation 2

As housekeeping supervisor in a resort, you are in the process of preparing the A.M. guestroom check report when you discover that room 2004 is occupied, although the night clerk's report that you received early in the morning indicated that the room was vacant. (a) What do you think could have happened for the discrepancy to exist? (b) What do you do from there?

Situation 3

As supervisor of the housekeeping evening shift, you receive a work order duplicate from the engineering department indicating that the painting job in the out-of-order room 2008 has been completed. The hotel will be at 100 percent occupancy that evening. (a) What steps will you take after receiving the information from engineering?

The Executive Housekeeper as Department Manager

The Westin Grand, Berlin, Germany.
Courtesy of Westin Hotels & Resorts.

CHAPTER OBJECTIVES

▶ Learn how management concepts apply to the position of executive housekeeper.

▶ Discuss the necessity of achieving high productivity in housekeeping while also considering the needs of the employees in the department.

▶ Understand the role of the executive housekeeper as department head.

▶ Explain the role of the executive housekeeper as department coordinator.

▶ List the managerial responsibilities of the executive housekeeper.

 ## OVERVIEW

This chapter explains how management concepts can be applied to the role of executive housekeeper. As a manager, you must be able to combine concern for production and concern for people in order to run the department effectively. The traditional functions of management can be followed as a guide to organize and coordinate the department, plan and direct activities, and control results.

As a department head, the executive housekeeper must be proficient in technical, people-related, and conceptual skills. As a manager, the executive housekeeper must understand the concepts of time management, problem resolution, quality control, and decision making, and operate within the precepts of industry-accepted codes of ethics.

MANAGEMENT CONCEPTS AS THEY APPLY TO THE EXECUTIVE HOUSEKEEPER

It is the responsibility of a manager to create and maintain an environment in which people can work toward the goals of the company. As the manager of the largest department in the lodging property, the executive housekeeper must possess strong managerial skills in order to perform this task well. Members of a management staff must be concerned with the productivity of the work force and people, and must be able to efficiently coordinate effort in the workplace.

Concern for Production

The overall goal of management in a profit-making operation is to increase the owner's equity by maximizing profits. So, in turn, one of the major concerns of the executive housekeeper should be to maximize the productivity and efficiency of housekeeping employees. Theoretical production and efficiency methods in the workplace were first explored at the turn of the century by **Frederick W. Taylor**, whose **classical scientific management** concepts, although developed under industrial conditions, can still be applied today in the lodging industry. Taylor analyzed jobs systematically to determine the amount of work that each employee could produce. He did so by measuring the performance of workers in a given period of time. This allowed management to set standards of production and require employees to reach the pre-established levels of performance in a certain number of hours. If the productivity levels were above the standard, management could choose to pay bonuses to workers as an incentive to maintain productivity quotas.

If the productivity levels were below the standard, production methods had to be improved.

This approach is still followed in well-managed housekeeping operations. For instance, the executive housekeeper can analyze the time required to efficiently clean one of the property's guestrooms and use that time as the department's standard for that task. When productivity and quality exceed the standards, special recognition or extra compensation could be given for maintaining the productivity quotas. If performance falls below pre-established levels, the section housekeepers would need to be retrained or the method used to clean guestrooms re-evaluated. This approach can foster productivity and increase the profits of the company which, in turn, could pay its employees higher wages.

Concern for People

Frederick Taylor's classical scientific management approach dealt with techniques to increase productivity in the workplace. At the time, workers had little reason to improve their productivity; on the contrary, they viewed the introduction of new machines and equipment to improve efficiency as a direct threat.

Toward the end of the 1920s, a new management approach developed as a result of experiments conducted in the workplace by **Elton Mayo**. The study concluded that factors other than the physical aspect of a job can have an effect on productivity, namely, the workers' social interactions and personal relationships. Mayo's study demonstrated that in order to increase productivity in the workplace, human relations factors must be considered. That is, an organization consists first and foremost of the people working in it and management must be greatly concerned with the social and psychological aspects of the relationship between the company and its employees. As a result, the **human relations management** approach was developed.

This approach can be easily understood and applied from a housekeeping management perspective. For instance, if the department manager does not consider the social needs of the workers a priority, workers in turn will not develop a sense of loyalty for their manager. If a houseperson who is scheduled to work the morning shift cannot find a babysitter for mornings, management should do everything possible to schedule this worker in the evening. If this were done, the employee would feel gratitude and therefore be more willing to return the favor by improving productivity. In other words, productivity can be greatly improved if management takes care of its workers.

The human relations theory allowed for an understanding of the dynamics of human behavior which led to the premise that management must be aware that workers, besides being units of production, are social entities in their own right.

Combining Concern for People and Concern for Production

Mayo's work provided a needed addition to scientific movement. Management, which until then perceived employees as mechanistic elements in the productive system, was now viewing workers as human components in the organization's social system. Although it is true that executive housekeepers must develop a keen sense for production in the workplace (after all, the main reason for lodging companies to stay in business is to generate a profit), they must also see housekeeping employees as individuals. Yet, without adequate productivity in the workplace, profits will be diminished, forcing management to pay insufficient wages and to provide inferior benefits.

Clearly, then, adding concern for people to the management equation is imperative. However, the real skill lies in finding a proper balance; for example, an executive housekeeper determined to please workers at any cost may not be totally successful, for employees easily sense when a manager is a "softy," not tough enough to have the work done fairly but efficiently. A case in point would be an executive housekeeper agreeing to pay too much overtime or allowing employees to call in with any excuse not to show up for work.

Coordination of Effort in the Workplace

Another function of management is to see to it that all parts of a working unit are integrated as a whole. **Henri Fayol**, of France, theorized that certain management principles can be applied to any type of business as well as to the various levels within the business.

These principles apply, therefore, to the lodging industry in general and to the housekeeping department in particular. Fayol's book, *Administration Industrielle et Generale*, originally published in 1916, was not adopted in the United States until three decades later. Fayol proposed that a manager must practice the following functions of management:

Planning

Organizing

Directing

Coordinating

Controlling

PLANNING

One of the main functions the manager of the housekeeping department must perform is deciding what tasks are essential at any given time to keep the department running at peak efficiency. As the occupancy of the property varies from month to month, and even from day to day, forecasting labor and supplies needs must be done in advance to minimize costs. The definition of planning is simple: deciding where one should go and how to get there. Planning, however, is not always easy for it requires the predetermination of strategies and policies necessary to fulfill company goals. When forecasting employees, for instance, the executive housekeeper must skillfully plan the scheduling of employees according to the property's upcoming occupancy. If the hotel is full, all employees are needed, but only part of the staff is required when the occupancy is low. Regarding material, lack of planning might result in purchasing excessive amounts of guest supplies, for example, which means tying up cash that might be needed to pay salaries or to purchase new bed linens. On the other hand, underestimating future occupancy may result in understocking supplies and running out of them when they would be most needed.

Creativity is an important element of the planning function; it requires the ability of a manager to develop and implement different, more efficient solutions to operational problems. A creative executive housekeeper is flexible in judging employee initiatives, encouraging workers to develop new ways to improve the efficiency of the department. A highly structured, bureaucratic housekeeping department might be efficient in production but would stifle or limit innovation. Creativity in planning should allow for diversity of ideas without attempting to rigidly structure the behavior of employees.

Planning involves the achievement of short- and long-range objectives. A **short-range objective** might be to bring down the labor cost by one percentage point next month. A **long-range objective** might be to increase the productivity of section house-keepers by 5 percent over last year's results by the end of the current fiscal year.

ORGANIZING

The organization of housekeeping is necessary in order to establish a pattern of relationships with other operational units and among the different components of the department itself. The organization of housekeeping includes the determination of tasks, skills, and personnel necessary to achieve the objectives of the department. It is the responsibility of the executive housekeeper to structure the department so that all work can be finished efficiently and on time. The first necessary step when structuring the housekeeping department is to determine the pattern of authority by drawing an organizational chart. This follows the principle of **unity of command** proposed by Fayol which states that workers should be given orders only by their own supervisor. To this effect, the **span of control** must be clearly defined; this relates to the number of subordinates that a supervisor can oversee effectively. In the housekeeping department, when employees are well trained and dependable, the span of control can be quite broad. In the case of new or untrained employees, the span of control should be narrow, usually four or five workers.

Defining relationships within the department is also important because a strong cooperation must exist among its different units. For instance, a sufficient amount of clean linen must be made available to section housekeepers during the morning shift to set up guestrooms as quickly as possible. However, if the soiled linen is not brought to the laundry room to be washed, dried, and ironed early in the day, the clean linen will not be ready on time.

Another organizational task is that of creating descriptions of the jobs to be done (list of tasks) and the qualifications of workers who are to perform the jobs. Matching the right person for each job that must be accomplished is a priority in the organization of the housekeeping department. For instance, section housekeepers in lodging properties must clean between 12 and 20 rooms on average in one 8-hour shift. The importance of selecting people who are physically able to perform this strenuous job is obvious.

DIRECTING

This managerial function involves achieving the goals of the department by explaining to employees what needs to be accomplished, then facilitating their efforts to do the job. Crucial to directing effectively is the ability of the manager to train, motivate, supervise, and discipline employees. Competent executive housekeepers will be able to reach higher levels of productivity from the housekeeping work force than managers who are not adequately trained to direct people.

Without proper direction, employees tend to duplicate efforts, focus on the wrong priorities, and relate efforts to the wrong purpose. An example of improper direction may be allowing section housekeepers to clean every guestroom (checkout and stay-over rooms alike) early in the morning when there are incoming guests waiting in the lobby to be checked in. Another example of poor management would be to play favorites with employees, which would lead to discontent among them. As a manager, an efficient executive housekeeper should emphasize both the economic-technical system and the human aspects of administration.

COORDINATING

If we compared the housekeeping department to an orchestra, coordinating would be the act of bringing all the instruments together to produce a fine piece of music, that is, matching the individual work of the staff to the common goals of the operation. The executive housekeeper must coordinate the procurement and distribution of materials, working schedules, and overall communication among the different units of the department. This function is carried out through a series of briefings, meetings, and committee work where daily operational matters, intradepartmental issues, and hotel-wide concerns are addressed.

Lodging operations require a large degree of interdepartmental coordination. It is the job of the executive housekeeper to integrate the department in the operation as a whole, making sure that the communication flows to and from housekeeping and the different operational units of the property. A case in point would be that of attending a meeting in which the arrival of a large convention to the hotel is discussed. It would be up to the executive housekeeper to learn about the number of people in the group, arrival time, the type of accommodation booked, and other requirements and communicate this information in due course to the housekeeping supervisors for proper followup.

Coordination can be achieved by linking all activities together under a central authority. In the housekeeping department, however, it would be difficult to cope individually with all the coordinating problems that might arise every day. The coordinating function must be supported by a system of procedures designed to carry out much of the routine work automatically, for instance, using forms, memos, and routing slips. It is also important to achieve voluntary coordination on the part of the housekeeping employees. If they see the need for coordination and they are willing to find means to integrate their activities with other participants, departmental coordination will be accomplished.

CONTROLLING

The purpose of control is to make operations more efficient and cost effective. This function involves measuring actual with expected standards established during the planning process and effecting necessary corrections if deviations from the standards are found. Feedback is an essential component in the control process. In housekeeping departments feedback should be sought from guests, employees and other departments of the lodging operation. Figure 2.1 is a sample of the control process, in which standards are set during the planning function, operations take place, feedback is obtained from different sources, an evaluation of results is conducted, and new standards are prescribed.

The need for executive housekeepers to control the activities of their department represents an important management function. Without controls there is no way of evaluating the degree in which the objectives set during the planning function are met.

In other words, the actual results need to be compared to desired or anticipated goals and standard of performance. Labor cost percentages are typical standards of control; if the labor cost was set in the budget at 18 percent of revenue and the actual labor cost is

FIGURE 2.1   The Cycle of Control

running at 22 percent, the results are over budget and some corrective measures must be taken.

Controlling also refers to the need to regulate and protect material and equipment. This can be accomplished by implementing stock pars and taking protective measures against theft, pilferage, and misuse. An effective quality control can also lead to significant saving in costs. For instance, controlling the quality of cleaning materials to be used in the housekeeping department can result in substantial savings of time spent in having the job done.

 ## THE EXECUTIVE HOUSEKEEPER AS DEPARTMENT HEAD

The position of executive housekeeper in the organizational structure of lodging operations is that of **department head** or member of the middle management team. In small properties, executive housekeepers report directly to the general manager of the establishment, while in large properties they report to the rooms division director.

Today's successful executive housekeeper requires skills beyond those of a person who is just in charge of keeping the place clean. An effective manager of the housekeeping department must be object-, people-, and idea-oriented.

Technical, People, and Conceptual Skills

Executive housekeepers cannot concentrate their managerial ability on technical skills alone—material, budgets, equipment. They also must concern themselves with people and with the conceptualization of notions about the resolution of management-related issues. Executive housekeepers must have a thorough knowledge of how the job is done and how the equipment works, and also be able to exercise leadership and influence people to have the work done while being sensitive to the employees' needs. At the same time, they must be able to analyze situations, implement change, and effect innovative ideas in the workplace.

Supervision

A supervisor is anyone whose responsibility is to supervise; therefore every manager is a supervisor. The definition of supervision is quite similar to that of management in that it is concerned with directing, facilitating, and monitoring the work of others in order to have the job done. The executive housekeeper's field of supervision encompasses three major components: the company's assets, the employees, and the guests. Poor supervision of employees may lead to preparing guestrooms inefficiently, which in turn may create customer disloyalty and an eventual loss of profits.

Executive housekeepers can effect supervision tightly or loosely. Supervision can be exacted by following prescribed rules and regulations or by allowing teamwork and decision making by line employees. In the latter case, workers are expected to exercise initiative and self-coordination. Whether to use one style or the other should depend on the composition of the work force. When there is a substantial turnover of employees and their working skills are weak, supervision should be tighter than when the work force is well trained and reliable.

Leadership

Providing leadership is one aspect of management. Leadership can be defined as "the ability to lead people to willingly perform in ways to achieve the organization's goals." One commonly encountered problem in the lodging industry is that of indifferent employees. Some of the reasons for this are the inadequate wages, poor benefits, part-time positions, and insufficient training so common to the industry. In spite of these obstacles, it is the task of hospitality managers to create an appropriate environment in which employees willingly display a positive attitude toward guests and fellow workers. This can be achieved through proper leadership.

There are three leadership styles generally used by leaders in human situations. In the **authoritarian style**, the manager who dictates the tasks to be performed and the ways to accomplish them assumes the determination of policies; input from subordinates is not sought. **The democratic style** of management takes place when all policies are reached after group discussion and decision, encouraged and facilitated by the manager. In the **laissez-faire style** subordinates have complete freedom for group or individual decisions where the manager does not take part in matters related to work. An executive housekeeper exerting the same leadership style in all circumstances will most likely fail to achieve optimum results in the workplace. As different problems require different solutions, a flexible approach should be used when leading people. For instance, if a houseperson refuses to perform a task necessary for the normal operation of the department, the manager should compel the worker to do the job. On the other hand, if the same houseperson is performing the job satisfactorily, the manager should allow the worker to do the job without interfering.

Several studies conducted to identify leadership traits have yielded a series of attributes inherent to their personalities. Successful business managers generally are well educated, self-assured, decisive, risk-takers, power-seekers, problem-solvers, and good in their relationships with people. Besides these attributes, executive housekeepers should be good motivators, good communicators, good delegators, and good administrators of their invested power/ authority.

Motivation

Employee motivation may be the greatest challenge that executive housekeepers can face. Managers should not always try to motivate workers directly; instead they should create the right environment for employees to motivate themselves. The first step is to establish a climate of mutual trust and respect, meaning that employees should never be looked down upon from a position of superiority. Instead, managers should be characterized as fair, caring, and approachable individuals. Good leaders must be capable of understanding people well and be sensitive to their individual needs and differences. Motivation is internal, complex, and individually patterned; what motivates one person might displease someone else, and vice versa.

Before attempting to motivate workers, the executive housekeeper must provide for the satisfaction of their basic needs, which according to **Abraham Maslow**, theorist of the humanistic movement, may be physiological, security-driven, social, self-esteem. and achievement-driven. It would be difficult to motivate someone feeling physiologically uncomfortable, for instance, a laundry worker laboring in a room without ventilation at 110-degree temperature. An employee working part-time without assurance of a guaranteed number of working hours per week might also be hard to motivate. The same is true for workers who are shunned by fellow employees because of their ethnic background, employees who feel unappreciated, and those who feel they are not challenged to their true potential. It is therefore the duty of the executive housekeeper as a leader to facilitate the fulfillment of the individual needs of employees prior to attempting to motivate them.

An effective, universal way of motivating people is providing them with equitable, if not generous, compensation. It is axiomatic to assume that employees are motivated to work because of a need for money to live. However, greater financial incentives may not necessarily be the only motivators in all cases. For instance, a worker with job security and sufficient compensation may need additional challenges to get motivated in the workplace. **Frederick Herzberg** worked on identifying the factors that motivate people. He proposed that employees may be motivated through job enrichment, that is, making the work meaningful. **Herzberg** found that factors people reported as providing job satisfaction include responsibility, achievement, personal growth, advancement, and recognition. From this theory it follows that executive housekeepers should provide workers with jobs that embody responsibility, interest, opportunity, and challenge.

Communication

The fundamental function of communication is to link people together in organizations in order to achieve a common purpose. The activity of a group would be impossible without good communication because without it coordination could not be effected. One of the attributes executive housekeepers must have is the ability to determine when and what to communicate to whom, as well as to know the available means for information transfer, including the use of both formal and informal avenues.

Communication depends on the way different people perceive messages, and even ideas. Workers of diverse geographical or ethnic backgrounds might interpret differently concepts such as "clean," "on time," or "efficient." Executive housekeepers must have the ability to convey messages to all employees so that they are unequivocally understood.

Housekeeping managers spend most of their working time talking and listening to others; in some cases communicating represents about 80 percent of the work day. This volume and intensity of communication requires that hospitality students become proficient in sharing meaning and understanding with others. There are four types of verbal communication: speaking, listening, writing, and reading. Speaking and writing are used to send messages, while listening and reading are used to receive them. Of all these, face-to-face communication is the most effective.

In order to avoid one-way communication, managers should strive to convey their message in such a way that employees feel free to express their feelings as well. There is a difference between getting someone to agree with the message sent and showing a willingness to accept possible disagreement. In the first case we are trying to communicate one way; in the second, we are being open to receive the employee's feedback in return.

Another condition for two-way communication is the ability to understand what someone is trying to say from that person's point of view. In other words, being able to empathize during a conversation is the key element for two people to understand each other.

There can be several roadblocks to effective communication. The **status barrier** can undermine willingness to listen patiently to workers who are perceived as having low social status, as, for example, the communication process that may take place between a section housekeeper and an engineer who might consider the former "unworthy" to listen to. In this case, it is better to use an impersonal mechanism like a work order to avoid any friction between departments. The **psychological barrier** can cause communication distortion when one of the communicators has a preconceived, negative perception of the other person. If front office personnel perceive housekeeping room attendants as "members of the cleaning brigade," they will always find reasons not to listen attentively to them. In this case, cross-training between the two departments will be necessary for all to understand the importance of the type of job performed by section housekeepers.

Communication breakdowns can also occur when people pass judgment in haste, when they seem unapproachable, or when they show displeasure at being interrupted. Cutting in with a quick judgment while workers are explaining something only shows a manager's inability to listen properly and will discourage two-way communication. Not having an open-door policy will discourage workers from engaging in informal conversation, which can be an effective way of learning what is on employees' minds. Interruptions are often nothing but unscheduled exchanges of important information.

Although many managers are good top-down communicators, they often don't have the patience or interest to listen to dissenting views or they don't have good listening skills. In the first case, managers must understand that any views expressed by any employee in the organization might be worth listening to. Managers who are incapable of listening should develop listening skills. Several types of listening are appropriate for different circumstances. **Active listening**, for instance, is necessary when an employee requests information leading to the resolution of a problem. In **passive listening**, on the other hand, the listener expects a nonjudgmental answer or acknowledgment. An employee who is complaining about the lack of cleanliness in the locker rooms requires active listening and specific answers. A worker lamenting the loss of a relative calls for passive listening and perhaps a word of encouragement.

Power/Authority

Power is the ability a person has to influence the behavior of others. When power is institutionalized in organizations, the ability to influence the behavior of others becomes a right. This established power is referred to as authority. The use of power should be administered wisely for individuals generally cannot grow and develop in an atmosphere of overwhelming authority. However, for repetitive work such as housekeeping's, well-defined procedures and a rather strong power base may be most appropriate.

Some managers may have an innate ability to do or affect something; others may resort to their invested authority to get things accomplished. Managers may exert their authority by coercion, reward, suggestion, persuasion, or emulation. **Coercive** and **reward power** refer to situations in which the manager administers punishment or recompense depending on the employee's behavior. Rewards and punishments should be administered fairly and be based on the behavior modification they may effect when applied to workers. **Suggestion** applies when the leader places an idea or proposition before a worker for consideration and possible action. If suggestion doesn't work, the manager may resort to **persuasion**, that is, advising or urging (rather than forcing) a person to do something. The best source of leader power is **emulation** in which workers want to equal or excel the behavior of a superior. Executive housekeepers who are experts in their fields and possess charismatic behavior generally fit this type of leadership.

Delegation

No one should attempt to accomplish effectively the duties of executive housekeeper without delegating to others some of the functions involved in the management of the department. Carrying out the responsibility of managing the housekeeping department requires the completion of numerous tasks, most of which are performed by assistants, supervisors, and hourly employees.

Delegation can be defined as the process of assigning work with the necessary authority and accountability to accomplish it effectively. In practice, the process of delegation involves the creation of a relationship in which authority and responsibility are shared between manager and employee to get the job done. When delegation takes place effectively, the manager is left free to coordinate the different activities of the department. There are four steps that must be followed when delegating tasks: defining the task, designating who is to perform the job, empowering the employee to do the job, and requiring accountability for it. Figure 2.2 is a delegation diagram showing a simple delegation process.

GUESTROOM INSPECTIONS
↓
will be accomplished by
↓
TEAM SUPERVISORS
↓
with corresponding
↓
EMPOWERMENT
↓
and adequate
↓
ACCOUNTABILITY

FIGURE 2.2   Delegation Diagram

Several methods of delegation can be used in the housekeeping department. The manager may decide to define the results expected after the task is accomplished. For instance, the section house-keepers will clean 15 guestrooms efficiently in one 8-hour shift. The manager may set performance standards to be met after the completion of tasks, for example, using guestroom inspection forms indicating levels of cleanliness and décor. The manager may also establish specific procedures to do the job; for instance, breaking down the way to clean a bathtub into components to be followed sequentially by section housekeepers. Some managers find it difficult to delegate authority to others, for reasons that may include lack of trust in employees, unwillingness to invest any of their authority in others, and enjoying hands-on work.

Executive housekeepers must understand that, although authority and responsibility may have been delegated, they are ultimately responsible for the acts of their subordinates. For this very reason, the process of delegation must always be carefully and efficiently administered. Responsibility is ultimately the superior's obligation and cannot be shifted to subordinates. The manager of housekeeping, employed by the company, cannot avoid total responsibility for the results of the department. If employees are negligent in their duties or upset guests, the executive housekeeper must answer to the rooms division director or general manager for these actions.

MANAGEMENT RESPONSIBILITIES OF THE EXECUTIVE HOUSEKEEPER

Beginning with Henri Fayol's proposition 100 years ago, the functions of management have been repeatedly listed with some variations, as planning, organizing, directing, and controlling. There are, however, several other management abilities that executive housekeepers must master to effectively fulfill the numerous responsibilities inherent in their positions. Among those, the management of time, the solution of operational and personnel problems, the achievement of quality, the practice of values, and the ability to make decisions are the most manifest.

Time Management

Time must be managed proactively by managers in order to be ready for upcoming events rather than having to react to crises. The tasks to be accomplished in the housekeeping department are so numerous that managers often find, to their dismay, that 8, 10, and even 12 hours of work per day are not enough to get the job done. In most cases, too many hours on the job leads to burnout and ultimately even resigning the position.

Job demands in the housekeeping department generally can be categorized into short-run, intermediate-run, or long-run time frames. The short-run demands include day-to-day matters of an operational nature, such as ensuring that the guestrooms are cleaned well and on time, that the soiled linen and napery are processed prior to distribution deadlines, that public areas and offices are cleaned before or after rush hour, and so on. Short-term demands usually require an intense interaction with employees as a large number of activities do take place at the same time.

Intermediate-run demands require planning and organizing activities necessary to maintain the cohesiveness and efficiency of the housekeeping department. The training and development of housekeeping employees and the preparation of labor and supply forecasts for upcoming events are typical examples of intermediate-run activities. These activities not only require downward communication but also lateral interaction with other departments of the property. For example, the arrival next month of a large convention would require a review with the sales and front desk departments of the specific steps necessary to coordinate this event.

Long-range forecasting is another important task for executive housekeepers, specifically in the preparation of annual budgets. This process requires the provision of resources for both capital and operational expenditures and foreseeing essential major maintenance and refurbishing projects. Long-run demands require substantial upward communication with the rooms division director, lateral communication with the controller and plant manager, and downward communication with the department supervisors.

The first step in managing time is to chart it. Having a time log such as a large calendar or wall bulletin board where the day's and week's activities are entered helps to plan ahead and to be aware of how much time each activity requires to be completed. Computer software such as Microsoft® Schedule can be equally effective. Tickler file systems and phone call screening are some practices that can save precious time.

Problem Solving

A problem in the workplace can be defined as any impediment or difficulty that interferes with the regular achievement of goals. Considering the unpredictability and immediacy of situations, the type of employees, and the pace of housekeeping operations, executive housekeepers must possess an extraordinary ability to solve problems swiftly and effectively without resorting to the "shoot-from-the-hip" approach.

The first step to effective problem solving is to identify the real issue. For instance, if the laundry department is chronically behind in producing clean linen, the laundry workers might be blamed for it, although the real cause could be obsolete laundry equipment. Once problems have been clearly identified, their solution can be attempted individually or collectively. When the solution seems clear and the manager does not see any need for the input of others, problems should be solved by the managers themselves. Such is the case when dealing with inanimate economic and technical aspects of operating the department. When the problem deals with human aspects, the task becomes more difficult and judgmental and usually needs the involvement of others. In collective problem solving, the manager's role is to foster ideas, then guide the process to its conclusion. Brainstorming is an effective technique aimed at eliciting group input by discussion in order to find solutions to problems.

The solution of problems can be facilitated by *empowering* employees to do whatever is necessary, within reason, to resolve problems for the guest rather than to shift the problem upward to management. Some workers may be reluctant to solve problems for fear of making mistakes or assuming too much authority. In these cases, employees need to be invested with some leeway to make their own decision in uncomplicated cases.

Total Quality Management (TQM)

Quality control has been a major concern in American businesses for a very long time, since companies long ago realized that quality standards for any given product are ultimately established by the customer. However, while manufacturing companies in general concern themselves mainly with the quality of mechanical processes, lodging operations must concern themselves with both product and service quality.

The principles of total quality management (TQM) that apply to housekeeping operations are having an understanding of customer requirements, measuring customer satisfaction, empowering employees, and focusing on the continuous improvement of the search for quality. Housekeeping managers in lodging operations must be aware of the expectations of the traveling public when staying in their properties. Cleanliness, firm mattresses, fluffy towels, appropriate amenities, and friendly service are generally ranked as top requirements for the American traveler. In locations where the customer base is different from the norm, surveys should be conducted to find out the expectations of guests. For instance, a property that regularly receives large numbers of tourists from Japan may want to know what pleases Japanese guests, whose tastes might differ from those of, say, Canadian customers.

Guests' input should be sought regularly to find out whether they are pleased with the accommodations and services offered. Comment cards and personal interaction with guests will provide the information the department needs to measure guest satisfaction. Although I have stayed in numerous lodging properties, including four- and five-star hotels and resorts, I have never been approached by a housekeeping manager or supervisor to find out if my room was prepared to my liking. These relationships with guests should be the rule in lodging operations rather than the exception.

Empowering employees to take initiative in customer satisfaction is essential to quality management. In order to achieve this, employees should be given greater decision-making latitude and be given twice the necessary training to enable them to make reasonable decisions. This TQM approach generally results in a streamlined chain of command and in workers taking responsibility for their own work performance.

The concept of TQM also implies that the process of striving for excellence is not finite—it is about constantly improving and innovating. Avoiding errors, not fixing them, should be a never-ending process. Well-implemented TQM programs can also provide tangible savings to housekeeping operations. For instance, section housekeepers who are committed to quality could conduct the final inspection of their own rooms before turning them to the front desk for occupation, thus eliminating the need for a designated inspector.

Ethical Values

It is the manager's obligation to follow those lines of action that are acceptable in terms of the values of society. The concept of ethics should therefore be mainly concerned with the social responsibilities of managers. The reality of it, however, is quite difficult to grasp because there are no nationally recognized ethical standards. With regard to the behavior of executive housekeepers as department managers, "ethics" could be referred to as high standards of professional conduct, affecting matters such as sexual harassment, equal opportunity, privacy rights, racial discrimination, and making decisions that affect people's lives fall within the realm of values in the workplace.

Some guidelines for ethical behavior in the workplace include:

1. Be honest in relationships with others.
2. Enhance the human dignity of workers.
3. Respect employees as individual human beings.
4. Understand the needs and concerns of employees.

5. Observe the law.
6. Be accountable for your decisions.
7. Create a good reputation as a manager.
8. Be fair and equitable.
9. Show integrity in business transactions.

The ethical reputation of companies is often determined by the behavior of the managers who work for them. Housekeeping managers should make reasonable efforts to foresee possible negative ethical consequences that would mar the reputation of their companies, their guests, and their subordinates.

Decision-Making

Choosing from among alternatives of a course of action is called decision-making. One of the executive housekeeper's central jobs is to prioritize what needs to be done, who will do it, where, and even how. The process of decision-making involves the identification of what needs to be accomplished, the search for possible alternatives, the evaluation of these alternatives, and the selection and implementation of the best one by which the job can be done. Managers should avoid making rapid-fire decisions that often fall short of the desired target.

Good managers often decide to accomplish a job cost-effectively in order to maximize profits; however, the needs, attitudes, and prejudices of people must be taken into account. For example, an executive housekeeper may decide to improve the labor cost percentage of the department by laying off two full-time workers and hiring four part-time employees without benefits to do the same job. While the results may be positive in the short run, the reaction of the remaining full-time workers may be quite negative as they might perceive the company as not taking the welfare of its people into account.

One way to improve decision-making is by getting employees involved in the process. This method usually draws on different viewpoints and motivates people to be cooperative in carrying out an idea. Indeed, some companies use the concept of **quality circles**, in which total worker involvement in the decision-making process as well as in matters related to production and quality is sought.

KEY TERMS

Abraham Maslow
classical scientific management
department head
emulation
Henri Fayol
Frederick Herzberg
human relations management
leadership styles
   authoritarian
   democratic
   laissez-faire
listening
   active
   passive

long-range objectives
Elton Mayo
persuasion
power
   coercive
   reward
psychological barrier
quality circles
short-range objectives
span of control
status barrier
suggestion
Frederick Taylor
unity of command

DISCUSSION AND REVIEW QUESTIONS

1. Why should executive housekeepers have great concern for production as well as for people in the workplace?
2. When planning activities in the housekeeping department, what could be a short-range objective? A long-range objective?
3. Describe the principle of unity of command and explain why it should be adopted in housekeeping operations.
4. Give a practical example of the control process as a management function in housekeeping operations.
5. When managing employees, what is the difference between authoritarian and laissez-faire styles?
6. Give an applied example of Maslow's basic needs theory and one of Herzberg's theory of motivation that relate to housekeeping operations.
7. When communicating verbally with employees, when would you listen actively and when passively?
8. What are the advantages and disadvantages of empowering hourly employees in the housekeeping department?
9. Explain a practical way of implementing total quality management (TQM) in the housekeeping department.

10. In your opinion, why should executive housekeepers follow an ethical code of professional conduct in the workplace?
11. Describe both an ethical example and an unethical example of the professional conduct of a housekeeping manager.
12. Why would you, as an executive housekeeper, adopt quality circles in your department?

MINICASES

Situation 1

George Sandoval, housekeeping manager at the Royal Hotel, wrote the following memo regarding operations in the laundry department of the hotel: "The level of productivity of laundry workers has been very low lately. On two occasions, there has not been enough linen to go around, the section housekeepers have had to wait for sheets and pillowcases to set up the beds. Beginning today, the 30-minute mid-morning break will be reduced to 15 minutes in order to increase productivity. I will be checking the laundry room often to make sure that everyone is on task at all times. We must have the clean linen out fast every morning!" (a) How would you evaluate George's attitude regarding his concern for production? (b) How would you evaluate George's attitude regarding his concern for people? (c) What would you have done in George's place?

Situation 2

After graduating from a hotel and restaurant management school, Christie Wilson accepted the position of assistant to the executive housekeeper at a mid-market hotel on the East Coast. Christie's responsibilities included supervising 80 housekeeping employees, filling in for team supervisors when they called in sick, conducting inventories, preparing weekly time cards, and assisting her boss in the overall management of the department. The first month was spent becoming familiar with the department procedures and getting acquainted with her fellow employees. After the training period, Christie got more and more involved with the routine duties of the housekeepers, housepersons, and laundry workers. If they had a problem, she would immediately get personally involved in finding the solution. In time, her performance began to deteriorate as she had to deal with the tasks described in her job description plus the problems her subordinates were having.

After a while, complaints began to pour in from the accounts department, the front desk, and top management about paperwork being backlogged and errors being committed regularly. Christie began to find herself becoming jumpy and restless at the onset of any minor crisis. Her employees started filing complaints with the executive housekeeper, who thought that Christie would work out her problems as she continued to gain experience on the job. This turned out not to be the case. After six months on the job, Christie had a nervous breakdown and decided that it was a mistake to have accepted the assistant manager position. (a) What did Christie do wrong from the beginning? (b) What recommendation do you have for Christie as she begins to look for another job with a lodging company?

Situation 3

You are a housekeeping manager in a resort in the Southwest. You have received several complaints about supervisor Johnson repeatedly asking female employees for dates after work. After discussing the problem with Johnson, he becomes defensive, saying that he will quit the job if you keep bothering him about his personal relationships with his fellow workers. Because Johnson is a very dedicated, productive employee, you decide not to pay any attention to the complaints lest you end up losing this otherwise excellent supervisor. (a) Are you behaving ethically in this particular situation? (b) Why or why not?

PART 2

Organization of the Housekeeping Department

Structural Planning
of the Housekeeping
Department

Westin Century Plaza Hotel & Tower,
Los Angeles, California. Courtesy of
Westin Hotels & Resorts.

CHAPTER OBJECTIVES

▶ Define the areas of housekeeping responsibility in large properties.
▶ Discuss the need for establishing area cleaning inventories, frequency schedules, and performance standards.
▶ Describe the process of dividing the guestrooms cleaning staff into teams.
▶ Explain the composition of a staffing matrix for a large hotel.

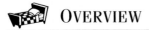 OVERVIEW

This chapter describes the structural planning of the housekeeping department beginning with the definition of its areas of responsibility. Although in small properties executive housekeepers may be in charge of servicing most areas, in large establishments the areas of responsibility should be limited to guestrooms, offices, public areas, back-of-the-house spaces, employee locker rooms and cafeteria, laundry and linen rooms.

Once the areas of responsibility have been established (what is to be cleaned), the executive housekeeper needs to determine how

53

often they are to be cleaned, and to what degree. The purpose of this planning activity is to provide workers with specific guidelines about how the different cleaning tasks should be performed. The property's guestrooms should then be divided into sections and the sections grouped into teams, determining how many teams will be needed to service the property while giving employees two days off every week. An example of a staffing matrix for large hotels is provided in this chapter.

 ## AREAS OF HOUSEKEEPING RESPONSIBILITY

When organizing the internal structure of lodging properties, the identification of cleaning and maintenance responsibilities for every area of the hotel is a prerequisite. All spaces of the property must be assigned by upper management to the different operating departments that are then charged with keeping their respective areas in a perfect state of cleanliness and maintenance. Ideally, in order not to leave any space unassigned, the various cleaning and mainte- nance area boundaries are marked on a copy of the property's blueprint.

The areas of responsibility of the housekeeping department will be different depending on the size of the property. In small lodg- ing operations the executive housekeeper is usually in charge of the cleaning and upkeep of most areas. In this particular case, very close cooperation between housekeeping and other departments is necessary to have the job done efficiently. For instance, if house- keeping is in charge of cleaning the banquet rooms, the manager needs to know the type and time of functions in order to provide the necessary service. In some cases, because the preparation and service of food begins very early in the morning and ends quite late in the evening, the cleaning function in food and beverage areas must be provided late at night.

In large properties, the division of work by area is spread out among the different operating departments. Often some of the cleaning functions—such as cleaning the kitchen, restaurant, and grounds—are contracted out to outside companies. Before contract- ing out cleaning tasks, it is important to obtain cost estimates from two or three different sources based on the size of the areas and the type and frequency of the cleaning desired. Once the contract has been signed, it is essential to check the quality of the work performed by the contractor. In no case should the cost of the services contracted be substantially higher than the cost of the same services performed by in-house personnel. An ideal division of work in large properties would keep the housekeeping department from having to clean areas that are operated by the food and beverage or engineering divisions. There are several reasons for this: the housekeeping department usually does not have the necessary technical resources, the time, nor the expertise to clean ovens, walk-in refrigerators, kitchen hoods, and swimming pools or to prune palm trees and trim rose bushes. An ideal distribution of cleaning and maintenance responsibilities in large hotels may be:

Area	Department Responsible
guestrooms, including hallways, vending areas, elevators, stairwells, and floor closets	Housekeeping
public areas, including lobbies, front desk, main entrance, corridors, restrooms, game and exercise rooms, and shops	Housekeeping
offices	Housekeeping
employee areas, including locker rooms, cafeterias, and restrooms	Housekeeping
laundry room	Housekeeping
linen room	Housekeeping
housekeeping storage areas	Housekeeping
recreation areas, including pools, tennis courts, volleyball courts, etc.	Engineering
grounds, including parking lot, parking garages, trees, landscaping, and sidewalks	Engineering
maintenance shop	Engineering
food and beverage service, including restaurants, coffee shops, bars, and cocktail lounges	food & beverage*
kitchens	food & beverage*
banquets, including ballrooms, meeting rooms, and exhibition halls	banquets

*Often, these outlets are contracted out to outside cleaning contractors. Cleaning areas of difficult accessibility, such as windows in high-rise buildings, may also be assigned to outside cleaning services.

Once the cleaning and maintenance responsibilities for all the areas of the property have been established, the respective department heads must plan the activities necessary for the upkeep of their areas, secure sufficient resources, and provide personnel to service them effectively.

Area Cleaning Inventories

The first step in planning the upkeep of the different areas assigned to the housekeeping department is to establish a list of the items that need to be regularly cleaned and maintained. A cleaning inventory list for guestrooms, for instance, will include all items that need to be cleaned, checked, and maintained in each room. The list should follow the sequence that section housekeepers keep when servicing guestrooms, for example, beginning with the entrance door to the rooms, standing lamps, window sills, furniture, and so on and ending with vacuuming the carpet. Another example of cleaning inventory would be that drawn for the lobby of the hotel, which might include not only furniture and fixtures but a water fountain, plants, bookcase, chandelier and so on. Area cleaning inventories can be combined with cleaning frequency schedules, including what needs to be cleaned and how often the items must be cleaned in one single document.

Cleaning Frequency Schedule

Once the area cleaning inventory lists have been prepared, the frequency for cleaning and maintenance of each item should be established. Figure 3.1 shows a sample of area cleaning inventory and frequency schedule. Generally items need to be cleaned daily, biweekly, weekly, monthly, and so on. Examples of daily service in the lobby area would be the windowsills; plants could be dusted twice a week, the water fountain polished once a week, the air vents on the wall once a month, and so forth. Besides cleaning items on a regular basis, most areas are **deep cleaned** once or twice a year. In this case, the cleaning crews scrape and scrub every nook and cranny until all surfaces are spotless. Deep cleaning projects gener-

ITEM	ACTIVITY	FREQUENCY
Carpet	Vacuumed	Daily
Furniture	Dusted	Daily
Furniture	Polished	Weekly
Chandelier	Dusted	Bi-monthly
Lamps	Dusted	Daily
Wood Paneling	Polished	Monthly
Sconces	Dusted	Weekly
Water Fountain	S/S Cleaned	Bi-weekly
Sand Ashtrays	Cleaned	Twice daily
Air Vents	Dusted	Monthly
Hallway	Stripped/Waxed	Monthly

FIGURE 3.1   Sample Area Cleaning Inventory and Frequency Schedule—
Lobby

ally coincide with low occupancy periods and are coordinated with repairs being done in the area by the engineering department.

Performance Standards

After compiling cleaning inventories and frequency schedules, performance standards must be established. Performance standards are used to inform subordinates of the equipment and supplies they must use to clean an item, of the method or way of doing the job, and of the expected cleaning outcomes. It is not good enough to tell section housekeepers and janitors to "clean well." "Cleaning well" may mean different levels of cleanliness to different people. An example of performance standard to clean a vanity top could be: "Spray all-purpose cleaner on the vanity top and wipe the surface clean with a sanitized rag, wiping it dry until no spots, marks, or specks remain."

The development of cleaning performance standards should be established keeping in mind the direct input of the workers who are assigned to do the cleaning. The written cleaning standards should be a part of the department's **standard operating procedures** (SOPs) and strictly observed during the training period of new employees. Properties that have written cleaning standards in place are able to measure employee performance by comparing the worker cleaning outcomes with the established standards.

 ## DIVISION OF GUESTROOMS

The assignment of guestrooms for daily cleaning is usually done randomly in small hotels. That is, the section housekeepers are gathered at the beginning of the shift and given a number of rooms to service on an individual basis. In large hotels, however, **housekeeping teams** should be formed to which the same sections of rooms are consistently assigned. There are several advantages to allotting the guestrooms to teams. Individual housekeepers take ownership of the rooms they clean day in and day out, showing pride for the work they perform, which increases their morale. Teams create a sense of unity, of common interests and responsibilities (esprit de corps) by which room attendants are less likely to let their partners down by calling in sick, thus improving attendance. A team may consist of four or five **section housekeepers**, a **team supervisor**, and a **houseperson**. The section housekeeper cleans guestrooms while the supervisor coordinates the work of the teams and inspects rooms. The housepersons assist in the work by providing the team with supplies, hauling the trash, vacuuming the hallways, moving heavy objects around, and so on.

Guestrooms are divided by creating a pictorial representation of all rooms and allocating a certain number of them to every section housekeeper of each team. Figure 3.2 shows a floor plan layout of a large hotel in which the sections have been delimited to include 16 rooms per room attendant. The criteria for guestroom cleaning workload vary from hotel to hotel depending on the size of the rooms, the number of furniture and fixture pieces to be cleaned, and the level of quality that management wishes to provide. Generally a property with small rooms allocates about 18 rooms per section housekeeper for an 8-hour shift. Properties with average-size rooms assign around 16, while establishments with large rooms or suites allocate about 12 units per shift.

As an example, a 400-room property that assigns 16 rooms to one section housekeeper and that groups the section housekeepers

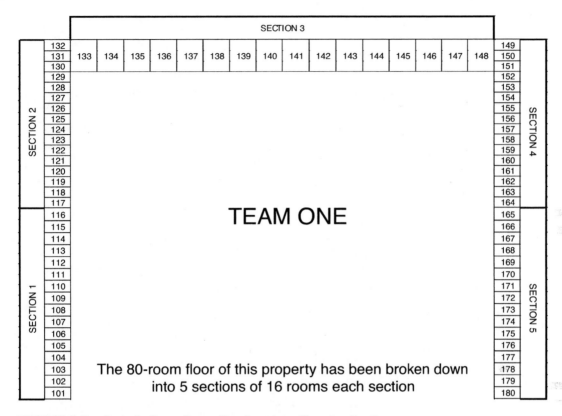

The 80-room floor of this property has been broken down into 5 sections of 16 rooms each section

FIGURE 3.2   Sample Guest Room Breakout into Cleaning Sections

in teams of 5 would have the following workload distribution at 100 percent occupancy:

Number of teams: **5** (400 ÷ 16 = 25; 25 ÷ 5 = 5)

Number of section housekeepers: **25** (400 ÷ 16 = 25)

Number of team supervisors: **5** (one per team)

Number of houseperson: **5** (one per team)

In this particular example, the assignment of five teams to clean the rooms works perfectly. But what would happen if the hotel continues to operate at 100 percent occupancy for some time? As the workers need to be given two days off per week to avoid overtime, the department will need a larger number of workers to substitute for those who are off. The problem becomes more complicated if the property operates an **on-premise laundry**. Let us suppose that this is the case and that the laundry is operated by one full team consisting of five section housekeepers, one supervisor, and one houseperson. In this case, as the hotel is open seven days a week and the employees work only five, the total number of teams, section housekeepers, supervisors, and housepersons needed to clean the guestrooms and operate the laundry will be as follows:

25 section housekeepers needed to clean the rooms + 5 to operate laundry = 30 workers
30 workers × 7 days per week of operation = 210 man/days
210 man/days ÷ 5 days per week employees work = 42 workers needed

The minimum number of teams and workers needed to cover guestroom cleaning and laundry operation is now:

Number of teams: **8** (42 ÷ 5 = 8)

Number of section housekeepers: **42**

Number of supervisors: **8**

Number of housepersons: **8**

The distribution of teams on any given day that the hotel is full will be:

Teams assigned to guestroom cleaning: **5**
(400 ÷ 16 = 25; 25 ÷ 5 = 5)

One team to operate laundry: 1

Two teams off duty: 2

Total teams   8

This example property will need eight teams to operate efficiently.

 ## STAFFING MATRIX

The internal organization of the housekeeping department follows the same pattern as that of the property as a whole. The chain of command begins with the executive housekeeper and goes on to encompass all employees in the department. Figure 3.3 is a typical organization chart for the housekeeping department of a large hotel. Besides the section housekeepers, supervisors, and housepersons needed to clean the guestrooms, and the laundry room workers, the housekeeping department needs additional personnel to service other areas of the property, such as offices, public and back-of-the-house sections, and linen room. The employees in the department's work force can be classified into **management, fixed, evening, laundry, and guestroom cleaning teams**. The executive housekeeper, housekeeping manager (assistant to the executive housekeeper), and laundry manager fall under management. These employees are salaried and are required to work a minimum of 40 hours each week. The housekeeping fixed employees are the janitors and the linen room attendants. These workers are usually hourly employees who are guaranteed 5 days' work regardless of guestroom occupancy. The reason for guaranteeing fixed work is that whether or not the guestrooms have been sold out, lobbies, offices and other

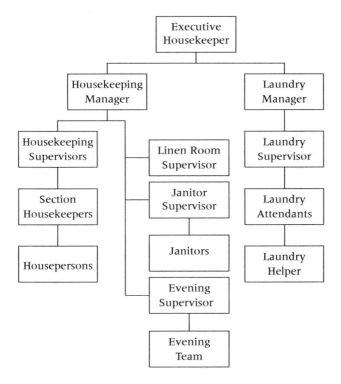

FIGURE 3.3　Sample Organizational Chart for the Housekeeping Department

front and back-of-the-house public areas must be serviced on a daily basis. The evening team takes over the duties of the department at the end of the morning shift when all regular teams clock off. The jobs generally assigned to the evening shift are cleaning late check-out and day-rate guestrooms, providing turndown service, counting soiled linen, servicing public and back-of-the-house areas, preparing carts for the morning shift, washing guestroom glasses, and filling out guest requests as the evening progresses. As with the janitors, the evening team is composed of hourly employees who are guaranteed 5 days of work regardless of occupancy. The guestroom cleaning and laundry teams are also composed of hourly employees, but the number of hours they are scheduled to work depends on the number of guestrooms sold daily. For instance, if the hotel is full all section housekeepers who are not off duty that day will be needed to clean all guestrooms, but if the occupancy drops to 80 percent, only enough section housekeepers to clean 80 percent of the guestrooms will be called to work. Figure 3.4 is a sample staffing matrix for a hotel with on-premise laundry that needs five regular teams to clean guestrooms, one laundry team, and two relief teams to cover days off.

KEY TERMS

deep cleaning	laundry team
evening team	management team
fixed team	on-premise laundry
guestroom cleaning team	section housekeeper
housekeeping teams	standard operating procedures
houseperson	team supervisor

DISCUSSION AND REVIEW QUESTIONS

1. What areas are generally assigned to the housekeeping department for daily upkeep in large lodging properties?
2. Why should executive housekeepers avoid the responsibility of having to clean food and beverage and engineering areas?
3. Which department should be in charge of cleaning the public restrooms in the lobby? The parking lot?

Management

1   Executive housekeeper
1   Housekeeping manager
1   Laundry manager

Fixed

1   Linen room supervisor
1   Janitor supervisor
4   Janitors

Evening Team

1   Evening supervisor
2   Section housekeepers
2   Janitors
1   Houseperson

Regular Team One

1   Housekeeping team supervisor
5   Section housekeepers
1   Houseperson

Regular Team Two

1   Housekeeping team supervisor
5   Section housekeepers
1   Houseperson

Regular Team Three

1   Housekeeping team supervisor
5   Section housekeepers
1   Houseperson

Regular Team Four

1   Housekeeping team supervisor
5   Section housekeepers
1   Houseperson

Regular Team Five

1   Housekeeping team supervisor
5   Section housekeepers
1   Houseperson

Laundry Team

1   Laundry supervisor
5   Laundry attendants
1   Laundry helper

Relief Team One

1   Housekeeping supervisor
5   Section housekeepers
1   Houseperson

Relief Team Two

1   Housekeeping supervisor
5   Section housekeepers
1   Houseperson

This staffing matrix covers all housekeeping positions for a lodging property with on-premise laundry that needs five regular teams, a laundry team, and two relief teams to operate. The property would also need a fixed team to service public areas, back of the house and offices, and an evening team.

FIGURE 3.4   Sample Staffing Matrix for the Housekeeping Department of a Large Property

4. What is the purpose of area cleaning inventories?
5. Why should cleaning frequency schedules be established for all areas?
6. What are cleaning performance standards?
7. Why is the formation of cleaning teams recommended in large housekeeping operations?
8. In a 450-room property with a workload criterion of 16 guestrooms to be cleaned by one section housekeeper per shift,

how many section housekeepers are needed when the property is 75 percent full?

9. In the same 450-room property, how many section housekeepers are needed when the hotel is at 100 percent occupancy?

10. Describe the fixed team as explained in this chapter.

11. In a lodging property with teams in the housekeeping department, why are relief teams needed?

12. Why are all janitors who are not off duty generally scheduled to work regardless of the property's occupancy?

 MINICASES

Situation 1

After graduating from a hotel and restaurant management school, Tim O'Regan is hired by a leading national lodging company. Tim is sent to a large, four-diamond property in the Southwest as executive housekeeper. Upon arrival he soon finds out that the areas of responsibility of the housekeeping department are different from those recommended by his professor in his housekeeping management class. O'Regan lists the distribution of cleaning and maintenance area responsibilities of the housekeeping department as follows: guestrooms, grounds, tennis courts, offices, ballrooms, public areas, linen and laundry rooms, and employee areas. If you were Tim O'Regan, how would you propose to upper management to redistribute the property's areas?

Situation 2

A 650-room resort in southern California has been operating the housekeeping department by assigning section housekeepers to clean the guestrooms at random. The department's supervisors would select different room attendants in the morning, assigning them to different floors every day. As a result, the section housekeepers did not take ownership of the rooms they cleaned, and morale as a whole was low. As the new assistant to the executive housekeeper, you are asked to organize the guestroom cleaning function by forming housekeeping teams. What steps would you follow to divide the 650 guestrooms into sections and teams?

Situation 3

How many teams (including relief) of six section housekeepers each would you need to form in the housekeeping department of a 576-room hotel if:

- **(a)** each section housekeeper cleans 16 guestrooms.
- **(b)** the hotel has an on-premise laundry that takes one team to operate.
- **(c)** the hotel is open 7 days a week.
- **(d)** the employees work 40 hours per week maximum.
- **(e)** you need to have enough teams to cover days off.

CHAPTER

4

Housekeeping Staffing Patterns

The Westin St. Francis, San Francisco, California. Courtesy of Westin Hotels & Resorts.

CHAPTER OBJECTIVES

- ▶ Discuss the importance of scheduling workers in the housekeeping department.
- ▶ Describe the process of setting up a Housekeeping Need Table.
- ▶ Explain how to define criteria for workloads.
- ▶ Explain how to set up Standing Schedules for the different housekeeping teams.
- ▶ Describe how the number of workers is adjusted daily based on occupancy.
- ▶ Discuss alternative methods of scheduling employees in the housekeeping department.

 ## OVERVIEW

The housekeeping department must prepare the rooms for incoming guests as soon as possible. Although guests are expected to check out around noon and to check in after 2 P.M., this is not always the case. It is not uncommon for convention and resort properties to have most of the guestrooms in the house depart at midday and receive a large number of guests right at the same time. When one considers that the rooms must be thoroughly cleaned and inspected in such a short period of time, it is clear that the scheduling of employees in lodging properties can be very difficult indeed. Because labor is the largest housekeeping expense, the executive house-keeper must be sure not to overschedule the department's work force, for calling too many employees to work results in decreased departmental profit. On the other hand, not having enough section housekeepers to quickly turn over ready rooms to the front desk will result in incoming guests having to wait in the lobby until enough rooms are available for check-in. Thus, understaffing the department to save on labor expense may also cause guest dissatisfaction and an eventual loss of business.

When scheduling workers, the executive housekeeper must combine the need to provide adequate coverage to clean the guest-rooms effectively with ensuring fairness to employees and achieving an adequate departmental profit.

 ## SECTION HOUSEKEEPER NEED TABLE

Scheduling employees for guestroom cleaning and laundry operation is done taking into account the property's daily occupancy. If the establishment is full today and at three-fourths capacity tomorrow, all guestroom cleaning and laundry personnel will be scheduled to work tomorrow but only 75 percent of the workers should be asked to work the day after. For example, a 400-room property that has 16 of its rooms cleaned by one section housekeeper in one 8-hour shift will schedule the room attendants on a particular week as follows:

Day of the Week	% Occupancy	Rooms to be Cleaned	Section Housekeepers
Monday	80	?	?
Tuesday	100	320 (400 × .80)	20 (320 ÷ 16)
Wednesday	75	400 (400 × 1.0)	25 (400 ÷ 16)
Thursday	90	300 (400 × .75)	19 (300 ÷ 16)
Friday	40	360 (400 × .90)	23 (360 ÷ 16)
Saturday	40	160 (400 × .40)	10 (160 ÷ 16)
Sunday	90	160 (400 × .40)	10 (160 ÷ 16)
Monday	?	360 (400 × .90)	23 (360 ÷ 16)

Criteria for Workloads

The number of rooms to be cleaned by each section housekeeper in an 8-hour shift varies from property to property, depending on factors such as the size of the rooms, number of breaks permitted per shift, the time allowed for lunch, the average number of people occupying one room, and the standard of cleanliness to be achieved. The **section housekeeper workload** may range from 12 guestrooms in suite hotels to 20 in budget motels. In this last case, allowing one hour for lunch and breaks, a section housekeeper must clean rooms at a rate of one for each 21 minutes ($21 \times 20 = 420; 420 \div 60 = 7$ hours).

Executive housekeepers should compile a **section housekeeper need table** establishing the number of room attendants required for each level of occupancy. The table can also be extended to include the number of hours that section housekeepers generate per day, per week, and per month. This information may be valuable to anticipate the **cost of labor** in any specific period of time. The cost of labor can be determined by multiplying the number of hours by the average hourly wage paid to section housekeepers. The accounting office provides the **average hourly wage** to the housekeeping department on a regular basis. Table 4.1 shows the number of room attendants needed per day at different levels of occupancy considering a workload of 16 rooms per section housekeeper in one 8-hour shift. The table also provides the hours of work generated per day, per week, and per month. As an example, let us consider an 80 percent level of occupancy. In this case, the number of rooms to be cleaned is 320 ($400 \times .80$); the number of section housekeepers needed to clean the rooms is 20 ($320 \div 16$); the number of hours worked for the day is 160 (20×8). If the same occupancy were considered for one week, the hours generated would be 1,120 (160×7); if the occupancy were 80 percent for one month, the hours would be 33,600 ($1,120 \times 30$). An estimated cost for section housekeepers can be anticipated by multiplying the forecasted hours by the average dollars per hour paid to these employees. For instance, if the average hourly wage paid to section housekeepers in this example was $5.95, the cost to clean guestrooms at 80 percent occupancy would be $952 per day ($160 \times 5.95$), $6,664 per week ($1,120 \times 5.95$), and $199,920 per month ($33,600 \times 5.95$).

TABLE 4.1   Sample Section Housekeeper Needs[a]

Percent of Occupancy	Rooms to Be Cleaned	Section Housekeepers Needed Day	Hours/ Day	Hours/ Week	Hours/ Month
100 (400 × 1.0)	400 (÷ 16)	25 (× 8)	200 (× 7)	1,400 (× 30)	42,000
95 (400 × .95)	380 (÷ 16)	24 (× 8)	192 (× 7)	1,344 (× 30)	40,320
90 (400 × .90)	360 (÷ 16)	20 (× 8)	160 (× 7)	1,120 (× 30)	33,600
85 (400 × .85)	340 (÷ 16)	21 (× 8)	168 (× 7)	1,176 (× 30)	35,280
80 (400 × .80)	320 (÷ 16)	20 (× 8)	160 (× 7)	1,120 (× 30)	33,600
75 (400 × .75)	300 (÷ 16)	19 (× 8)	152 (× 7)	1,064 (× 30)	31,920
70 (400 × .70)	280 (÷ 16)	18 (× 8)	144 (× 7)	1,008 (× 30)	30,240
65 (400 × .65)	260 (÷ 16)	16 (× 8)	128 (× 7)	896 (× 30)	26,880
60 (400 × .60)	240 (÷ 16)	15 (× 8)	120 (× 7)	840 (× 30)	25,200
55 (400 × .55)	220 (÷ 16)	14 (× 8)	112 (× 7)	784 (× 30)	23,520
50 (400 × .50)	200 (÷ 16)	13 (× 8)	104 (× 7)	728 (× 30)	21,840
45 (400 × .45)	180 (÷ 16)	11 (× 8)	88 (× 7)	616 (× 30)	18,480
40 (400 × .40)	160 (÷ 16)	10 (× 8)	80 (× 7)	560 (× 30)	16,800
35 (400 × .35)	140 (÷ 16)	9 (× 8)	72 (× 7)	504 (× 30)	15,120
30 (400 × .30)	120 (÷ 16)	8 (× 8)	64 (× 7)	448 (× 30)	13,440
25 (400 × .25)	100 (÷ 16)	6 (× 8)	48 (× 7)	336 (× 30)	10,080
20 (400 × .20)	80 (÷ 16)	5 (× 8)	40 (× 7)	280 (× 30)	8,400

[a]For a 400-room property with a workload criteria of 16 rooms cleaned by each room attendant in one 8-hour shift.

 ## STANDING SCHEDULES

The function of scheduling workers in the housekeeping department is of great importance. The manager must juggle several factors in order to protect the interests of the company, fulfill the individual needs of the workers, and provide guest satisfaction. To protect the company's interests, the manager must schedule the minimum number of workers to achieve an optimum labor cost percentage, because the more employees called to work, the greater the payroll cost will be. At the same time, employees have all types of individual requests; some of them may prefer to have weekends off, others may insist that they will not settle for less than rotating days off, others will need fixed days off every week to match those of their spouse. In any case, scheduling must always be done keeping in mind the ultimate goal of providing efficient service to the property's guests.

The first step in housekeeping scheduling is to prepare a matrix showing the scheduled consecutive days off for the **guestroom cleaning teams, laundry teams**, and **relief teams**. Figure 4.1 shows the scheduled days off for a 400-room hotel that needs a total of five regular teams for guestroom cleaning, one team to operate the laundry, and two relief teams. The relief teams cover the days off of the regular and laundry teams and have two consecutive days off themselves. In this sample case the largest occupancy occurs Monday through Thursday while the weakest days are Friday through Sunday (common in most business properties). If occupancy were consistently high seven days a week, a third relief team might be necessary to cover 5 additional days of work. In the example shown in Figure 4.1, Team One is off Saturday and Sunday and is covered by Relief Team One. Relief Team One also covers one of the days off of Team Three (Wednesday) and is off itself on Thursday and Friday.

After the standing team schedule is done, a similar matrix should be prepared for the two consecutive days off of the fixed and evening teams. Figure 4.2 shows a sample **standing schedule** for these teams. In this example, the days off of the Linen Room Supervisor and the Evening Team Supervisor are covered by the Housekeeping Manager (Assistant Executive Housekeeper). An alternative to this would be to hire a relief supervisor to cover these shifts.

 ## ADJUSTED DAILY SCHEDULE

The purpose of standing schedules, as described above, is to designate which days the working teams are off and which days they are scheduled to work. However, in most cases guestroom occupancy in the lodging industry is never constant. For this reason, whenever occupancies are below 100 percent, the number of section housekeepers must be adjusted down accordingly. For example, the sample team standing schedule described in Figure 4.2 indicates that on Mondays teams One, Three, Four, Relief One, and Relief Two are scheduled to work. If each team consists of five section housekeep-

TEAM	MONDAY	TUESDAY	WEDNESDAY	THURSDAY	FRIDAY	SATURDAY	SUNDAY
One	ON	ON	ON	ON	ON	OFF / R-1	OFF / R-1
Two	OFF / R-1	OFF / R-1	ON	ON	ON	ON	ON
Three	ON	ON	OFF / R-1	OFF / R-2	ON	ON	ON
Four	ON	ON	ON	ON	OFF / R-2	OFF	ON
Five	OFF / R-2	ON	ON	ON	ON	ON	OFF
Laundry	ON	ON	ON	ON	ON	OFF / R-2	OFF / R-2
Relief 1	ON	ON	ON	OFF	OFF	ON	ON
Relief 2	ON	OFF	OFF	ON	ON	ON	ON

The relief teams (R-1 and R-2) cover the days off of the regular and laundry teams.

FIGURE 4.1 Sample Team Standing Schedule

POSITION	MONDAY	TUESDAY	WEDNESDAY	THURSDAY	FRIDAY	SATURDAY	SUNDAY
Linen Room Supervisor	OFF / HM	OFF / HM	ON	ON	ON	ON	ON
Janitor Supervisor	ON	ON	ON	ON	ON	OFF	OFF
Janitor 1	ON	ON	OFF	OFF	ON	ON	ON
Janitor 2	OFF	OFF	ON	ON	ON	ON	ON
Janitor 3	ON	ON	ON	ON	OFF	OFF	ON
Janitor 4	OFF	ON	ON	ON	ON	ON	OFF
Evening Supervisor	ON	ON	ON	ON	OFF	OFF / HM	OFF / HM
Section Housekeeper 1	OFF	OFF	ON	ON	ON	ON	ON
Section Housekeeper 2	ON	ON	OFF	OFF	ON	ON	ON
Houseperson	ON	ON	ON	ON	ON	OFF	OFF
Evening Janitor 1	OFF	OFF	ON	ON	ON	ON	ON
Evening Janitor 2	ON	ON	ON	ON	ON	OFF	OFF

The housekeeping manager (HM) covers the days off of the linen room supervisor and the evening supervisor.

FIGURE 4.2 Sample Fixed and Evening Team Schedule

ers and each one cleans 16 rooms, the number of guestrooms that could be cleaned on Mondays is 400 (5 × 5 × 16). But what if the occupancy for Sunday night was just 80 percent? In this case the number of rooms that need to be cleaned Monday is only 320 (400 × .80) and the number of section housekeepers needed to do the job would be just 20 (320:16). The standing schedule must therefore be adjusted to reflect only the number of section housekeepers needed to clean the rooms occupied. Figure 4.3 is a sample **adjusted**

Date: _____ Monday, September 3 _____

Estimated Occupancy: _____ 80% _____

Rooms Occupied: _____ 320 _____

TEAM	HOUSEKEEPING NEEDED	SCHEDULED TO WORK	EXTRA DAY OFF
ONE	4	Erika Kate Melanie Jennifer	Maria
R-1	4	Onida Angela Atsuko Kellie	Lupita
THREE	4	Pat Dawn Amie Teri	Fernanda
FOUR	4	Deliah Ana Isabel June	Marjorie
R-2	4	Patty Mariann Romilly Kelly	Rachelle
LAUNDRY	4	Ramsey Meagan Char Sara	Bethany

FIGURE 4.3   Sample Adjusted Schedule

daily schedule showing the section housekeepers per team who are scheduled to work at 80 percent occupancy and those who are given an extra day off as there are not enough rooms to be cleaned by the entire crew. In this particular example, the adjusted schedule indicates that one section housekeeper of each team is given an extra day off on this particular day. The decision of who stays home when the occupancy is below 100 percent is generally made by the team supervisor by asking for volunteers among the team members or by following a sequential order. In Figure 4.3 Maria, Lupita, Fernanda, Marjorie and Rachelle of the guestroom cleaning teams, and Bethany of the laundry team, have either volunteered to have an extra day off or asked to stay out because it was their turn to do so.

The adjusted schedule includes the laundry team whose workers are also scheduled according to the property's occupancy. The standing schedule must be posted the day before, prior to the end of the morning shift so that the workers know whether they are scheduled to work the following day. The estimated occupancy for the day is obtained from the front office, which usually is able to provide an accurate forecast based on reservations on hand, weather conditions, events taking place in town, and historical data from the same day in previous years. On some occasions, however, upon opening the department early in the morning it may be found that the actual occupancy of the hotel differs substantially from the estimated forecast posted on the adjusted schedule the previous day. In this case, the opening supervisor should attempt to adjust the number of workers required to clean the number of rooms actually sold. This is usually done by calling the workers by phone. When the actual occupancy is above the forecasted estimate, the supervisor needs to ask those section housekeepers who were given a day off to come to work; when the actual occupancy is below the forecasted estimate, the supervisor needs to ask some of the scheduled section housekeepers to stay home. If, after all attempts are made, the number of workers is above the maximum needed, they can be assigned to extra work in the department; for instance, deep cleaning of rooms or public areas. If the number of workers is below the maximum needed, the supervisor can assign janitors, housepersons, laundry or linen room personnel to clean guestrooms. As a last resort, the department may have to incur overtime.

When the employees of lodging properties are unionized, daily scheduling must comply with the specifications of the contract in force. For instance, the contract may stipulate that workers are guaranteed 40-hour work weeks or that employees are not allowed to do any type of work other than that which they were hired to do.

Rotational Schedules

An alternative to standing schedules is rotating forward the teams' days off by one day each week. This means that if Team One was off Monday and Tuesday this week, next week the team will be off Tuesday and Wednesday. The only advantage of **rotational schedules** is to ensure that all teams will eventually have a weekend off. On the other hand, the disadvantages are substantial; workers will not be able to commit themselves to activities outside the workplace, they will not be able to secure stable babysitting help, or it will be impossible for them to have the same day off as their spouses. For example, a student who must attend classes on Tuesdays and Wednesdays will not appreciate having rotating days off at work. A working mother who relies on sending her child to a nursery Monday through Friday might not be able to find child care on weekends. A worker who needs Wednesday and Thursday off to match her husband's days off will not be willing to work these days.

Alternative Scheduling Methods

FOUR-DAY WORK WEEK

Some large lodging properties have adopted a **four-day work week** system consisting of 10-hour shifts each working day. This type of schedule enables housekeeping employees to have more leisure time, to reduce time and expenses commuting back and forth to work, and to decrease child care by one day per week. Companies can benefit too by decreasing employee meals and uniform cleaning costs. However, the system, raises the question of whether workers can endure 10-hour shifts without decreasing their normal productivity and quality of work. A section housekeeper who must clean 16 rooms in 8 hours (30 minutes per room on the average) would have to clean 20 rooms with the 10-hour shift system, which could affect the morale of the employees in the long run. Some properties have found that using the four-day work week system has not decreased guest satisfaction while showing positive responses from their staff and substantial payroll savings.

PART-TIME WORKERS

Lodging properties may resort to hiring employees who are willing to work less than 40 hours per week, such as semi-retired people or college students. In this case, the company will profit by reducing costs for items such as employee benefits and overtime. On the other hand, **part-time workers** are usually less reliable because their stake in the job is less substantial than that of full-time workers, which may create scheduling difficulties.

FLEXIBLE WORK HOURS

In smaller properties employees may be allowed to begin and end their shifts at times convenient to them. Needless to say, this system will appeal to workers and increase their morale. On the other hand, the coordination of tasks in the department can become a nightmare if the employees are allowed too much flexibility. The system of **flexible work hours** could be adopted in properties where the arrival and departure of guests is predictable, such as in small highway motels where most check-outs take place early in the morning and most check-ins occur late in the day.

JOB SHARING

The purpose of **job sharing** is to allow two or more employees to accomplish a job regardless of who does it at any particular time. Although this system may be quite appealing to workers, the loss of supervisory control is very obvious. Job sharing could be adopted in small properties when the employees are well known to the manager and have proven to be reliable.

GUESTROOM TEAM CLEANING

Some recent surveys of housekeepers have shown that pairing room attendants for guestroom cleaning may improve productivity and enhance morale. On the other hand, **guestroom team cleaning** may have the risk of collusion and lower productivity by having two largely unsupervised workers in each other's company. An advantage of team cleaning could be improved security, as having two housekeepers working together may deter assaults by other employees or guests. In cases where the two workers are a good complement to each other, team cleaning might achieve higher levels of productivity and increased levels of morale, while in instances where the personality of the team members is incompatible the results would be the opposite.

EXTENDED TIME OFF

Some properties experience intense occupancy fluctuations during the year. While all workers are needed during peak season, during off-season there might be only sufficient occupancy to require a skeleton crew. One way to solve this problem is to schedule workers on the basis of seniority, but this would necessarily result in losing those employees being laid off. A better arrangement is to have the staff agree on sharing the work. This can be done by asking all employees to work two weeks and take two weeks off during low season. When on layoff periods, employees are eligible to collect unemployment insurance in most cases.

KEY TERMS

adjusted daily schedule   laundry team
average hourly wage   part-time worker
cost of labor   relief teams
flexible work hours   rotational schedules
four-day work week   section housekeeper need table
guestroom cleaning teams   section housekeeper workload
guestroom team cleaning   standing schedule
job sharing

DISCUSSION AND REVIEW QUESTIONS

1. Explain why the scheduling of section housekeepers is based on the property's occupancy while the scheduling of janitors is not.
2. What factors determine the workload criteria for cleaning guestrooms?
3. If the workload criteria for cleaning rooms in a lodging property is set at 15 rooms per 8-hour shift and each section housekeeper is allowed one half hour for lunch and one 20-minute

break per shift, what would be the average number of minutes that each section housekeeper should take to clean one guest-room?

4. How can an executive housekeeper determine the cost of labor for section housekeepers in one particular week of work?
5. What are the advantages of adopting a system of permanent standing schedules versus a system of rotational schedules?
6. Considering standing schedules, what role do relief teams play?
7. Why must standing schedules be adjusted for occupancy on a daily basis?
8. If you were to adopt a four-day work week in the housekeeping department that you manage, what would your major operational concerns be?
9. One way to reduce labor cost is to hire part-time workers because they do not receive as many benefits as full-time employees are entitled to. Why then are executive housekeepers reluctant to hire large numbers of part-time workers?
10. What are the disadvantages of allowing housekeeping workers to use flexible hours in large lodging operations?
11. Describe an ideal situation in which you might decide to adopt job sharing in a housekeeping department that you manage.
12. Explain the advantages and disadvantages of adopting guest-room team cleaning in housekeeping operations.

 MINICASES

Situation 1

You have just been hired as Assistant Executive Housekeeper of the 600-room Cactus Resort in the Southwest. The section housekeeper workload per shift is 14 rooms and the average number of hours worked is 8 hours. Your immediate boss, Mr. Brown, has been asked by the General Manager to provide the cost of labor for the housekeeping department for the upcoming month of June. The occupancy percentage for the hotel has been estimated to be 88 percent. Mr. Brown entrusts you with the job of working out the cost for the section housekeepers needed to clean the guestrooms in June, informing you that the average section housekeeper hourly wage next month is $6.05 per hour worked. What would your response be?

Situation 2

On Wednesday, June 5, you are asked to prepare the adjusted daily schedule for Thursday, June 6 for the same property as in Situation 1. The forecast received from the front desk indicates that 519 rooms will be occupied Wednesday night. How many section housekeepers will you need to show up for work on Thursday morning to service the estimated occupied rooms?

Situation 3

As Executive Housekeeper of a casino hotel in Reno, Nevada, you have been notified by management that your department is to establish a four-day work week. The rationale behind this decision, according to your boss, is that the company will have increased labor and employee benefit savings; that the staff will have fewer personal expenses; that there will be a decrease in absenteeism; and that the department turnover will be reduced.

In spite of your company's enthusiasm, some questions will come to your mind. Specifically: Will my section housekeepers be able to clean 18 guestrooms per shift instead of the 14 rooms cleaned now in 8 hours? Will the quality of service be impacted? How many older employees would I lose with this new system? Will morale be damaged? Will productivity be decreased?

Armed with the potential advantages that the new method might bring, you decide to "sell" the idea to your staff. Prepare a memo to be included in everybody's paycheck explaining to your employees the new system and how you think they might benefit from it in the long run.

PART 3

Technical Skills
Management

Management of Inventory and Equipment

The Westin Osaka, Japan. Courtesy of Westin Hotel & Resorts.

CHAPTER OBJECTIVES

▶ Learn how housekeeping material is classified.
▶ Define the concepts of fixed and operating assets.
▶ Explain the difference between capital expenditure and operating budgets.
▶ Discuss the function of purchasing material in the housekeeping department.
▶ Explain how housekeeping inventories are conducted.
▶ Describe the purpose of conducting inventories.

 OVERVIEW

The amount of material used in the housekeeping department is considerable, ranging from guestroom furniture and accessories to departmental equipment and supplies. An important function of executive housekeepers is to classify all items into categories and subcategories as a first step to control cost, procurement, and usage. Costs are controlled by using budgets, which are yearly plans of operation used for the allocation of resources that itemize estimates of expense and income. This chapter includes a format for house-keeping budgets.

This section also explains the importance of the purchasing function in housekeeping, how to ascertain the value of goods, and how to assign purchasing specifications to products. The control of inventories, involving buying, receiving, storing, issuing, and cost accountability is also discussed.

 ## CLASSIFICATION OF MATERIAL

The administration of housekeeping material is an important component of the overall responsibilities assigned to executive house-keepers. This administrative function refers to the adequate selection and purchasing of supplies and equipment, their proper use, and suitable control of the amount of money invested while ensuring the existence of a sufficient amount of goods to supply the needs of the property. The classification of material is a prerequisite to the process of controlling the large number of items used in the house-keeping department.

Housekeeping material is divided into two major categories: **fixed assets** and **operating assets**. Fixed assets comprise house-keeping items that have a long-term life span, generally over one year. Fixed assets usually cost over $100 and are depreciated at the end of the fiscal year. Depreciation means that the company reduces the value of assets during the period of the assets' estimated useful life. For tax purposes, depreciation is a tax allowance that can be set aside by the company year after year for replacing the items once they can no longer be used. Table 5.1 lists material that is commonly categorized under fixed assets in housekeeping operations. Fixed assets are subcategorized into **F.F.&E.** (furniture, fixtures, and equipment), **software**, and **department equipment**. Items that have a 5- to 7-year life span are categorized under F.F.&E., such as beds, chairs, paintings, mattresses, and television sets that are used in guestrooms, public areas, and staff areas. Software items comprise guestroom fixtures of a textile nature that are not bed linens or bath linens, such as curtains, bedspreads, pillows, and blankets. The life span of software items is usually 3 to 5 years. Heavier, mobile equipment used in the housekeeping department for cleaning or transportation purposes is generally classified under department

TABLE 5.1   Sample Classification of Housekeeping Fixed Assets

F.F.&E. *(Guestroom, Public and Staff Areas)*	Software *(Guestroom)*	Department Equipment *(Housekeeping Department)*
Furniture	Accent curtains	Glass washers
Armoires	Blackout curtains	Hampers
Boxsprings	Bedspreads	Laundry equipment
Beds	Blankets	Maids' carts
Chairs	Comforters	Rotary floor scrubbers
Chests of drawers	Pillows	Pile lifters
Couches	Sheers	Sewing machines
Desks		Shampooers
Dressers		Vacuum cleaners
Employee lockers		Wheelchairs
Hutches		
Nightstands		
Sofa beds		
Tables		
Fixtures		
Accessories		
Ceramic ornaments		
Lamps		
Lighting fittings		
Mirrors		
Paintings		
Equipment		
Clock radios		
In-room safes		
Minibars		
Telephone sets		
Television sets		

equipment. The life span of these items is between 3 and 7 years. Included under this subcategory are items such as vacuum cleaners, shampoo machines, glass washers, and so on.

Operating assets include items under the control of the executive housekeeper that are generally used in the day-to-day operations of the department. They are considered cost items whose money outlay is charged to operating expenses. An important characteristic of operating assets is that it must to be regularly inventoried. Operating assets are usually categorized into **cleaning supplies, linens, uniforms,** and **guest supplies**. The category of cleaning supplies includes every one of the items used for cleaning purposes, for example, cleaning solutions, disinfectants, polishers, brooms, mops, and rags. The classification of linens encompasses the subcategories of **bed linen** and **bathroom linen**. The subcategory of bed linen includes sheets and pillowcases and that of bathroom linen comprises towels, washcloths, bath mats, and washable shower curtains. The category of uniforms is self-explanatory, including apparel used in the housekeeping department by supervisors, section housekeepers, housepersons, laundry, and linen room personnel. Operating assets items used by guests are listed under guest supplies. This category is usually subdivided into two classifications: **non-reusable** and **reusable items**. Non-reusable guest supplies include soaps, pens, paper items, mints, etc. Items that can be used again, such as ashtrays, clothes hangers, and wastebaskets fall under the reusable subdivision. Table 5.2 is a sample list of items generally classified as operating assets.

The executive housekeeper is ultimately responsible for the control of assets in the housekeeping department. The control of expenses of fixed and operating assets is achieved by maintaining budgets, sound purchasing procedures, and inventories.

 ## CAPITAL EXPENDITURE AND OPERATING BUDGETS

Every lodging property is allocated with the necessary fixed and operating assets prior to its opening to the public. The costs of the initial allocation of material are itemized on a **pre-opening budget** that includes all inventory requirements to open the property and commence operations. Once operations begin, budgets for fixed and operating material items necessary for operating the property during the next twelve months must be prepared. The budget used to record the fixed assets needed for the upcoming fiscal year is called the **capital expenditure budget**. This budget is relatively easy to compile; it consists of a list of the number of fixed assets (F.F.&E., software, and department equipment) required by the housekeeping department, their individual prices, and the sum total for all items listed. Table 5.3 is a sample capital expenditure budget for a lodging property.

TABLE 5.2   Sample Classification of Housekeeping Operating Assets

Cleaning Supplies	Guest Supplies	Linens	Uniforms
All-purpose cleaner	*Non-Reusable*	*Bed*	All housekeeping
Bowl cleaner	Bath soap	Pillowcases	department personnel
Brooms	Candy mints	Sheets	
Buckets	Coffee/Tea		
Cleaning rags	Facial tissue	*Bathroom*	
Disinfectants	Hand soap	Bath mats	
Furniture polish	Laundry bags	Bath towels	
Germicidals	Matches	Hand towels	
Laundry chemicals	Notepads	Shower textile	
Metal polishers	Pens	curtains	
Mops	Postcards	Washcloths	
Rubber globes	Sanibags		
Scrubbing pads	Stationery		
Spray bottles	Toilet seat bands		
Window cleaners	Toilet tissue		
Wringers			
	Reusable		
	Ashtrays		
	Bibles		
	Coat hangers		
	Do-not-disturb signs		
	Glasses		
	Ice buckets		
	Loan items		
	Shower rubber mats		
	Shower plastic curtains		
	Trays		
	Waste baskets		
	Water pitchers		

Operating budgets are also prepared annually for the property's fiscal year operation. In large properties, the housekeeping operating budget is part of the **rooms division operating budget,** which includes both the front desk and the housekeeping departments. Unlike capital expenditure budgets, operating budgets have a direct relationship to the day-to-day revenue resulting from the sale of guestrooms. The rationale behind this approach is to limit operating costs to a predetermined percentage of the generated

TABLE 5.3   Sample Yearly Capital Expenditure Budget**

15 armchairs at $405 each[a]	$6,075
1 oak bookcase[b]	790
25 extra firm, queen-size mattresses at $380 each[c]	9,500
10 metal employee lockers at $325 each[d]	3,250
1 wet vacuum[e]	490
400 guestroom coffee makers at $33 each[f]	13,200
Total	$33,305

**Description and specifications of all items is enclosed.
[a]Addition of one armchair to all suite rooms.
[b]Bookcase to be installed in lobby.
[c]Replacement of mattresses in third-floor queen rooms.
[d]Addition of 10 lockers in employee locker room.
[e]Needed by laundry room.
[f]Addition of one coffee maker to all guestrooms.

revenue. For example, assuming that the housekeeping department is expected to expend 1.2 percent of sales on guest supplies, if the daily room revenue is, say, $20,000, the cost of guest supplies should be $240 (20,000 × 1.2%). If the revenue is $18,000, the cost should be $216 (18,000 × 1.2%), and so on. The cost percentage assigned to each operating budget expense category is based on the cost history of the property, the quality of the products used, and the pay scale and types of benefits that employees receive. The housekeeping categories used by the housekeeping department usually include: housekeeping **salaries and wages, payroll taxes and benefits**, and **other expenses**. Salaries and wages include those of the entire housekeeping department; payroll taxes and benefits include the operator's share of additional costs related to payroll; the category of other expenses encompasses any other cost incurred by the housekeeping department that is not payroll-related. Table 5.4 is a sample rooms division operating budget for one month for a large hotel where the items related to housekeeping have been listed in bold. Under Other Expenses, the cost of outside services, telephone, postage, printing and stationery supplies, uniforms, and incentive plan, is usually shared by the housekeeping and front office departments.

TABLE 5.4   Sample Rooms Division Operating Budget

Rooms Division Department
Month of March 1999

	$	%
Revenue		
Total rooms sales	544,509	100.5
Allowances and rebates	2,709-	.5-
Net room sales	541,800	100.0
Salaries and wages		
Front Office	24,925	4.6
Housekeeping	43,890	8.1
Total salaries and wages	68,815	12.7
Payroll taxes and benefits		
Payroll taxes and employee relations	19,393	3.6
Employee meals	2,680	.5
Total payroll taxes and benefits	22,073	4.1
Total payroll and related	90,888	16.8
Other expenses		
Travel commissions	11,110	2.1
Outside services	160	
Cleaning supplies	1,085	.2
Linen replacements	3,795	.7
Guest supplies	6,550	1.2
Glassware	200	
Window washing		
Telephone	2,650	.5
Postage	50	
Printing and stationery supplies	1,625	.3
Uniforms	180	
Laundry supplies	1,630	.3
Incentive plan	1,600	.3
Shuttle van expense	3,026	.6
Total other expenses	33,661	6.2
Total expenses	124,549	23.0
Departmental profit	417,251	77.0

PURCHASING HOUSEKEEPING MATERIAL

The function of buying goods in lodging institutions is a highly specialized job. Buyers must be knowledgable about the items they purchase, be familiar with the market, and know how the materials are produced and marketed. The process of buying material for the housekeeping department involves finding the best sources of supply at the most satisfactory prices and obtaining the quality and quantity that the property requires. Although cost is always an important consideration, it should not take precedence over the quality of the product and the service of the company that sells it. Buyers should understand how to conduct **value analyses**. First, the performance of the products' components is evaluated by identifying their essential, desirable, useful, and unnecessary characteristics. Then the buyer must find the products with the most essential and desirable quality factors. The value function can be quantified by the ratio Q/P, where Q = quality and P = price. Although not always possible, the goal of the buyer should be to keep the value of products as high as possible by increasing Q while keeping P down.

The buying function in lodging chains is often centralized. Items like soap, linen, mattresses, pillows, furniture, and fixtures are procured by the company's purchasing department and shipped to the different units on request. Purchasing in large independent properties is done by the **purchasing agent**, who is a specialized buyer in charge of procuring products for all departments in the property. Smaller properties often allow the department heads to purchase goods for their respective areas of responsibility. In any case, it should be the job of the executive housekeeper to always pre-test and approve all items used in the housekeeping department and decide the quantities and the specifications of the products to be bought. It should not be the job of the purchasing agent, or any other person for that matter, to purchase material and supplies without the consent of the executive housekeeper. It is also important to solicit the input of janitors, section housekeepers, housepersons, and laundry personnel on the appropriate characteristics of the items that in the end are to be used by them.

All merchandise purchased should have precise specifications, which are descriptions of the products' quality and factors that should reflect precisely the performance needs for each particular institution. Specifications should be stated clearly, giving the information needed to assure proper identification. A specification should include:

1. the name of the product: *bed sheets.*
2. the amount to be purchased: *12 dozen.*
3. the grade or brand desired: *180 threads per square inch.*
4. container size: *3 dozen cartons.*
5. the unit on which prices are to be quoted: *dozen.*
6. the specific factors needed to obtain the exact item: *made in USA, sanforized, 50/50 blend, queen size, etc.*

Some specifications are generally the same for several properties. For example, a good detergent should be used in all laundry operations. Other specifications are different, depending on the type of property where they are to be used. For instance, a luxury resort does probably require the best bed linen money can buy, while a small, inexpensive motel may just need bed linen of fair quality.

Before buying a product, prices should be obtained from at least three different vendors. Figure 5.1 is a sample **shopping form**

Item: _____

	PRICE	**QUALITY**	**SERVICE**
VENDOR 1			
VENDOR 2			
VENDOR 3			

FIGURE 5.1   Sample Shopping Form

that can be used for every product before it is purchased. Product price and vendor dependability and service should be reviewed once or twice every three months. Purchasing decisions should be made based not only on price but on quality, suitability, and storage availability as well.

There may be three types of entities involved in the purchasing function: producers, middlemen, and consumers. Producers manufacture the items to be sold and sometimes sell the products directly to the consumers. Middlemen may bring the different commodities to their own warehouses from which they distribute them to consumers or act as order takers and have the goods shipped directly from the manufacturer. Middlemen always add a charge to the product's price. Usually, the fewer middlemen through which a product passes, the lower the price. However, although purchasing directly from the manufacturer may be less expensive, very often lodging properties benefit from buying through brokers (middlemen) because these can provide better service and in some cases employee training at no cost. Another disadvantage from buying directly from manufacturers is that they often require the purchase of large quantities of goods. In this case, the money saved because of lower price is upset by the cost of having assets tied down for long periods of time.

There is great competition among purveyors of cleaning and guest supplies. Some will lower their prices initially to obtain the property's account. Others may offer prizes or kickbacks to get their foot in the door. Executive housekeepers should be aware of these often unethical tactics and decline any "free" personal gifts.

If the executive housekeeper needs to order products directly from a manufacturer, filling out a formal purchase order may be necessary. The **purchase order** is, in essence, a sales contract stating the specifications of the product to be delivered and the conditions involving payment. When the merchandise has been previously bought by the property's buyer and stored in the main storeroom, the housekeeping department usually needs to fill out a **requisition form** before the products can be obtained.

Executive housekeepers should always be on the lookout for new items on the market. Testing for new, better, or less expensive products often leads to improving the department's bottom line. The salespersons who visit the property on a regular basis may be a reliable source of product information and often have considerable experience in solving most cleaning or laundry problems encountered during operations.

 ## INVENTORY CONTROL

The functions of purchasing, receiving, storing, issuing, and accounting for housekeeping material must be managed efficiently. The range of inventory used in the rooms division of lodging operations is quite large, varying from textiles, guestroom furnishings, and amenities to sophisticated department equipment and supplies.

The executive housekeeper must control the function of purchasing by defining clearly what is to be procured, who will be in charge of the buying, what specifications are to be considered, and what quantities will be needed. The person in charge of purchasing must consistently provide the needed quantities of products in housekeeping inventories. Although in some cases purchasing is done by the corporate office or by the property's purchasing agent, the executive housekeeper is ultimately responsible for the cost and results of what is purchased. For some products, linen for instance, **pars** need to be established; for others, for example soaps and paper products, **maximum and minimum quantities** are set up. Pars can be defined as the number of required on-hand items to perform housekeeping operations. In the case of linens, for instance, the optimum number of pars is 4. This means that ideally the property should have on hand one set of sheets and pillowcases set up in the guestroom beds at any given time, another set being laundered, an additional set ready to go in floor closets and room attendant carts, and one final set on reserve. For guest and cleaning supplies, the maximum quantity is the greatest number of units that should be in stock at any given time, while the minimum quantity refers to the fewest number of units. For example, the maximum and minimum number of cases of soap could be 35 and 25 respectively. That means that if at any given time the soap inventory is above 35, the product is overstocked. On the other hand, if the number of cases falls below 25, additional supplies must be ordered. This system eliminates the risk of overstocking or of running out of products.

The receiving function of goods ordered must also be controlled. Unless adequate inspection and receiving procedures are used, the best purchasing system may fail because it is at this point that determination must be made of whether or not the products meet the specifications and quantities of the order previously placed. Failing to inspect the merchandise adequately may result in higher costs, lower quality, theft, and fraud. On receiving a shipment, the goods should be compared with those listed on the receiving sheet or purchase order to verify the correctness of the delivery. If the goods meet the pre-arranged requirements, they are accepted by signing the invoice or delivery memo. If the products do not meet inspection requirements, they should be refused and a notation indicating the reasons for refusing the delivery made.

The function of storing merchandise must also be controlled adequately. Access to storerooms must be limited to authorized personnel only. The storeroom should be locked off-hours and a record should be kept of the person entering it and of the merchandise taken. Valuable items like towels and some guest supplies should be stored in an area that remains locked at all times. The storage area should be designed to hold the specific products stored in it; bottom shelving levels should be at least 10 inches off the floor to ensure adequate ventilation and to allow for cleaning underneath. A rotation system should be established by which oldest stock is placed in front and issued first.

In large properties, housekeeping items may be stored in the main storeroom. In this case, the housekeeping department will need to fill a requisition form to request products. Every requisition should bear the signature of a person designated by the executive housekeeper to sign it. Nothing should be requested without an approved signature. When products are stored in the housekeeping department, issuing controls must also be established so that the merchandise is handed out to authorized personnel only. Floor closet storage should also be locked at all times and access limited to the section housekeepers, housepersons, or supervisors in charge of the area.

To account for the cost of housekeeping operating assets used, physical inventories are conducted regularly, in most cases monthly. Linens, uniforms, and cleaning and guest supplies inventories are taken by counting all items on hand and listing them on a physical inventory form (Figure 5.2). Laundry chemicals may be included in the cleaning supplies category or counted separately for better control. The purpose of taking physical inventories is to find out what amount of items for each category is on hand and to work out its

Type of Product: *Laundry Chemicals*				Month: *March*
Product	**Unit**	**Amount in Storage**	**Market Price**	**Total**
Detergent	case	75	$ 90	$ 6,750
Neutralizer	case	31	65	2,015
Softener	case	35	55	1,925
Bleach	case	15	12	180
Starch	pail	5	126	630
				Total $11,500

FIGURE 5.2   Sample Physical Inventory Form

current market value. Once the value of items used is ascertained, the costs are expensed against the revenue produced for the same period and the percentages obtained compared to the amounts budgeted for the different categories. For example, let us assume that the projected percentage of laundry chemical supplies for the month of March 1999 had been set at 1.2 percent of room sales and that the cost of laundry chemicals used in that month, according to the physical inventory, was $6,960. If the guestroom revenue was $600,000, the control performance of the housekeeping department would have been good (600,000 × .012 = 7,200), the department having actually spent $240 less than projected (7,200 – 6,960 = 240). The cost of items used is determined by adding the total purchases during the month to the opening inventory and subtracting the merchandise on hand as per the physical inventory for every category. For instance, in the case of laundry chemicals:

beginning inventory on 3/1	$15,800
purchases for the month	2,900+
total	18,700
physical inventory on 3/31	11,740–
cost of inventory used in March	6,960

The property's controller will then divide the cost of inventory used ($6,960) by the rooms revenue ($600,000) to find out the percentage cost of laundry chemicals used during the month ($6,960 ÷ $600,000 = 0.012, or 1.2%). The controller will then compare the result to the percentage budgeted for the month to find out whether the expense has been controlled effectively by the housekeeping department, in this case below budget.

Physical inventories are difficult to conduct as all items that need to be accounted for must be counted one by one. In the case of linens, for instance, linens are found in guestrooms, laundry room, linen room, floor closets, room attendant carts, etc. Figure 5.3 is a sample linen inventory sheet that provides information about loss of items and total inventory value. The first section indicates the items on hand at the time of the last physical inventory, to which new purchases made during the month are added. The new total, minus the discarded items during the same month, indicates the items that should be on hand. The second section reflects the actual items on hand at the time of the physical inventory. The third section indicates the losses for the month and the current market price of the different items. The next step consists of finding out the value of the inventory on hand and the number of items of each category that need to be ordered to bring the inventory to the pre-established par.

To keep tight control on valuable items, for example imported chocolates for special guests, a **perpetual inventory** system may be implemented. A perpetual inventory is a form where items received and issued are recorded every time a transaction occurs. The form shows the quantity that should be on hand at all times. If the number of items on the balance does not correspond with the number of items on the shelf, the possibility of pilfering exists.

There are several software programs on the market that can be used to track inventory supplies and generate reports detailing con-sumption of supplies. Software packages can also provide order pat-terns, delivery schedules, and supply quantity levels by vendor.

 KEY TERMS

bathroom linen	linens
bed linen	maximum quantity
capital expenditure budget	minimum quantity
cleaning supplies	non-reusable items
department equipment	operating assets
F.F.&E.	operating budget
fixed assets	other expenses
guest supplies	par

Housekeeping Linen Inventory

Inventory Date: _____

Prepared By: _____

PREDICTED INVENTORY (should have)	WHITE SHEETS	PILLOWCASES	BATH TOWELS	HAND TOWELS	WASHCLOTHS	BATH MATS	POOL TOWELS	CREAM SHEETS	MATTRESS PADS
1. Last Inventory (Date)									
2. New Received									
3. Sub-total (1. + 2.)									
4. Discards									
5. Total (3.–4.)									
TODAY'S INVENTORY (have)									
6. In Guestrooms (1 par)									
7. In Laundry									
8. In Storage (Floor Closets)									
9. In Storage (Reserve)									
10. In Storage (Carts)									
11.									
12. Total on Hand (add 6. Through 11.)									
13. Losses (5.–12.)									
14. $ Value per Item									

FIGURE 5.3   Sample Inventory Form

KEY TERMS (continued)

payroll taxes and benefits
perpetual inventory
pre-opening budget
purchase order
purchasing agent
requisition form
reusable items

rooms division operating budget
salaries and wages
shopping form
software
uniforms
value analysis

DISCUSSION AND REVIEW QUESTIONS

1. Explain the difference between housekeeping fixed assets and operating assets.
2. Why are fixed assets depreciated while operating assets are not?
3. Which are the three categories into which fixed assets are generally subdivided?
4. Executive housekeepers need to request expenditure allocations each fiscal year to run the housekeeping department. What are the two budgets used to request those allocations?
5. What is the difference between non-reusable and reusable housekeeping items?
6. In which subcategory would you classify a case of hand soap? Would a case of hand soap fall under a fixed or an operating budget? Why?
7. In large lodging properties, which two departments are included in the rooms division operating budget?
8. Buyers of housekeeping equipment and supplies need to be aware of the equation $V = Q/P$. Explain what the equation represents.
9. In a 150-room lodging property with two queen-size beds in each room and two sheets per bed, how many sheets do you need to have in stock for a 4 par?
10. As executive housekeeper of a lodging property, how much should you spend on cleaning supplies in a fiscal year period if the projected yearly revenue is $6,150,000 and the expenditure percentage for this category had been set at 0.3 percent of the revenue?

11. What was the cost of the linen expenditure in May if the beginning inventory on May 1 was $13,000, the purchases for the month were $2,500, and the physical inventory taken on May 31 was $12,900?

12. Prepare a sketch of a perpetual inventory showing the following transactions and the inventory balance on May 31:

> May 1:   112 bottles of French perfume on hand
>
> May 7:   6 bottles issued
>
> May 13: 15 bottles issued
>
> May 18: one bottle was found broken (unusable)
>
> May 20: 1 case with 25 bottles purchased
>
> May 25: 20 bottles issued

 MINICASES

Situation 1

As a new housekeeping manager of a large lodging property, you are asked to classify the material in your department to facilitate inventory-taking and budgeting procedures. As a first step, you check out the storeroom, and find the following items:

> bedspreads, rubber gloves, mattresses, towels, bath mats, brooms, pillows, candy mints, one minibar, vacuum cleaners, houseperson coveralls, furniture polish, all purpose cleaner, washcloths, cleaning rags, one sewing machine, ashtrays, waste baskets, bed sheets, clock-radios, blankets, toilet tissue, facial tissue, television sets, ice buckets, pillowcases, stainless steel cleaner, various laundry chemicals, window cleaner, curtains, plastic shower curtains, two boxes of guest stationery, and three boxes of company letterheads.

Classify the above items into fixed assets or operating assets. Within these two categories, subcategorize the items into F.F.&E., software, department equipment, cleaning supplies, guest supplies, linens, or uniforms. Furthermore, classify the guest supplies found into reusable and non-reusable.

Situation 2

After taking a monthly physical inventory in a housekeeping department, it was found that the cost of merchandise used during the month was as follows:

Cleaning supplies	$4,050
Linen replacements	3,125
Guest supplies	5,900
Laundry supplies	1,975

The pre-established percentages of revenue for the four categories were: cleaning supplies 0.6%, linen replacements 0.7%, guest supplies 1.2%, and laundry supplies 0.3%. If the rooms revenue for the month was $580,000, by how many dollars were each of the categories under or over budget?

Situation 3

On May 31, you have been assigned to conduct the following tasks:

(a) Take a physical inventory of linens in the housekeeping department.
(b) Ascertain the losses of each linen category for the month.
(c) Prepare a list of items needed to bring the numbers up to par. The pre-established par for all items is 3.5.

One par consists of:

800	bed sheets
800	pillowcases
800	bath towels
1,600	hand towels
1,600	washcloths
400	bath mats
200	pool towels

The beginning inventory for all items at the beginning of May was:

2,700	bed sheets
2,850	pillowcases
2,550	bath towels
5,650	hand towels

5,490 washcloths
1,385 bath mats
  660 pool towels

No items were discarded in May. The physical inventory showed the following amounts:

2,700 bed sheets
2,825 pillowcases
2,390 bath towels
5,585 hand towels
5,310 washcloths
1,370 bath mats
  620 pool towels

Courtesy of La Quinta Inns, Inc.

Characteristics of Housekeeping Equipment and Supplies

CHAPTER OBJECTIVES

▶ Define the basic characteristics of housekeeping fixed assets.
▶ Emphasize the importance of maintaining interior design consistency throughout the property.
▶ Describe the cleaning supplies most commonly used in lodging properties.
▶ Discuss strategies to be followed in purchasing housekeeping chemicals.
▶ Explain how to handle and store chemicals.
▶ Learn about non-reusable and reusable guest supplies.
▶ Discuss issues regarding uniforms.

OVERVIEW

One of the responsibilities of the executive housekeeper is to administer and maintain all assets allocated to the rooms division of lodging properties. In order to accomplish this task, executive housekeepers must know the characteristics of all items under their control as well as their cleaning peculiarities.

It is also important for executive housekeepers to understand the purpose of cleaning chemicals and to be aware of the dangers that they pose to employees who have not been effectively trained to use them properly. Federal regulations must be adhered to when handling and storing housekeeping chemicals.

This chapter also deals with the topics of guest supplies and uniforms, explaining the main characteristics of bathroom and guestroom amenities, non-reusable items, and how to deal with employee uniform procedures.

HOUSEKEEPING F.F.&E., SOFTWARE AND DEPARTMENT EQUIPMENT

Executive housekeepers must administer and maintain their properties' fixed assets classified as Furniture, Fixtures and Equipment (F.F.&E.), Software, and Department Equipment. Although new establishments are usually handed over to the management team equipped with all items needed for operation, the executive housekeeper is directly involved in the replacement, refurbishing, and upkeep of most fixed asset items in the property. For this reason, executive housekeepers must have appropriate knowledge of the assets that are under their control.

Design

Regardless of their type of service, lodging properties must maintain interior design consistency standards throughout the building. Whether a property has been classified as economy, mid-market, or luxury, its guestroom and public area design, color patterns, fabric and upholstery quality, and overall appearance must befit the category they represent. Doing piecemeal refurbishing or renovating must always be avoided. Colors, for instance, must be **complementary**. In general, blue is a complement of orange, green of red, and yellow of violet. Using several light tints and shades of the same color makes rooms seem larger, while full-intensity hues tend to make the room seem compact. Adjoining walls should be painted the same color to provide a sense of continuity. When covering walls, smaller prints should be used in small rooms and in all cases, color patterns should be complementary in fabrics, wall coverings, and carpets. Earth tone colors which often used in **art deco** design, such as ocher, mauve, and burgundy, are quite popular in guestroom and lobby outlines. These soothing colors, when combined with terracotta vases, lamp bases, and statuettes, are often found in classic settings and are generally pleasing to most guests.

Surfaces look better and last longer when finished with durable materials like marble, granite, and corian. Public areas should be attractively decorated and furnished with special touches to please guests. For instance, lobbies may be fitted with fireplaces, bookcases, and live plants to make them seem more homey and inviting to travelers.

Furniture

Executive housekeepers are generally responsible for the refurbishing and upkeep of the furniture in guestroom, public, and employee areas. Furniture should be solidly built, easy to maintain, functional, and attractive. It is not advisable to purchase pieces of furniture directly from a catalogue; instead, the executive housekeeper should carefully examine samples to ensure that the products have been built to withstand repeated rough use. All furniture tops should be plastic-laminated or finished with water-repellent polyurethane to avoid scratches, rings, and stains caused by abusive treatment and spilled liquids. Desk chairs should have padded backs to provide comfort to guests and prevent wood from hitting desktops. Furniture dotted with glides or casters will prevent carpet damage when pushed or pulled around the room.

Luggage racks are better if built-in and fitted with wall-protecting panels, as there is a greater likelihood that the luggage will bump against and deteriorate walls when detached racks are used. Desks should be large enough to accommodate a desktop computer and a fax machine. TV/VCR units should be an actual piece of furniture, rather than simply a conventional metal stand, and should be fitted with 180-degree swivels so that guests can see the screen from anywhere in the room. **Case furniture** such as chests of drawers, credenzas, armoires, desks, and bureaus also should be purchased with durability in mind. Drawers should be equipped with nylon ball bearings and slide glides so that they don't jam when opening and closing. In general, guestrooms should provide a warm residential look; for instance, love seats and arm-chairs can replace the standard chairs so often found in hotel rooms.

UPHOLSTERY

Upholstery fibers may be natural, synthetic, or plastic. Natural fabrics, such as cotton, linen, silk, and wool, are rich looking and long wearing but expensive and delicate to maintain because they stain easily. Synthetic fibers are less expensive and easy to clean but they are less elegant and more likely to generate static electricity. Often, upholstered materials are a blend of natural and synthetic fabrics. The greatest advantage of upholstery plastic materials such as vinyl is that they can be easily cleaned by just wiping with a soapy cloth; however, they generally have a duller appearance than natural or blended materials.

Upholstery fabrics should be strong enough to withstand repeated shampooing. Treating fabrics with soil-retardant sprays can decrease the need for dry-cleaning the material. It is also important that upholstery fabrics be treated with flame-retardant finishes.

Before putting upholstered furniture fabrics into use, they should be pretested to ascertain the best way to clean the pieces without causing shrinkage or discoloration. Some fabrics can be cleaned with solvent, others can be cleaned with water and detergent, and some only allow for vacuuming. In general, synthetic fabrics such as nylon and plastics such as vinyl are the most stain-resistant and easy-to-clean upholstery materials.

BEDS

Beds are the central attraction in guestrooms and often a big selling point for travelers when choosing a lodging property. When asked to pay an average of $70.00 per night per room, guests expect to receive a clean, well-maintained sleeping area and a comfortable bed.

In commercial operations, beds consist of a frame to support the springs and mattresses and unattached headboards. Bed frames usually consist of metal bars with legs attached to each corner or of a metal or wood platform. The main advantage of platform frames is that room attendants don't have to vacuum underneath the box frame, thus saving time when cleaning the room. Headboards are mounted on the wall and should match the general design of the room's furniture.

It is important to know the composition of the **bed structure** of each property in order to figure out the maximum number of people that the property can house. Knowing the different types of beds and how many guests can stay in the rooms will help executive housekeepers plan for bed and bathroom linen and supplies. Table 6.1 shows the different types of beds normally found in lodging properties.

Another type of sleeping equipment is the **mobile bed**. Families on vacation and traveling high school or college groups often require additional sleeping accommodations in guestrooms. The **rollaway**, or bed on wheels, consists of a folding frame with an attached bed spring body. The mattress in rollaways must be made of latex foam or have very light, flexible innersprings so that they too can fold with the frame. Because rollaways are unable to provide a comfortable surface to hold the weight of an adult person, they should be recommended only for children or young people to avoid legitimate complaints about the property's not providing adequate accommodation. **Cribs** are also essential to have in order to accommodate infants or young children. While cribs should be collapsible to save storage space, their extension mechanisms should be kept in good working order to prevent the crib from collapsing when being used.

Dual-purpose sleeping equipment is common in guestrooms. These pieces of furniture provide both seating space and extra sleeping capacity, eliminating the need to roll in a mobile bed on short notice. Sofas, couches, chair-beds, and in-wall beds are the most common dual-purpose pieces of furniture found in lodging properties. Sofas, couches and chair-beds convert into beds by removing the cushions and pulling out the folding frame and mattress or by dropping the back to the level of the seat. In-wall beds, also called **Murphy beds**, are concealed in the wall behind a panel,

TABLE 6.1 Sample Bed Structure in Lodging Properties

Type	Standard Size (inches)	Number of People per Bed
Single	38 × 74	One
Twin	42 × 76	One
Double	54 × 76	Two
Queen	60 × 80	Two
King	76 × 84	Two

giving the room the appearance of a studio or parlor rather than a bedroom. The wall is balanced in such a way that it can be swung open with a gentle pull on a handle.

BOX SPRINGS

The main purpose of bed box springs is to act as shock absorbers between the mattress and the bed frame itself. Box spring coils are more rigid than those of mattresses to provide a firm base for the mattress to rest on. Besides cushioning the mattress, box springs increase the height of beds, giving them a more elegant look.

MATTRESSES

Surveys of favorite guest amenities conducted regularly by hospitality magazines consistently show that guests put comfortable mattresses at the top of the list, second only to cleanliness. Most mattresses used in lodging operations are of the **innerspring** type; they have metal coils that support the weight of the sleepers while conforming to their body contours. The strength and number of coils determine the mattress firmness, which may range from medium to super firm. Heavy-gauge steel wire coils are best, allowing for weights to flex down a specific area without disturbing the space surrounding the pressure points. This allows for two persons of different weights to lie side by side and each get different levels of buoyancy. The firmness of the mattress is determined by the gauge of steel used, the number of turns of each coil, and the way the coils are attached to the mattress frame. Preferably, the springs should be encased in fabric pockets to provide independent coil action, rather than being attached to each other with wire or hooks. Good mattresses have sufficient padding to cushion the springs beneath and provide a smooth surface. The padding should be nonallergenic and comply with the government flame-spread regulation, which states that a lighted cigarette should not be able to ignite the insulation. The recommended way to purchase mattresses is to inspect a cutaway section to make sure that the padding is sufficiently dense, that the coils are of fine quality and closely spaced, and that the covering fabric is well attached to the main body.

Lodging properties may also use foam mattresses, especially for their rollaway beds. The synthetic material used in this type of mattress is usually latex foam or urethane. Although less expensive, rubber mattresses do not provide the adequate firmness expected by an adult guest, nor do they last nearly as long as those built with innersprings.

Water-filled mattresses (waterbeds) became quite popular with the public when they were first used in the 1960s, but they soon proved to be inconvenient with lodging operators because they often leaked and because the water had to be heated, which became costly. Although today's waterbeds are efficiently built with individually filled cells that do not need to be heated because of an insulating foam layer, there doesn't seem to be a great demand for them from lodging guests. Lodging properties, however, should have a few waterbeds to fulfill the request of interested travelers.

Fixtures

Guestrooms and lodging property lobbies are also furnished with accessories such as mirrors, decorations, pictures, and lights, to complement the furniture. The color and style of fixtures should be balanced with the overall room décor; a vermilion vase, for instance, will probably not match a surrounding of pale yellow hues. The amount, style, and quality of furnishings will dramatically affect the appearance of rooms. For instance, strategically placed mirrors can give small rooms an illusion of depth; serene motifs in paintings will provide a feeling of tranquillity; triple magnification makeup mirrors and wall-mounted hair dryers in bathrooms are a welcome amenity; a well-stocked mahogany bookcase in the lobby will provide a homey feeling to guests who enjoy reading.

CARPETS

Beautiful carpeting can enhance the appearance of lodging properties and make a lasting impression on guests. On the other hand, discolored, worn, or dirty carpets are usually sources of guest complaints. The first step in selecting the right carpet is to match its color, texture, and pattern with the design of the area where it is to be installed. Then, other factors need to be considered, such as determining the anticipated level of wear and tear caused by the intensity of traffic, the location of the carpet, and the budget allocated for it. When heavy traffic is expected, carpets should feature strong resistance to abrasion, as well as texture retention and anti-soiling and staining characteristics. The location of the carpet should determine specifications such as enhanced colorfastness, anti-microbial protection, resistance to snags, and resilience under rolling loads. Besides durability and stain resistance, carpets in lodging properties should be capable of withstanding repeated cleaning treatment.

Before purchasing carpet, be sure you fully understand the warranty coverage offered by the manufacturer or installer. Warranties for commercial carpets should include protection for wear and tear, colorfastness (fading from sunlight and atmospheric contaminants), tuft bind deterioration, static charges, backing strength, raveling of seams and edges, and any other manufacturing defects.

Carpets must be professionally installed in order to comply with the manufacturer's instructions. If carpeting is not installed properly, it will buckle and wear out fast. One important component of the installation process is to use a quality carpet cushion or pad that will prolong the life of the carpet. In general, denser, thicker pads yield better results than thinner, softer ones by holding their shapes longer and being more resistant to dirt and stains. In back-of-the-house areas that are subject to traffic of heavy carts and where an impression of luxury and coziness is not necessary, carpets may be glued directly to the floor.

Carpets should be dense to the point of not showing the backing when bending a piece with both hands with the pile facing up. In woven carpets the density of the pile is measured by the number of lengthwise yarns in a 27-inch width of carpet. In tufted carpets, the density (gauge) is measured by the number of tufts per widthwise inch expressed in fractions where the numerator of the fraction indicates the number of inches and the denominator the number of tufts. A gauge of 3/40, for instance, indicates that there should be 40 tufts in every 3 inches of carpet. Another way of ascertaining the quality of a carpet, all things being equal, is by its **face weight**, or its number of ounces of yarn per square yard. The greater the face weight, the better the quality.

Two types of fibers are used in carpet construction: natural and synthetic, each one having peculiar characteristics and a number of usage advantages and disadvantages. Wool is a soft-to-the-touch, durable, resilient but expensive natural fiber that has been used in carpet making for centuries. Because of its absorbent fibers, wool is susceptible to damage from strong chemicals and has poor abrasion resistance. Most fibers used in carpets today are made of **nylon**, which has a high crush resistance and therefore long life.

Nylon also has a high melting point, which prevents marks caused by objects dragged across the carpet. Nylon fibers can be treated with chemicals to effectively prevent their soiling and staining. Carpets made with a blend of wool and nylon offer an excellent combination of the best qualities inherent in these fabrics.

The best characteristic of **polypropylene (olefin)** is that it doesn't absorb moisture, thus resisting stains and eliminating the need for much of the otherwise required maintenance. Because of its resistance to sun fading, olefin is recommended for outdoor carpeting. In general, solid colors in all carpets, especially light colors, show more dirt, which requires frequent vacuuming.

Executive housekeepers should have sufficient knowledge of carpet construction to ensure that the right carpet is selected for each area in the property. There are three main elements in the composition of carpets: the **pile**, or face; the **backing**, or material to which the pile is secured; and the **padding**, or cushion on which the carpet rests. Most commercial carpets are **tufted**, that is, the yarn is threaded through the backing material to form loops. The backing material usually is woven **jute** or polypropylene with a layer of adhesive latex extended over the material to anchor the tufts. Knitted carpets are made by interlacing together the pile yarn and the backing. The process of embedding the pile fibers electrostatically into a layer of adhesive material applied to the backing is called **flocking**. Weaving is the old-fashioned way of making carpets using conventional looms. The yarns are interlaced together to form the pile and the backing. As with linen, the yarns woven lengthwise are called the **warp** and the yarns going across are the **wefts**. The process of making carpets by compacting the fibers and the backing by mechanically punching them together is called **needle punching**.

LIGHTING

Improper lighting in rooms may discourage guests from staying in a particular establishment. Guests, particularly business travelers, expect to find adequate lighting to be able to work over flat surfaces such as tables and desks, or to read in bed or sitting on a couch or armchair. Lights of adjustable intensity should be placed strategically so that guests can arrange their preferences to suit their needs; for example, subdued lighting for relaxation or bright lighting for working or entertaining friends. Having three-way lamps or lights activated by rheostats give guests the option to set the mood of the room to their liking. Floor lamps are not recommended in guest-rooms because they can be easily knocked over and they create tripping hazards. Desk lamps should have the on-off switches at the base to reduce the risk of guests burning their fingers on the light bulb or upsetting the shade's balance when reaching around to locate the switch. Lampshades should be made of plastic rather than paper or fabric for longer life. When choosing fluorescent lighting, warm rather than cool light-giving units should be installed to avoid harsh tones of light. Pink incandescent light bulbs provide tones that enhance the appearance of guests when they look at themselves in the mirror. One advantage of fluorescent lights is that they use less energy and last longer than regular bulbs. In all cases, sufficient wattage must be provided in lamps that guests will use for reading or working purposes.

Equipment

Long gone are the days when hoteliers could sell rooms equipped with a minimum of basic features. Today's business traveler is putting a new spin on the concept of guestroom equipment. Lodging chains that cater to corporate clientele offer in-room or satellite office support services including computers and fax and copy machines. Guestrooms are often equipped with multi-line tele-phones complete with voice mail and PC compatibility; some hotels even provide cellular phones and 24-hour access to translators and information in other languages. Office centers are fitted with high-tech office support equipment, such as computers with desktop publishing, video room, and drafting center. Most hotels today offer TV in-room movie channels, and several chains have added VCRs in the rooms, together with video tape movie vending machines located in the lobby that guests can operate with their credit cards.

Refrigerators and microwave ovens are quite common in suite hotels, and coffeemakers, together with selections of coffee and tea blends, are now available in the rooms of most properties. Wide-screen television sets and high-quality clock radios are a must in four- and five-diamond properties, as are in-room safes.

In-room strongboxes are seen as a last-ditch defense for the guests' personal belongings, including items as large as laptop computers. The locking systems of in-room safes range from ordinary keys to programmable pushbuttons, magnetic-lock devices, and the guest's credit card. Some microprocessor safes automatically lock for 30 minutes after four false attempts to open them. Besides being a great convenience for guests who don't want to line up for safety deposit boxes, in-room safes are effective against thieves and even employees who may use stolen keys to burglarize rooms. Valuables can be stored by guests themselves and remain secure during trips to the pool, jogging around the block, or going out to dinner. Some safes have built-in memory, which enables the front office personnel to read the date and time of the most recent safe openings and closings. This can provide convincing evidence in case of a loss claim against the property.

Some upscale lodging properties, particularly resorts and first class hotels, offer minibars in their guestrooms and suites. Stocked with beverages and snacks, minibars can be profitable because guests are often tempted to have a last drink before going to bed or first thing in the morning. Fully automated minibars can electronically sense when an item is removed, sending the corresponding charge to the guest's room account. Nonautomated units must rely on the honesty of the guest to notify the front desk just before checking out if goods have been consumed.

Software

Depreciable fixed assets that are not furniture or equipment, such as bedspreads, mattress covers, blankets, pillows, and window coverings may be categorized under the classification of software.

BEDSPREADS

As with mattresses, bedspreads should be purchased with the qualities of durability, comfort, maintenance, and fire safety in mind. Bedspreads are an important component in the décor of guestrooms and should complement the motif, color, and design of the room. Fabrics made of 100 percent polyester offer excellent resistance to fading, staining, shrinking, and wrinkling. Woven fabrics perform better than knitted ones, which can make pattern colors appear faded if the knit loosens. **Polycottons**, a blend of polyester cotton, are less expensive than fabrics made of 100 percent polyester, but their life span is shorter, they have fewer fire-retardant qualities, and they fade more easily. While the normal recycling life span of a good bedspread should be at least 5 years, polycotton bedspreads only last from 2 to 3 years.

Other factors to consider when specifying bedspreads are their fill and seaming. Fill is one of the key elements that determines the appearance of bedspreads. The number of ounces of fill per square yard should be 7 or more. Noncompressed fills are better than mechanically packed fills because of their ability to spring back to its original loft is greater.

Wide, seamless bedspreads are preferred to those constructed with seams because they don't come apart as easily. Bedspreads can be large enough to reach to the floor or just to cover the mattress. In this case a pleated cloth skirting called a **dust ruffle** may be placed between the mattress and the box spring to extend around the sides and foot of the bed. Washable bedspreads should be purchased with the guarantee that they will not shrink, fade, or wrinkle. Par levels for bedspreads should be one plus 10 percent to allow for washing and replacement.

BLANKETS

The purpose of blankets is to act as insulators. A heavy blanket does not necessarily keep the warmth of the body from escaping through it. On the other hand, a material (even if it is light) that is tightly woven will retain body heat. However, all blankets should be porous enough to allow any moisture buildup under them to escape to the surrounding air. Wool is a delicate natural fiber that is very warm but that requires extreme care when laundered. Cotton, on the other hand, washes easily but it is a poor insulator and shrinks up to 15 percent if not purchased preshrunk. Synthetic fibers such as **acrylics** and **polyester**, if properly constructed, are suitable to commercial operations. Acrylic fibers are warmer than polyester but not as strong.

Because guests may fall asleep while smoking in bed, blankets should be fire retardant. The size of the blanket should be large enough to cover the length and width of the mattress and have some additional inches for tucking. Blankets that are too short will wear out from constant tugging by the guests.

MATTRESS COVERS

All mattresses should be fitted with moisture-proof covers at all times to prevent staining. Vinyl plastic covers are impermeable and can be washed like any other fabric. Their use is recommended for cribs or small cots for young children and hospital beds. Felt pads made of moisture-proof, flame-retardant, 100 percent polyester resist shrinkage and are quite durable. Quilted all-cotton pads are very comfortable but have a tendency to shrink and pucker after a few washings.

PILLOWS

Comfortable pillows are a necessary complement to comfortable mattresses. It is advisable to provide two pillows per person for most guests like to prop them up high to watch television in bed. Most commercial pillows are filled with synthetic fiber, mainly polyester. Synthetic pillows are quite common in commercial properties because they are inexpensive, easy to launder, and nonallergenic. When purchasing pillows, it is important to make sure that the fill is of good quality so that it springs back into shape easily; lumpy, heavier fills are an indication of inferior grade. The synthetic covering of the pillow must be fire retardant and stain proof and able to withstand frequent washings.

Pillows with natural fills such as down and feathers are very expensive, particularly goose down. Lodging properties should stock a few natural-fill pillows to meet the occasional request for them. Because of the price, down and feather pillows should be provided to guests on a loan basis, that is, a record should be kept in the housekeeping department of the room number where the pillows were delivered and then should be recovered after the guest's check-out.

WALL COVERINGS

The first consideration for selecting wall coverings is that they match the general décor of the room; the second, and just as important, consideration is their durability and ease of maintenance. The two most common forms of wall coverings are paint and vinyl. The paint used to finish walls should be easy to wash with soapy water and of very good quality so that the surface doesn't require repainting after a short period of time. Vinyl wall coverings are available in several thicknesses to suit the area to be covered; for instance, walls covered with thin layers are vulnerable to bumps from baggage and carts and should be used only to cover no-traffic areas. Heavier vinyl can withstand heavy impacts and can be used over surfaces susceptible to abrasion. Although far more expensive than paint, vinyl wall coverings generally pay for themselves because they require very little maintenance. Vinyl coverings are made by laminating the material to cotton or polycotton backings and are glued to walls using an adhesive paste. To prevent mildew from loosening the vinyl from the adhesive, the glue should contain a mildew-cide. Fabric wall coverings can provide rooms and hallways with a luxurious, elegant look but they should be avoided in commercial operations because of the difficulty of cleaning or replacing them when soiled. Wallpaper should be used only if it is stain- and water-resistant and allows for damp cleaning with soap and sponge.

Service areas, busy hallways, and elevators where carts and dollies may gouge the walls should be protected with rubber or heavy vinyl cove base and wall guards. Corner salients should be reinforced with thick plastic corner guards.

WINDOW COVERINGS

Most windows in guestrooms are covered with curtains and sheers. Windows in offices, lobbies, and employee areas are usually fitted with vinyl blinds.

Because of their susceptibility to fading, fabrics used for curtains must be resistant to direct sunlight. As curtains attract dust and odors, they require frequent washings and dry cleaning; for this reason, it is advisable to purchase good-quality, vinyl-coated fabrics that can retain their shape and color for long periods of time. Curtains should be flame retardant to comply with local fire departments specifications.

Drapery can be simple or quite ornate. Valances, and shirred or pinch-pleated fabrics, can add elegance and warmth to rooms, although they will require more cleaning time to keep them dust free. In all cases, the curtain rods and cords must be sturdy to avoid damage; having batons instead of cords may reduce the chance of breakage.

Department Equipment

Besides F.F.&E. and software material, the housekeeping department needs major pieces of equipment to clean guest, public, and employee areas and to transport clean and soiled linen, trash, and supplies. In all cases, the department equipment used in house-keeping should be of heavy-duty quality, able to withstand rough and continuous use. Often, purveyors of chemical supplies also carry a complete line of equipment. In some cases, manufacturers have their own representatives who will describe the machines and demonstrate their performance.

Perhaps the most significant piece of housekeeping equipment is the housekeeping cart. Usually, one cart is assigned to the cleaner of each section of guestrooms (the section housekeeper) and one to each janitor. The cart should be large enough and have enough shelves to carry a full complement of supplies needed in each working shift in order to avoid unnecessary trips to the linen room for additional supplies. Although sturdy, the cart must be light and maneuverable enough to be pushed by one person from door to door and from floor to floor, including pushing it into and out of service elevators. The cart should be contoured with rubber bumpers to protect walls and wall corners and have casters with brakes of superior quality. Some carts can be purchased with side panels that can be locked in order to prevent linen and guest amenities from being exposed to whomever walks past them, thus eliminating theft. If fitted with laundry and trash bags, these should be made of heavy-duty material to withstand hard use. Plastic baskets or **caddies** containing guest amenities and cleaning supplies are generally placed on the top shelf of carts.

Vacuums

Several types of vacuum cleaners are used by housekeeping. One requirement common to all of them is that they be heavy-duty and powerful enough to provide efficient, one-pass cleaning. The typical vacuum cleaner used in guestroom carpet cleaning is upright, with one or two motors. The dual-motor type has one motor to drive the beater brush and another to provide the suction. Some useful characteristics of commercial vacuums are as follows: having collector cups or zipper receptacles instead of paper bags (some models can be messy and difficult to empty, in which case it is better to use disposable bags), long electric cable, wraparound bumpers, secondary filters to protect the vacuum motor, adjustable brush settings, three-position handles, and self-lubricating brushes. Some vacuums are incorporated into the housekeeping cart. This arrangement, however, may cause some difficulties. Because the hoses must be long enough to reach all corners of the room, suction power may be reduced. And since the vacuum must be operated in hallways, the noise permeates throughout the area. Also, because the machine is attached to the cart, repairs and maintenance are more difficult to perform on site than in the engineering shop.

Large-area vacuums are used in hallways and lobbies that contain extensive areas of carpeting. In very large ballrooms and meeting rooms, vacuums with 30-inch brushes should be used. These high-power machines can operate at 1,200 rpm and are able to service 14,000 square feet of surface per hour. **Wet/dry vacuums** are designed for wet pickup on any type of hard flooring surface. Equipped with a wide squeegee, they can be used to remove liquids when hard floors are stripped or for any kind of liquid absorption. **Back vacuums** worn by the housekeeper, are convenient for dusting and cleaning vertical or high surfaces and fixtures, especially curtains, drapes, and wall coverings. Back vacuums are light, quiet machines equipped with adjustable straps and hoses that can be expanded to three times their normal length.

FLOOR MACHINES

Floor machines are designed to mechanically polish, buff, strip, scrub, grind, sand, burnish, and shampoo surfaces. Usually one multipurpose machine can be used for several tasks by changing the pad as needed to accomplish the task at hand. **Burnishers** are used when the property has large areas of terrazzo or tile floor. These machines are capable of burnishing up to 30,000 square feet per hour. **Polishers** are heavily weighted machines used to grind, sand, and polish marble and other stone floors. **Scrubbers** are used to automatically scrub hard or resilient surfaces by applying a stripping solution and recovering the liquid as the machine is pushed along the surface. Large scrubbers feature 40-gallon stripping solution and recovery tanks, a 34-inch self-propelled scrubber, 37-inch squeegee assembly, and can service 44,000 square feet per hour. **Extractors** are used to clean carpets and rugs. The simplest and least expensive consists of a machine with two tanks—one that holds the cleaning solution and one that collects the suctioned liquid. A better version has a beater brush attached to the wand to deepen the penetration of the cleaning solution into the carpet fabric. **Self-contained extractors** are very convenient to operate as they don't require a wand or hoses. The best models have four-phase cleaning action (spray, scrub, rinse, and extract in one pass) with a spray power of 100 PSI. Self-contained carpet extractors are also available with dry foam instead of liquid solution.

Other Department Equipment

When large lodging properties use drinking glasses made of glass (rather than plastic), glass washers are necessary. The practice of washing housekeeping glasses in the kitchen's dishwashers is not an effective one as it is usually seen as an "encroachment" by the food and beverage department personnel. When operating a glass washer, the right type of detergent and the correct water temperature as determined by the local health department must be provided.

Rather than transporting trash, soiled linen, and supplies in plastic bags, lodging properties should use light trucks or **hoppers**. This is preferable to hauling material in bags carried over the shoulder, especially along public hallways.

 CLEANING SUPPLIES

Cleaning supplies are categorized under operating assets and are included in the property's operating budget. Cleaning supplies comprise the chemicals necessary to perform the myriad cleaning jobs throughout the property and the nonchemical utensils needed to apply, scrub, rub, cleanse, wipe, etc. the chemicals onto all types of surfaces. There are several hundred manufacturers of cleaning chemicals, each of which markets and sells countless products. The responsibility of selecting and using the right chemicals rests with the executive housekeeper.

Purchasing Supplies

In large properties, the purchasing function, including housekeeping products, is performed by the **purchasing agent**. However, it should be up to the executive housekeeper to determine what products to use in the department, and to inform the purchasing agent of the specifications and characteristics required for the supplies to be bought. Because marked differences exist among products, before choosing cleaning supplies they should be tested by the employees who will use them regularly. Janitors, housepersons, and section housekeepers must agree that the products chosen will be effective. An agreement should be made between the department and the vendor to train workers, at no cost, on how to use the cleaning supplies properly.

As with many other products, price should be only one of the factors regarding the purchasing decision, the others being availability, service, and quality. For instance, if a product is difficult to obtain, if the purveyor doesn't provide training and technical support, and if much larger quantities than a more expensive one have to be used, you might not obtain the expected value from it. Shopping for cleaning supplies must be done competitively; that is, trying to obtain the best price for the same or comparable product. When asking for a product quotation, the executive housekeeper must be very specific regarding its packaging, composition, and concentration. Figure 6.1 is a **competitive shopping form** on which the price, service, and other remarks are kept for cleaning supplies of similar quality from at least two different vendors. Product prices should be obtained once every two or three months. In practice, it is common to select one vendor for most cleaning supplies needs, while keeping abreast of new products and prices offered by competitors.

	UNIT	**VENDOR 1**	**VENDOR 2**	**REMARKS**
All-purpose cleaner	*gallon*			
Liquid degreaser	*gallon*			
Disinfectant spray	*6-ounce can*			
Deodorant spray	*8-ounce can*			

FIGURE 6.1   Sample Competitive Shopping Form

It is important to designate specific days and time to receive salespeople. Placing orders by phone can help save time, although direct contact with vendors is essential as they generally are specialists in their fields and therefore are able to suggest the solution to severe cleaning problems. Periodic shipments of supplies may be arranged for those products used in large quantities; however, in no case should vendors be allowed to place an order without the direct approval of the person in charge of purchasing.

Because the cleaning supplies market is quite competitive, it is common for vendors to offer free items and personal prizes to the person in charge of buying. It is only ethical to assume that any discount or give-away should benefit the property and not the buying individual. Accepting gifts or kickbacks should be prohibited, so for example if a vendor gives the purchasing agent tickets for an upcoming football game, the tickets should be rejected or, if accepted, raffled off among all employees.

Bulk purchasing of chemicals generally allows for great savings in price to the housekeeping department. There are, however, serious disadvantages with buying chemicals in large quantities. For instance, overbuying products may mean having to store them for long periods of time, tying up resources and space. Chemicals may also deteriorate while in storage and actually be more labor intensive. For example, decanting a liquid from a 55-gallon drum into smaller containers may take a considerable amount of time. Human error when mixing concentrates and water or causing spills may also be a considerable disadvantage. Although **pre-measured chemicals** are ready to be used as purchased, thus not requiring much handling, their higher cost is a disadvantage. The fact that they generate a lot of trash as they are used is also an inconvenience. In-house **chemical dispensers** or mixing stations can be a good alternative to both bulk and pre-measured products. The dispensers, plumbed to hot or cold water, can automatically mix bulk chemicals, eliminating human error and labor cost from the process.

Housekeeping Chemicals

The three major purposes of chemicals used in the housekeeping department are to remove dirt, to destroy harmful microorganisms, and to preserve and beautify furniture, fixtures, and surfaces. Chemical cleaners are manufactured to remove soils from surfaces through chemical action. The stronger the chemical is, the better effect it will have on getting the job done. The strength of cleaning chemicals is measured on the **pH scale**. pH is the symbol for the logarithm of the reciprocal of hydrogen ion concentration in gram atoms per liter. For example, a pH of 5 indicates a concentration of .00001 atoms of hydrogen ions in one liter of solution. The scale goes from 1 to 14, 1 indicating a very acidic solution, 14 a very alkaline solution, and 7 a neutral solution. Cleaning chemicals that have been enhanced with alkalis or acids to strengthen their cleaning powers can be dangerous to humans and often cannot be used on certain surfaces. A neutral cleaner can be used for all types of jobs but its cleaning power is limited.

The executive housekeeper should have adequate knowledge of the department's needs to select cleaning chemicals appropriate for each type of cleaning job to be performed regularly in the housekeeping department. Generally speaking, high-alkaline cleaners are effective degreasers while acidic cleaners are good for fighting lime and rust, which are always found in urinals and toilets. Another name for cleaners is **detergents**. Detergents act chemically to emulsify dirt, holding it in suspension so it can be removed away from the surface. Synthetic detergents are easy to rinse off and often have excellent cleaning, deodorizing, and germicidal characteristics. Most cleaning detergents are made from mineral oils. **All-purpose cleaners** have neutral pH-balanced formulas for general-purpose cleaning jobs. They usually are synthetic detergents, often vegetable oil based, of which pine oil is very popular because of its pleasant scent and strong deodorizing power. All-purpose cleaners may have corrosion inhibitors to protect metal surfaces. **Single-purpose cleaners** are heavy-duty cleaners used for specific cleaning jobs. Abrasive cleaners are cleaning powders or pastes combined with silica for tough cleaning jobs. These cleaners will scratch soft surfaces like fiberglass or porcelain. Gentler cleansers made with nonscratching calcite instead of silica greatly reduce their abrasive action. Degreasers are highly effective cleaners, often biodegradable, that remove grease, tar, ink, food deposits, smoke film, fats and other grimy soils. Degreasers can be highly effective on concrete floors. It is important to remember that some products advertised as degreasers may be toxic and therefore not suitable for use on kitchen surfaces.

Although most all-purpose cleaners can be used as deodorizers, stronger chemicals are needed to counteract stale odors. Deodorizers, or air fresheners, should neutralize odors without adding strong perfume scents in the space to be deodorized. Deodorizers can be purchased as mists, wall and urinal blocks, cup and wick, and aerosols. Glass cleaners are ammonia- and alcohol-based products that clean and provide a protective coating to glass surfaces. Glass treated with good-quality glass cleaners resist fogging caused by moisture and temperature changes and in some manner repel dust, dirt, fingerprints, and smudges. Most glass cleaners can also be used as multipurpose cleaners on chrome, stainless steel, enamel, formica, ceramic tile, and other washable surfaces. Metal cleaners are nonscratching products that remove rust, tarnish, corrosion, and grime from metal surfaces and fixtures. These products can be used on brass, stainless steel, copper, chrome, and aluminum materials. Metal cleaners can be purchased as liquids, aerosols, pastes, and cotton wadding.

Another purpose of housekeeping supplies is to beautify surfaces and fixtures. Furniture polishes are liquid waxes or oils or silicone-based sprays designed to protect and give shine to wood, leather, vinyl, metal, and plastic surfaces. When pigments are added to liquid furniture polish, the product helps cover nicks and scratches in wood furniture, paneling, and floors. Most metal surfaces can be dusted, cleaned, and polished with metal polishes. Strong liquid metal polishes can remove rust, corrosion, tarnish, and grime from brass, stainless steel, copper, chrome, and aluminum. Cream polishes are quite effective in cleaning sterling silver, silver-plated utensils, nickel, and pewter.

RESTROOM AND BATHROOM CLEANERS

Strong acidic cleaners are needed to clean away lime and rust deposits in restroom and bathroom fixtures. Bowl cleaners may contain hydrochloric or phosphoric acid to cut scale and calcium deposits with little or no scrubbing. Milder bowl cleaners are nonacid and nonabrasive, designed not to etch or pit porcelain fixtures, but their cleaning power is lower. Most toilet cleaners kill bacteria and viruses, including the HIV-1 virus, on contact. Janitors and section housekeepers should be trained well in how to handle these powerful products. Acidic bowl cleaners, for example, should not come in contact with metal attachments, stone, or tile surfaces. Public and employee urinals are usually deodorized and disinfected with paradichlorobenzene blocks that neutralize offensive odors.

Graffiti removers consist of a gel formula that effectively effaces ink, crayon, lipstick, some spray paints, magic marker, and bumper stickers from most hard surfaces. These powerful products should not be used, however, on rubber, vinyl, plastic, or painted surfaces.

Besides cleaning, housekeeping chemicals can be used to control and kill pathogenic bacteria by sanitizing and disinfecting surfaces and utensils. Disinfectants are germicidal chemicals that kill microorganisms and prevent them from multiplying. Often, germicides are combined with chlorinated liquid detergents to act both as germ killer and cleanser, making them effective against many forms of microorganisms, including salmonella, fungi, and a broad range of viruses. Aerosol disinfectants are generally much stronger as they are able to eliminate most bacteria and viruses such as herpes simplex, influenza, and HIV-1. Hand soaps are also important in fighting contagious diseases. Liquid soaps used by employees in back-of-the-house areas should be antimicrobial and capable of reducing nosocomial infections caused by the fungal organism *candida albicans*. Guest liquid soaps should be formulated with emollients to soften the skin, have a pleasant fragrance, and produce a rich lather.

FLOOR CARE CHEMICALS

Hard and resilient floor cleaners must be pH neutral, that is, mild enough to clean dirt from surfaces without affecting polymer finishes, sealers, and shines. Floor cleaners are water- or vegetable oil-based and can be applied to synthetic surfaces, marble, terrazzo, and other washable floors. Stronger solvent-based cleaners, capable of erasing heel marks, rubber burns, tar, and grease from concrete and hard wood surfaces are very effective but will affect the floor finish when applied. **Strippers** are chemicals used to remove and clean old floor finishes prior to rewaxing, resealing, or refinishing them. These products penetrate and emulsify worn wax buildup, polymer and acrylic finishes, and surface dirt deposits. After the floor has been stripped, the alkaline residue should be neutralized with a **neutralizer rinse** prior to applying a new finish. Floor **sealers** are used to protect porous surfaces such as concrete, terrazzo, wood, and marble from staining. Stronger sealers have a substantial amount of solids and are formulated to fill scratches and provide a base for floor finishes. Some sealers can coat and polish surfaces at the same time. Resilient floor finishes usually contain detergent-resistant acrylic polymers. Good products are burnishable and resistant to scuffing and black marks, acting both as sealers and finishes.

CARPET CHEMICALS

Carpet shampoo is marketed under many commercial brands, and its composition can be different as well. Some shampoos are water-based and are a blend of polymers, biodegradable surfactants, and solvents. Soil-retarding carpet shampoos provide a fluorochemical barrier to protect against dirt, dust, spills, and stains. Defoamers are silicone foam suppressors used to eliminate foam from the recovery system of steam cleaners. Anti-static sprays are designed to eliminate static electricity buildup on wool and synthetic carpets caused by foot traffic or low humidity. Spot removers are concentrated formulas used to pre-spray carpets before shampooing to remove tar, grease, lipstick, graffiti, and food or beverage stains.

Cleaning Accessories

The number of nonchemical cleaning supplies in the housekeeping inventory can be substantial, ranging from broom to wringer. Upright brooms are sold under several denominations, such as janitor, warehouse, household, lobby, porter, and whisk brooms. In all cases, upright brooms should be heavy duty and have wire bands to help retain their shape. Push brooms usually consist of a combination of horse hair and synthetic fibers. For durability, the broom block should be attached to the handle by a sturdy metal brace. Wet mops also come in a variety of forms: four-ply cotton-synthetic fiber blend mops have good absorption; mops with looped ends are more durable than cut-ended. Some brands feature mildew- and bacteria-resistant mops with scrubber headbands and double banding. Tight twisted, string-style eight-ply mops are specially designed for floor finishing applications. Mop buckets/wringers come in different shapes and forms as well. Dual bucket systems consist of two overlapping buckets mounted on a mobile platform with casters; one bucket holds the cleaning solution and the other carries the rinse water for better sanitation. Heavy-duty plastic buckets are preferable to zinc ones as they are quieter, have no corrosion, and will not dent.

HANDLING AND STORING CHEMICALS

Hazardous materials are dangerous as they can harm both workers and property. Knowing how to safely handle, mix, and store them can protect employees, guests, and the company from explosions, fires, environmental contamination, higher insurance premiums, and costly litigation. Besides being dangerous, chemicals are expensive and strict guidelines should be followed to hold employees accountable for their proper dilution and use.

Hazard Communication (HazComm)

In order to protect workers from unsafe working conditions, the Occupational Safety and Health Administration (OSHA) requires that employees handling chemicals are informed of the risks that these chemicals pose and that the employer provides appropriate training on how to use them safely. Failure to comply with OSHA's HazComm regulations may result in fines if inspections of the property indicate that the directions have not been followed. HazComm requires that a list of all hazardous chemicals used in the housekeeping department be compiled and kept updated. The executive housekeeper must then develop a program to let all employees be aware of, and alert to the hazardous materials they will come in contact with, teaching them about their specific characteristics and dangers. The program may include lectures provided by distributors of chemical products, videos, discussions, and hands-on demonstrations. Other important steps include ensuring that all containers of chemicals are properly labeled and that workers follow approved disposal procedures. The label must state the name of the chemical, hazard warnings, and the manufacturer's name and address. Because people who work in housekeeping maybe unable to understand English, labels with color codes or signs are strongly recommended.

Workers should wear the right personal protective equipment when handling certain chemicals—mainly gloves, face masks, and goggles. Mixing or combining hazardous materials must be done strictly following the manufacturer's guidelines. Acids and caustics, for instance, can cause violent reactions when combined. Transferring liquids from one container to another can produce flammable vapors that can ignite easily. Worker exposure to hazardous materials may cause allergies, such as eye, nose, and throat irritation, skin rashes, anxiety, and nausea. In severe cases, chemicals may cause dizziness, vomiting, blindness, and even death.

Besides complying with OSHA's regulations, the housekeeping department must display a list of all the chemicals used, specifying information about the manufacturer, the product's hazardous ingredients, its physical and chemical characteristics, flammability, recommended handling, health hazards, and what to do in case of ingestion, fire, or explosion. This information is obtained from the manufacturers' **material safety data sheets** (MSDT) provided when the product is purchased. Employees working with chemicals should be required to read and understand product warning labels. The list must be updated and made available to employees at all times. Chemicals should never be stored near food products but in separate storage, preferably under lock and key. Flammable liquids and sprays should be stored in a cool, dry place away from heat and sunlight. Enclosing them in metal lockers is best, in order to avoid possible fires from spreading. Acid chemicals should be stored separately from each other. Detailed information on how to be in compliance with HazComm standards may be obtained from the Superintendent of Documents, Government Printing Office, Washington D.C.

 ## GUEST SUPPLIES

Lodging companies provide their guests with guestroom items intended to make their stay as convenient and comfortable as possible. These items also raise the guests' perceived value for the rate paid when occupying a room or rooms.

Non-reusable Supplies

Also called **amenities**, non-reusable supplies are items that guests are expected to use up or may take away with them when at the end of their stay. Tables 6.2 and 6.3 are limited lists of bathroom and guestroom amenities commonly supplied by lodging properties. Finding the right amenities for a property must be a calculated

TABLE 6.2   Sample Bathroom Amenity Items

After-shave lotion	Hand lotion
Bath gel	Hand soap
Bath salts	Mouthwash
Bath soap	Nail clippers
Body lotion	Perfume
Body powder	Razor
Cologne	Scissors
Cosmetics	Shampoo and conditioner
Deodorant	Shaving cream
Fabric wash	Shower cap
Facial tissue	Suntan lotion

endeavor; the higher the room rate is, the more luxurious amenities should be. Conversely, rates paid by guests in economy properties do not allow for providing them with extravagant supplies. But, in all cases, today's travelers have come to expect the best possible amenities for the type of establishment they patronize. For example, guest surveys indicate that about 75 percent of respondents rank bathroom amenities as "extremely" or "very desirable" attributes when traveling on business, second only to the property's full-scale services. Overall, a property's amenities figure very high in the total sum of what a particular establishment represents to the traveler, who often equates the facility's image with the amenities provided.

TABLE 6.3   Sample Guestroom Amenity Items

Bathrobe	Mints
Candy	Notepads
Chocolates	Pens
Coffee and tea	Postcards
Cookies	Sewing kit
Corkscrew	Shoe horn
Flowers	Shoe mit
Fruit	Slippers
Laundry bags	Stationery
Matches	

BATHROOM AMENITIES

Some lodging properties offer guests their own private-label products, stamped with the company's logo, because they can be customized to fit their clientele needs or because in most cases the cost is less. Others opt for adopting brand names, arguing that guests instantly recognize and prefer the quality of national and international brand amenities. The basic bathroom amenities for most properties are deodorant and hand soaps, shampoo and conditioner (often provided combined in one container), shower caps, and paper products.

Soap bars should be of reasonable size, usually 1.5 ounces for bath and ¾ ounce for facial. Shampoo and conditioner should be provided in easy-to-open bottles with large tops or snap caps, as packets are very difficult to tear open with soapy hands. Shower caps are a necessity for guests to shower or bathe without wetting their hair if they so desire. Luxury properties usually provide sophisticated products like almond oatmeal and glycerin soaps, fancy toiletries, all-inclusive lost luggage kits, and ecologically sensitive, all-natural items, packaged in recycled paper printed with soybean inks and wrapped in parchment to emphasize minimal paper use.

Paper products must be of premium quality. The facial tissue must be soft, absorbent, and durable, preferably with 2-ply rather than one. Bath tissue should have a large number of sheets per roll so that less time is spent refilling dispensers. Adequate thickness and strength, as well as softness, are also necessary.

GUESTROOM AMENITIES

Upscale lodging establishments outdo each other by offering a vast range of amenities aimed at pampering their guests while they relax in their rooms. Today's hoteliers view personal-care amenities as a positioning tool for their lodging properties, in that the more plentiful and novel they are, the higher value for the rate paid is perceived by guests.

Coffee makers, together with several blends of gourmet and decaffeinated coffee and a variety of teas, are common. Besides the typical candy placed on the pillow at turndown-service time, companies are adding specialty confections, such as Belgian and Italian chocolates or fancy fortune mints described as "rectangles attractively wrapped with witty fortunes and/or proverbs inside the wrappers." Chocolate chip and oatmeal cookies, cosmetics, and safe-for-all-fabric stain removers are just a few of the $300-million-a-year products that the industry invests in indulging guests.

Reusable Supplies

Depending also on the quality of lodging establishments, reusable supplies can range from the barely essential items offered by economy properties to the highly sophisticated, state-of-the-art technology found in first-class establishments. Supplies provided by most lodging properties are coat hangers, ice buckets, wastebaskets, ashtrays, Bible, and, recently, electronic equipment.

Coat hangers should be made of wood or hard plastic instead of flexible wire. Hangers with ball tops rather than hooks are usually not taken by guests, although some travelers find it difficult to fasten them to the lip on the closet rod. Women's hangers with skirt clips are designed for garments that hang better clipped than on a bar. Hangers are also available with clamping trouser bars to assure guests that the clothing will stay in place. Ice buckets are preferable if they are insulated with polyethylene liners and have a lid; stainless steel buckets are very durable and have a stylish look. Providing tongs with the ice bucket is a nice touch. Rather than plain-looking rectangular rubber wastebaskets, oval fireproof ones made of metal with simulated grain leather are more elegant. For smoking rooms, heavy crystal ashtrays with beveled edges are best. The Gideons, a nonprofit organization, provide free of charge guestroom Bibles on request. The appearance of all guest supplies is greatly enhanced by imprinting the property's or chain logo on them. The cost of logo items taken as souvenirs may be compensated by the advertising effect they will have when seen by members of the family and friends proudly displayed in the guests' own residences.

Today's guests, particularly business travelers, expect to find a wide selection of in-room electronic equipment. Computers with Internet access, fax machines, voice mail, video-cassette players, and high-quality stereo receivers are an important part of the selection of amenities that technology-minded guests hope to find in lodging properties.

LINENS

See Chapter Seven for a complete discussion of linens.

UNIFORMS

Uniforms for section housekeepers and housepersons should be functional, good-looking, and comfortable, with sleeves that allow for ease of movement. Badly designed, unstylish uniforms can affect the workers' morale and lower the property's image. Because of turnover, smocks, shirts, and pants must be easily alterable and able to stand frequent washings. While 100 percent cotton uniforms are comfortable to wear, they usually shrink, wrinkle, and cost more. Polyester/cotton blends are wrinkle-, shrink-, and soil-resistant, less costly, and easier to wash.

It is important to establish an adequate par of employee uniforms so that each worker is provided with a clean, fresh-looking outfit each day. The executive housekeeper should have on hand enough sizes of uniforms to fit all employees at any given time. The sight of large-frame employees clad in small-size clothing and small-frame workers wearing large-size uniforms should be avoided. In large properties, when the housekeeping department is in charge of keeping and maintaining uniforms for other departments, it is advisable to assign a specific employee for this particular task. In this case, a large, secure storage space and a commercial-size sewing machine for repairs and alterations should be provided. Uniformed departments, such as front desk and porters, often require outfits that need dry cleaning. Having uniforms dry-cleaned outside of the property can be quite expensive, so the purchase of a dry cleaning machine for employee and guest clothing should be considered.

In order to save space, capital investments, and labor costs, some properties may resort to having uniform services provided by companies that furnish a five-par of uniforms for each full-time employee on a weekly basis. Although quite convenient, this service may cost the property a considerable amount of money. The executive housekeeper must analyze the cost of purchasing, laundering, and maintaining uniforms in-house and that of having the service provided by an outside contractor. If the cost of the latter is substantially greater, the service should be conducted on the property.

One way to maintain adequate control of employee uniforms is to make each worker responsible for his or her outfit. A good procedure is not to issue a clean uniform unless the soiled one is returned. When employees are dismissed, their final checks should be retained until their uniforms are accounted for. If employees are required to clean their own uniforms, the law requires that they be compensated for the cost they incur.

KEY TERMS

acrylics
all-purpose cleaners
amenities
art deco
backing (carpet)
back vacuum
bed structure
bulk purchasing
burnishers
caddies
case furniture
chemical dispenser
competitive shopping form
complementary colors
crib
detergents
dual-purpose sleeping equipment
dust ruffle
extractors (carpet)
face weight (carpet)
flocking
HazComm
hopper
innerspring
jute
large-area vacuum

mobile beds
MSDT
Murphy bed
needle punching
neutralizer rinse
nylon
padding (carpet)
pH scale
pile (carpet)
polishers
polycotton
polyester
polypropylene (olefin)
pre-measured chemicals
purchasing agent
rollaway bed
sealers
single-purpose cleaners
scrubbers
self-contained extractors
strippers
tufted
warp
weft
wet/dry vacuum

DISCUSSION AND REVIEW QUESTIONS

1. Why is it important for executive housekeepers to maintain a consistent interior design pattern in lodging properties?
2. What are the advantages of using synthetic fibers in furniture upholstery?
3. What is the number of guests that a property with the following bed structure can lodge (see Table 6.1)?

   80 rooms with one king-size bed in each room

   75 rooms with two double-size beds in each room

   50 twin-bedded rooms

   150 rooms with one queen-size bed in each room

4. If you were in charge of selecting the carpet for the guestroom hallways of your hotel, which carpet characteristics would you require from the purveyor?
5. What are the advantages of selecting a carpet made of olefin fiber?
6. What par level would you establish for bedspreads in your lodging property?
7. What is the difference between a back vacuum and a wet vacuum?
8. What are the advantages and disadvantages of purchasing cleaning supplies in bulk quantities versus pre-measured cleaning supplies?
9. What is the purpose of using a neutralizer rinse when stripping a floor?
10. **(a)** What is the purpose of HazComm?
    (b) How would you, as an executive housekeeper, comply with HazComm in your housekeeping department?
11. As executive housekeeper of a four-diamond convention property located in a major city on the West Coast, what bathroom amenities would you recommend for the guests staying in your establishment?
12. Which are the advantages and disadvantages of having a property's uniforms furnished by an outside contractor?

MINICASES

Situation 1

You have been requested by the rooms division director of your property to take over the job of carpeting the foyer of the establishment where you work as executive housekeeper. You anticipate that the area will be subject to heavy traffic, including that of the baggage carts used by the porters. Write a letter to a carpet dealer stating your requirements regarding characteristics of the carpet you need, warranties you want, as well as other specifications. Request description of the product and price quotation for the carpet.

Situation 2

After graduating from a hotel administration program you have been hired by a lodging company and sent to open a 300-room mid-market property located by a major highway near Houston, Texas. The marketing plan focuses on attracting transient travelers on their way into and out of Houston, families, and some corporate business from three nearby office buildings. Upon your arrival at the property you are asked to list and describe the specifications of the reusable guest supplies needed for each guestroom. Do so.

Situation 3

(For the same property as in situation 2.) The opening date for the property is at hand and you have not yet been provided with the HazComm standards distributed by the Superintendent of Documents of the Government Printing Office. You want to be in compliance with OSHA's HazComm regulations and decide to take care of all requirements regarding handling and storing of hazardous chemicals and employee training. List all steps taken and present a copy of all announcements that you would post on employee bulletin boards regarding HazComm.

Linen
Management

The Sheraton New York. Courtesy of
Starwood Hotels and Resorts
Worldwide, Inc.

CHAPTER OBJECTIVES

▶ Describe the characteristics of bed and bath linen, napery, and shower curtains.
▶ Provide purchase specifications for linen items.
▶ Discuss issues and develop criteria related to linen procurement.
▶ Learn about establishing linen pars in lodging properties.
▶ Discuss the importance of effecting linen controls and conducting physical inventories.

OVERVIEW

The management of linens in lodging properties is an important component of the regular duties of executive housekeepers. There are several characteristics inherent to linens that must be understood when purchasing them, such as their composition and construction. For instance, buying durable-press, chemically treated fabrics that require no ironing will allow for substantial labor savings in the department. Once the characteristics are understood, purchasing specifications within budget parameters may be established.

The establishment of pars for each linen item on the property is critical. Having an inadequate supply of sheets, for example, would leave section housekeepers idle while waiting for laundered linen to make the beds. Overstocking a linen inventory, on the other hand, would mean tying down resources for long periods of time.

Because of the common losses of linens due to pilfering and misuse, inventories must be taken regularly in lodging properties. This chapter explains how to conduct physical counts of bed and bath linens and recommends issuing and storage procedures to control the shrinkage of these products.

 LINEN CHARACTERISTICS

The category of linens encompasses bed sheets and pillowcases, described as **bed linens**, and towels and bath mats, described as **bath linens**. Other guestroom textiles (pillows, bedspreads, bed covers, mattress covers, etc., have been described in Chapter Six under the category of software). The management of linen inventories in lodging operations is always assigned to executive housekeepers. Expenses for linens in the rooms division budget is substantial, usually second only to the cost of salaries and wages. When the property has food and beverage outlets, such as banquets, restaurants, and coffee shops, the housekeeping department is usually in charge of laundering napkins and tablecloths. However, the expense of the **napery** (name that describes these items) is not allocated to the housekeeping department budget but to that of the food and beverage department.

Bed Linens

The fabric for bed sheets and pillowcases is usually made of a blend of 50 percent of the natural fiber cotton and 50 percent of the synthetic fiber polyester. Fabrics made solely of cotton are not recommended for commercial use because they are not as durable as those blended with synthetic fibers; in some cases, a 50/50 blend cotton/polyester can last three times longer than full cotton. Usually, sheets made with blended fabrics can withstand over 500 washings, while all-cotton sheets begin to deteriorate after 200 washings.

Other disadvantages of cotton-only bed linen are that it absorbs more water, it shrinks, and it wrinkles in larger proportions than do the blends. Because full-cotton fabrics retain more water when being laundered, the drying time is longer, which means higher energy and labor costs. While fabric blends do not necessarily need to be ironed after washing, 100 percent cotton material must be pressed.

QUALITY

All other factors being equal, bed linen fabrics are better when their **thread count** is denser. Thread count is the number of threads per square inch of material. Commercial linen should have at least 180 thread count per square inch, represented as T = 180, in order to withstand multiple washings. Obviously, materials with a T count higher than 180 are preferable to those with a lower T count. Another method of ascertaining quality is to compare the amount of weight it takes to tear an 1 inch by 3 inch piece of fabric. All other factors being equal, the fabric that has a higher **tensile strength** is of better quality.

The way in which the cotton fibers have been prepared before spinning also determines fabric quality. Carded fibers are rougher to the touch and less durable than combed fabrics. Bed linen textiles made with carded fibers are called **muslin**; fabrics manufactured with combed fibers are called **percale**. Sheets and pillowcases made of percale fibers are of better quality, and therefore more expensive, than those made of muslin.

The way fabrics are woven is also an indicator of quality. **Plain-weave** textiles are made by interlacing the vertical thread (**warp**) with the horizontal yarn (**weft**). When the weft threads are woven by crossing the warp to produce an effect of parallel diagonal lines the fabric is called **twill**. Because of the extra diagonal pattern, twill fabrics are denser, more durable, and therefore more expensive than plain-weave fabrics. Before linens are sold to commercial and residential buyers, the fabric is washed and treated with chemicals to give the cloth a shiny look. Linen is usually shipped in cartons containing lots of 12 units.

SIZE

Sheets and pillowcases must fit the mattresses and pillows they are to cover. Although several sizes of mattresses are used by lodging operations, executive housekeepers should limit the number of sizes in order to minimize the cost of sorting, counting, and storing them. The standard sheet sizes usually used in lodging properties are twin, double, queen, and king. The sizes for pillowcases are standard and large (see Table 7.1). The size (in inches) of the sheets should not include the top and bottom hems.

Bath Linens

Towels, washcloths, and bath mats are made of a pile fabric with loops on both sides called **terry cloth**. The **ground warp**, or main body of the item, usually consists of a blend of two parts polyester and one part cotton. The **pile warp**, or yarn making the loops on both sides of the material, is made of 100 percent cotton fibers for full absorbency. The four narrow, flat side edges of the item with no pile warp are called the **selvage**. The selvage prevents unraveling.

QUALITY

All other factors being equal, the quality of terry cloth is determined by the weight of the item. The heavier the item, the thicker it will be. Good terry has double-thread loops for extra absorbency. Bath mats are made with extra heavy terry and are therefore more expensive.

TABLE 7.1   Sample Guestroom Linen Sizes

	Size (inches)
Sheets	
Twin	66 × 104
Double	81 × 104
Queen	90 × 108
King	108 × 110
Pillowcases	
Standard	20 × 30
Large	20 × 40
Bath Linen	
Bath towel (standard)	20 × 40
Bath towel (large)	24 × 50
Hand towel	16 × 26
Washcloth	12 × 12
Bath mat (standard)	18 × 24
Bath mat (large)	20 × 30

SIZE

Terry cloth items come in several sizes, depending on the type of lodging property. Standard sizes in inches may be: 24 by 50 for bath towels, 16 by 26 for hand towels, 12 by 12 for washcloths, and 20 by 30 for bath mats. Luxury, over-size towels, sometimes called bath sheets, may be as large as 36 by 70 inches (see Table 7.1).

Napery

Because executive housekeepers are in charge of laundering table linens, they are often involved in selecting and purchasing napery. In properties offering restaurant, coffee shop, room service, and banquet services, the amount of napkins and tablecloths used every day can be substantial.

QUALITY

Like bed linens, blended fabrics last longer than full-cotton materials. The least expensive material used in napery is **momie cloth**. This fabric is usually a plain weave 50/50 cotton/polyester blend that wears well. More high-end restaurants may use **damask**, a twill-woven fabric blend, with a glossy, silky appearance. While momie cloth is made of carded cotton, damask is made of combed fiber that is more elegant and lasts longer than momie cloth. As for bed linen, napery should be ordered preshrunk and nonfading.

SIZE

The drape of a tablecloth should be level with the chair's seat or fall at least 12 inches below the table's edge (Table 7.2 provides some common tablecloth and napkin sizes).

Shower Curtains

Some lodging properties use shower curtains made of natural fibers. The advantage of this type of shower curtain is that they can be laundered at every guest's check-out, but on the down side, because they are light, they flap when the shower is turned on and don't contain the water within the tub. Most shower curtains are made of synthetic fibers such as vinyl or nylon. Nylon shower curtains

TABLE 7.2   Sample Napery Sizes

	Size (inches)
Tablecloths	
Table for 2	54 × 54
Table for 4	64 × 64
Table for 6	72 × 72
Table for 8	90 × 90
Napkins	
Regular	17 × 17
Large	22 × 22

are resistant to mildew and don't become brittle over time. Often, shower curtains consist of a nylon curtain on the outside and a vinyl liner on the inside for better protection against soap stains.

 LINEN PURCHASING

Linens can be purchased directly from the mill or through a linen broker. Orders placed with the mill must be for large quantities and may take considerable time to be delivered. For smaller orders, fast delivery, and dependable service, lodging properties usually purchase linens from local or regional brokers who will make frequent scheduled calls on the property.

As with many other products, minimum standards for linens have been established by the federal government. The American Standards Association can provide the Minimum Performance Requirements for Institutional Textiles on request. The standards provide information about desirable characteristics of linen products regarding shrinkage, strength, and so on.

The main factors to consider when purchasing linen are, in this order: durability, laundry costs, and purchase price. These three factors can be used to ascertain the **cost per use** of an item. The cost per use of an article refers to the true cost of using an item. Although this method is quantifiable, its practicality is doubtful due to the difficulty of determining exactly the durability and laundry costs of linens. For example, although the life expectancy of a towel can be pre-established by the manufacturer, the final results are generally a direct cause of factors such as the chemicals used to launder the item, the number of times the item has been pre-soaked for stains, the temperature of the water, and so forth. Students, however, should be instructed on how to ascertain the cost per use of articles so they understand that the purchase price is not the most important factor to be considered when buying linens.

The cost per use of an item is arrived at by multiplying the total number of washings expected of the item (its life expectancy) by its weight in pounds, times its pre-established laundry cost per pound, plus the purchase price of the article, divided by the same life expectancy. Thus, cost per use =

$$\frac{\text{Weight in pounds} \times \text{laundry cost} \times \text{life expectancy} + \text{purchase cost}}{\text{Life expectancy}}$$

For example, the laundry cost of a towel weighing 1.7 pounds has been determined at $0.15 per pound. The towel's life expectancy is 240 washings and its purchase price, $6.50. The cost per use of the towel is $ 0.282 [(1.7) × (.15) × (240) + (6.50) = 67.7; 67.7 ÷ 240 = 0.282].

It is evident from the application of this formula that the purchase price should not be the most important consideration when purchasing linen; rather, the life expectancy and the laundry cost are the critical factors to be kept in mind.

Linens should be purchased **sanforized**, meaning that the fabric has been pre-shrunk at the source and therefore will not shrink considerably after the first washing. In order to minimize labor costs, the material should be purchased as "durable press" or chemically treated to require no ironing after laundering. White is the most common color choice for bed linens because they don't fade after several washings as dyed fabrics usually do.

Linens that have minor imperfections, hardly detectable by guests, are sold as **seconds**. It is common for lodging properties to save considerable costs by purchasing items marked as seconds. For instance, towels with an uneven selvage sold as seconds do not lose absorbency in any way and can be perfectly used as firsts.

Whether or not to use towels with the property's or chain's monogram or logo woven on them should be decided by upper management. Logoed items are often taken by guests as souvenirs, which may cost the company a considerable amount of money over time. On the other hand, management may consider the loss a matter of marketing and may be willing to incur extra expenses for the sake of advertising the property or chain.

Dyed linens must be of very good quality to ensure that the colors do not fade after repeated washings. Improper laundering procedures also contribute to color fading; too much bleach used to remove stains, for instance, can make a dyed item look lighter than items that have not been pre-treated before washing.

Smaller properties that don't have on-premise laundry may rent linens from companies that deliver on a daily basis. Most establishments, however, own their own bed linen and napery, in order to minimize costs and control quality. Companies or very large properties that order linen products directly from mills to minimize linen cost should plan ahead as much as possible to allow for possible long delays in production. Keeping track of linen usage in low and high occupancies during the year can help implement annual reordering plans on a regular basis. For example, a large property in Phoenix, Arizona, with a full occupancy from October through April and a lower occupancy thereafter, may have two large standing orders for bath towels to be delivered in November and February and two smaller orders in May and August. In all cases, any linen order should be equal to the par stock level minus the linen on hand at any given time:

Order = Par Stock – Linen on Hand

It is important to check carefully shipments of linen to verify that the goods received match the goods originally ordered. The executive housekeeper is usually in charge of placing new linen in use when items are below par, as revealed by physical inventories or when linens are discarded because of unsalvageable stains, damage, or excessive wear. New linens not in use should be under lock and key and their quantities recorded on a perpetual inventory where new deliveries are added on and issues subtracted.

Par Levels

Lodging establishments must carry enough linen inventory to ensure that sheets, pillowcases, towels, bath mats, napkins, and tablecloths are available when needed. In properties where the linen stock is under par, the labor cost is usually high. This may occur if section housekeepers have to wait until linen is available to make up the beds and fit the bathrooms with clean towels and bath mats. It may also be the case that the laundry room needs to work round the clock to launder the soil linen, which will require overtime pay and cause a faster deterioration of linen and equipment. On the other hand, too much linen inventory will mean tying down resources that might be needed elsewhere.

The amount of linen needed to outfit the property at 100 percent occupancy is defined as one **par**. The number of pars that lodging establishments require differs from property to property, depending on such factors as the output capacity of the laundry, the overall occupancy percentage of the establishment, the rate of replacement of worn, damaged, or stolen linen, and so forth. Another factor is the number of times the sheets are changed in guestrooms. First-class hotels insist in changing the bed linen daily, whether the guest stays over or not; others will change sheets every other day if the guest stays on. Other properties may follow the environmental protection trend to limit the use of water and laundry chemicals and place cards asking stay-over guests to notify housekeeping or the front desk if they want sheets changed daily. Although this system helps the property to lower the number of pieces to be laundered, it can cause some operational problems. Given the high rate of check-ins and check-outs, communicating daily to the section housekeepers which beds should be changed and which should not can be a logistic nightmare.

In normal circumstances, the "ideal" number of pars for bed linen and terry items is four, distributed as follows: one par in the guestrooms, one in the floor service stations and carts ready to be used, one in the laundry room being washed, and one in reserve. A property operating with a par of four will need to stock four pieces of every item needed to set up one guestroom times every guestroom in the property.

Most lodging properties use two sheets per bed and provide two bath towels, two hand towels, and two washcloths per guest. Occasionally, a third sheet—sometimes called snooze sheet—is set over the blanket to protect it from overuse. One bath mat is needed per bathroom. Figure 7.1 shows how to ascertain the linen requirements for a 500-room property that has 200 rooms with one king bed, 200 rooms with two queen beds each, and 100 twin-bedded rooms. Each guest is provided with 2 pillows, 2 bath towels, 2 hand

500-room property with: 200 king rooms
200 Q/Q rooms
100 Twin-bedded rooms
Linen distribution per room: 2 sheets per bed
2 pillows per guest
2 hand towels per guest
2 washcloths per guest
1 bath mat per room
Maximum houseguests: 1,400 (400 + 800 + 200)
3.5 par for all items

SHEETS

Room type	# of beds	× 2 sheets	total	× par	total sheets
King	200	2	400	3.5	1,400 king-size
Queen	400	2	800	3.5	2,800 queen-size
Twin	200	2	400	3.5	1,400 twin-size

PILLOWCASES

Maximum House guests	× 2 pillows	total	× par	total pillowcases
1,400	2	2,800	3.5	9,800 pillowcases

BATH TOWELS

Maximum House guests	× item per guest	total	× par	total towels
1,400	2	2,800	3.5	9,800 bath towels
1,400	2	2,800	3.5	9,800 hand towels
1,400	2	2,800	3.5	9,800 washcloths

BATH MATS

Number of bathrooms	× 1 bath mat	total	× par	total bath mats
500	× 1	500	3.5	1,750 bath mats

FIGURE 7.1   Sample Linen Calculation Work Sheet

towels, and 2 washcloths. All rooms have one bathroom. The pre-determined par for this property was set at 3.5.

The par for table linen depends mainly on the number of covers served at each meal period and the output frequency of the laundry. For tablecloths, a par of four per each table in the restaurant is usually sufficient. For napkins, a par of four per number of covers served is also recommended. For instance, a restaurant with

70 seats and a diner turnover of 2.3 for lunch and 1.75 for dinner will need to establish a par of 1,134 napkins:

Type of service	Number of seats		Diner turnover		par	Total napkins needed	
Lunch	70	(×)	2.3	(×)	4	=	644
Dinner	70	(×)	1.75	(×)	4	=	490

 LINEN CONTROL

The loss (shrinkage) of linen in lodging properties can be staggering. Wear and tear, permanent stains, theft by guests and employees, and the use of towels, washcloths, and napkins for cleaning purposes are the main causes of linen loss. Employees and guests are fond of stealing the property's linen, especially if marked with the company's monogram. Misuse is also widespread; for example, polishing shoes, wiping all kinds of stains, and handling kitchen utensils with washcloths and napkins are common. Two basic steps to help minimize linen pilfering and misuse are providing the kitchen and cleaning staff with sufficient cleaning rags and establishing effective security measures. Cleaning cloths can be purchased directly from vendors or made on-premise from discarded linen. One way for employees to distinguish the difference between cleaning cloths and usable linen is to permanently dye the rags so that workers can be easily spotted when using the wrong items. Linen theft can be prevented by establishing security controls and by adopting a system of communication between housekeeping and the front desk by which the desk is rapidly notified of missing items from check-out rooms. The cost of the missing linen can be added to the guests' folio before checkout or charged to their credit card if they have already departed. However, being overzealous about controlling linens can be counterproductive and result in excessive labor costs. For instance, keeping track of linen in large properties by requiring section housekeepers to exchange soiled items removed from guestrooms for clean ones can be exceedingly time consuming. A more efficient method of linen control consists in spot-counting the linen issued and received in the laundry to and from a particular section or floor. This may show a difference large enough to be worth investigating.

A control of damaged linen should also be in place. Careful records of discarded linen are necessary for inventory purposes as well as to ascertain if the number of damaged items is too high. In this case, the quality of the linen purchased and the laundering procedures should be closely investigated. Laundering fabrics improperly or over-using potent chemicals will wear linen quickly. Damaged linens can be repaired only in very few cases; for instance a torn sheet should be sewn only if the seam can be hidden by tucking it under the mattress. The cost of having a seamstress in the housekeeping department is in most cases prohibitive, so it is usually less expensive to buy new linen than to have the old item repaired. Figure 7.2 is a sample form for discarded linens.

STORAGE

Soiled and clean linens should be secured at all times, in dry, well-ventilated spaces. After hours, the laundry and linen rooms must be kept locked. Likewise, the floor closets where linen is stored and the service carts carrying linen should also be under lock and key. After laundering, linens should be moved out of the laundry room where the humidity is usually high. If possible, sheets should be left to rest overnight from the time they have been washed until they are used again. This "breathing time" before putting it back into use is necessary to smooth out wrinkles.

Issuing

In order to exert control, clean linens should be stored in a central area, usually the housekeeping **linen room**. Here, section housekeepers are provided with clean linens according to the room occupancy of their respective sections. At the end of their shifts, their service carts are returned to the linen room where they are restocked again. In properties where the use of floor closets is necessary, a par for each closet should be established to keep the right amount of linen in every floor. At the end of the regular shifts, the evening crew will restock the floor closets for the next day's work. Overstocking floor closets or food and beverage outlets for the convenience of housepersons, section housekeepers, and food service personnel should be avoided.

DATE	Bath Towels	Hand Towels	Wash-cloths	Bath Mats	King Sheets	Queen Sheets	Twin Sheets	Standard Pillowcases	Large Pillowcases	Crib Sheets
Total Discarded										

Discarded Items From _____ to _____

FIGURE 7.2 Sample Linen Discard Form

Inventories

Once proper control of linens has been established, physical inventories must be regularly conducted. The two main purposes of physical inventories are to ascertain linen losses (shrinkage) and to determine the amounts of items needed to bring the stocks to their original pars. Lodging properties usually conduct linen inventories semi-annually or quarterly. If the losses are severe, inventories are taken monthly to determine where and how the losses are taking place.

Physical inventories are time-consuming and difficult to take because the procedure involves counting all items in the house, one at a time. In addition, the counting must be done off-hours, at the end of the normal workday when all guestrooms are made up and no laundering is taking place. Usually, two-person teams are formed, in which one person calls out the items and the other writes down the amounts. Often, a representative of the controller's office is present to guarantee that the results are accurate. When counting bed and bath linen, distinctions must be made for all sizes. Obviously, all items in all locations of the property must be counted. These, generally include

▶ Guestrooms
▶ Laundry room
▶ Linen room
▶ Floor linen closets
▶ Section housekeeper carts
▶ Soiled linen ready to be laundered
▶ Made-up mobile bedding

Count forms should be used at every location and all totals transferred to a **master inventory list** whose totals will indicate the existing inventory of all items, the losses for the month, and the amounts needed to restock the property. Figure 7.3 is a sample master inventory form that can be summarized as follows:

> beginning inventory (of each item counted)
> + purchases for the month
> − documented discards for the month
> = amounts that should exist
> − current physical inventory (total on hand)
> = losses (shrinkage)

par stock (of each item counted)
– total on hand
= amounts needed
– amounts on order
= need to order

The controller will multiply the number of items on the "losses" line by price to find out the total loss of linens for the month in dollars. Most properties assign full market price to new linen in stock but not yet used and half price to linen in use. The total value of all linens in stock is determined as follows:

$$(\text{Linen in use} \times \text{its original price} \div 2) +$$
$$(\text{new linen} \times \text{market price}) = \text{linen valuation}$$

The items calculated on the "need to order" line will be the number of items that need to be procured to bring the property to its original par. If the losses for the month are abnormally large, an investigation of the causes will be in order. In this case, an inquiry of possible pilfering, theft, quality of the products purchased, laundry chemical quality, laundering procedures, and improper use of the linen must be conducted. In any case, if the linen monthly percentage cost calculated by the controller is above the budget target, efforts must be made to bring the percentage down in subsequent months.

In order to avoid running out of linen, large properties or group of properties under the same management generally place orders, strategically timed throughout the year, directly from mills. Based on past history, the establishments forecast linen needs semiannually or quarterly and have standing orders placed one or two years ahead of time. Preplanned purchases of linens can represent great discounts, as opposed to a rushed-in order to the regional broker with the inherent substantial middleman surcharge.

 KEY TERMS

bath linen	damask
bed linen	ground warp
cost per use	linen par

INVENTORY DATE: _____

ITEM	Bath Towels	Hand Towels	Wash Cloths	Bath Mats	King Sheets	Queen Sheets	Twin Sheets	Standard Pillowcases	Large Pillowcases	Crib Sheets
1. ITEM										
2. BEGINNING INVENTORY										
3. PURCHASES										
4. SUBTOTAL 2 + 3										
5. RECORDED DISCARDS										
6. TOTAL 4–5										
7. GUESTROOMS										
8. LAUNDRY ROOM										
9. LINEN ROOM										
10. FLOOR LINEN CLOSETS										
11. CARTS										
12. SOILED LINEN										
13. ON ROLLAWAYS, CRIBS, ETC.										
TOTAL ON HAND 14. ADD 7 THROUGH 13										
15. LOSSES 6–14										
16. PAR STOCK_____ TURNS										
17. AMOUNT NEEDED 16–14										
18. ON ORDER										
19. NEED TO ORDER 17–18										

FIGURE 7.3 Sample Master Inventory List

linen room
master inventory list
momie cloth
muslin
napery
percale
pile warp
plain-weave
sanforized fabric

seconds
selvage
tensile strength
terry cloth
thread count
twill
warp
weft

DISCUSSION AND REVIEW QUESTIONS

1. Explain why fabrics made of 100 percent cotton are not recommended for commercial use in lodging properties.
2. What are the advantages of selecting bed linen made of 50/50 cotton/polyester blends in commercial operations?
3. Two methods of ascertaining quality of bed linen fabrics are the thread count per square inch and the tensile strength of the material. Describe both.
4. (a) What is the difference between muslin and percale?
   (b) If you were to decide between purchasing muslin or percale and price was not a determining factor, which material would you choose? Why?
5. What is the purpose of the selvage in terry cloth items such as towels and bath mats?
6. Why would a tablecloth made of damask be of better quality than another made of momie cloth?
7. What would the cost per use be of a linen item that weighs 3 pounds, has a laundry cost of 2 cents per pound washed, has a life expectancy of 300 washings, and costs $7.25?
8. Why is it recommended to purchase sanforized linens?
9. What is one par of king sheets in a property that has 100 rooms with one king bed each, and 300 rooms with two queen beds each? All beds are made up with 2 sheets.
10. What are the advantages and disadvantages of purchasing linen from a linen broker rather than directly from a mill?
11. What is (are) the purpose(s) of conducting physical inventories in lodging properties?
12. What formula is commonly used in lodging properties to calculate the linen valuation?

 MINICASES

Situation 1

Having been appointed assistant to the executive housekeeper of a new property in Denver, Colorado, you have been instructed to present the initial opening inventory for bed linen (sheets and pillowcases). The bed structure of the property is:

> 25 suites with one king-size bed and one double-size couch each
>
> 200 rooms with two queen-size beds each
>
> 100 twin-bedded rooms

Each bed is made up using two sheets. Two large pillows will be placed on each king-size bed, one large pillow on each twin bed and couch, and two standard-size pillows on each queen-size bed. The par for all items is 3.5.

Situation 2

You have been assigned to control the linen inventory of a 500-room resort on the West Coast. The loss of linen in the property has been exceedingly high since the hotel opened two years ago. Compile a list of possible causes for the linen losses and describe the methods that you would put in place to curtail the loss for each one of the causes identified.

Situation 3

On August 31, as the executive housekeeper of the Royal Hotel in San Antonio, Texas, you have taken the monthly inventory for sheets, and determined that the total number on hand is 5,715. The Royal has 400 rooms with two queen-size beds. Each bed is set with two sheets. The pre-established par for sheets is 4. The beginning inventory on August 1 was 5,500. The hotel did purchase 40 dozen sheets on August 18. Twenty-eight damaged sheets were discarded during the month. There are 12 dozen sheets on order.

Find: (a) shrinkage for the month;

        (b) number of sheets that you need to order to bring the stock to par.

Laundry Room Management

Hapuna Beach Prince Hotel, Hawaii.
Courtesy of Westin Hotels & Resorts.

CHAPTER OBJECTIVES

▶ Describe the process of planning on-premise laundries.
▶ Discuss the main characteristics of laundry equipment.
▶ Explain the operation of laundries, from the collection to the finishing of linens.
▶ Provide benchmarks for linen cost controls.
▶ Learn about staffing the laundry room.

OVERVIEW

The operative success of on-premise laundries depends on the adequate planning of the facilities based on a detailed analysis of the property's needs. Planning a laundry includes its design and space allocation, the selection and layout of equipment, and the initial staffing and training of workers. This chapter describes the main characteristics of washers, dryers, and ironers, and lists the chemicals used in the washing process. Laundry operation, from the collection to the finishing of linens, is also explained.

Students are provided with percentages based on national averages to approximate laundry costs in five categories: labor, linen replacement, energy, laundry chemicals, and other costs. Some considerations are provided for smaller companies that contract out their laundry services, emphasizing that executive housekeepers should be closely involved in the contract closing as they will have to live with the agreement once it is signed. Consideration is also given to staffing and training of laundry personnel.

 ## PLANNING THE LAUNDRY

Most large lodging properties process their linens in on-premise laundries (OPL). There are some compelling reasons why laundries are built within the property over having the products processed by an outside company. Some of the advantages are substantial reduction of costs, control over linen quality, and better product availability. The annual savings of an on-premise laundry versus a service linen company can be as high as 50 percent. By having an OPL, operators can also eliminate pick-up and delivery times and lengthy turnaround cycles. In cases where laundry companies do not deliver on time, the housekeeping department personnel must wait until the products are delivered in order to finish the daily tasks of making beds, fitting the bathrooms with towels, or providing the food and beverage division with napkins, tablecloths, and uniforms. Other advantages of on-premise laundries are having control of the laundering and handling of linens to conform with recommended hygienic standards and increasing the life of the linen by adopting efficient processing procedures.

Setting up a laundry room requires a detailed analysis of the property's needs. Poor planning may result in inadequate space to perform daily operations, insufficient equipment to keep up with the volume of linen to be washed, too small drains to funnel away the discharged water, poor working conditions caused by inadequate ventilation, and so on.

Design of the Laundry Room

The first step in designing the laundry consists of building a facility that has enough capacity to process the maximum amount of linen that the property can generate per day. Ample space should be allocated to install all equipment required and to provide an area large enough for clean and dirty linen to be easily separated. The space allocated varies with the size of the property and can range from 1,000 square feet in small properties to over 20,000 square feet in larger operations. The laundry room should be equipped with enough washers and dryers to process all items that the rooms and food and beverage divisions will require at 100 percent occupancy without incurring overtime or running the laundry operation round the clock.

The design should anticipate all mechanical, electrical, and ventilation installation connections for the equipment as well as identify the optimal location of drains for washers and soak sinks. If water restriction in the area is severe or if the water costs are high, a system for recycling washer rinse water can be installed. These water recovery systems route rinse water from the washer's dump valve into a recovery tank to be reused in the wash cycles. Over 25 percent of water usage can thus be saved.

The **selection and specifications of the equipment** depend on the type of linens to be laundered. For instance, a lodging property with restaurants and banquet department should have extra washers to process food and beverage napkins and tablecloths; a property offering in-house dry cleaning service will need to install dry cleaning equipment; an establishment that uses no-iron sheets may not require a **mangle** to iron these items. Choosing the right linens will result in substantial savings of equipment and labor costs. Most nylon and polyester/cotton blend fabrics require less washing and drying time, and do not need to be ironed. One negative aspect, however, of synthetic fibers is their sensitivity to high washing and drying temperatures.

Once the equipment has been selected it should be installed to allow for the best possible **layout**. An adequate work-flow pattern should be designed to provide an efficient distribution of space and avoid worker cross-traffic. Ideally, the work flow should follow a circular pattern in the following order: laundry room entrance → soak sinks → washers → dryers → mangle(s) → sheet folder stand → folding table → shelves and mobile racks → laundry room exit. Figure 8.1 provides a typical floor layout for a laundry room using three washers, six dryers, one mangle, and other additional equipment. The soiled linen can be sorted out, pre-soaked if necessary, washed, dried, ironed, folded, and stored for immediate use without workers bumping into each other because of a cross-traffic pattern.

FIGURE 8.1   Sample Laundry Room Layout

Because laundry operations are conducted in a hot, humid environment, sufficient exhaust capacity should be provided to draw out the moist air. Because of frequent liquid spills, the floor of laundry rooms should be waterproofed and consist of a nonslippery material. Adequate drainage should be provided to dispose of runoffs caused by water-soaked linen and possible washer overflows.

Laundry rooms must be well lighted so stains, spots, and shades in linens can be easily detected. A minimum of two feet of space between all machines and walls should be allowed to facilitate cleaning and repairs.

Washers

With the introduction of microprocessor controlled machines, washing linens has been greatly simplified. Gone are the days when loading detergent in the machine and setting water temperatures and time cycles were done by hand. Instead, these functions are done automatically by programmed processors that regulate the amount of soap to be injected in the machine, activate thermostats, and control the machines' timers. Smaller washers, for instance 18-pounders, operate on the same principles as conventional residential machines; that is, the soiled linen is placed in the machine's receptacle and agitated through washing and rinsing cycles. The washer finally spins the moisture out and the load is ready to be transferred to a dryer. Larger washers, however, are built with high efficiency and productivity in mind in order to maximize laundry outputs. Some washer-extractors, for instance, feature single-pivot tilts to facilitate loading and unloading, high-speed extract to reduce drying and ironing time, and thermal cool-down to eliminate wrinkles. The tilt feature minimizes operators' fatigue and back stress, helping the establishment keep its people by making the job easier.

The incorporation of microprocessors to washer-extractors has also simplified operations and ensured consistent, reliable results. Some machines offer over 20 pre-set wash programs that can be activated at the touch of a button. These machines can be pre-programmed with washing formulas specifically designed for hospitality linen; thus, a lodging property can have different pre-programmed formulas for bed linen, terry cloth, napery, and greasy kitchen aprons and rags. Large washer-extractors may be comprised of two or more separate pocket cylinders that allow different loads to be processed at the same time. Some lodging chains that operate a central laundry serving several establishments, and therefore process over 2,000 pounds of linen per hour, use **tunnel washers**. Tunnel washers have several chambers that enable the machine to process multiple loads simultaneously.

Investing in washer-extractors with high G-force (spinning power) can result in as much as 30 percent savings in time and energy. The lower the water retention of the fabrics is, the less time and energy consumption that will be needed during drying and ironing. For example, machines with greater than 200 G-force will reduce substantially the gas or electricity used during the drying process over 90 G-force washer-extractors. Operators of lodging facilities should install washing equipment with extraction flexibility, as all fabrics do not have the same extract G-force requirements. For instance, an extraction force of 90 is ideal for permanent press and blends, while a 140 G-force range is necessary for hard-to-dry items such as blankets, spreads, and mattress pads. Because of the high gravitational force exerted by these powerful machines, large washer-extractors must be professionally anchored onto the laundry floor. When located near guestrooms, washer-extractors should be well cushioned to avoid excessive noise or floor vibration.

Estimating the number and size of washers to be installed in a property depends on the type of linen to be processed, the desired number of hours within which the linen must be finished, and the **linen poundage** of the establishment. A lodging property with food and beverage facilities should have at least three washers installed, one for bed linen, one for terry cloth, and one for tablecloths and napkins. These three different kinds of linen require different **washing formulas** because of the different composition of the fabrics and the type of soiling that must be laundered. For instance, napkins and tablecloths are usually soiled with fats and oils, while guestroom linen usually has different types of stains.

The number of hours allocated for daily laundering is also a key factor for sizing laundries. If it is determined that 1,500 pounds of linen should be processed in 8 hours, it would be necessary to have twice as many washers as needed to launder the same amount of linen in 4 hours.

The linen poundage is the weight of one par of linen: that is, the maximum output for peak business period or the weight of all items that need to be processed at 100 percent occupancy. Using the same example as before, a lodging property with three 50-pound washers and ½-hour washing cycles would theoretically require 5 hours to process 1,500 pounds of linen ($3 \times 50 = 150$; $150 \times 2 = 300$; $300 \times 5 = 1,500$). If the linen poundage to be washed in the same period of time had been 3,000, a double number of washers would have been required. Table 8.1 shows how to calculate the linen poundage of a 400-room hotel that has 100 rooms with one king-size bed in each room, 200 rooms with two queen-size beds in each room, and 100 twin-bedded rooms. The poundage is calculated by multiplying one par of linen by the respective weight of each piece of bed and bath linens used in the property.

Assuming that this lodging property has no food and beverage outlets, theoretically only two washers would be needed to process bed and bath linens separately. However, having a small commercial top-load washer as a backup unit for smaller or emergency loads would be a wise step to take. Washers can be purchased from 50-pound to 500-pound and over. Choosing the right capacity washers is also important; using too many small machines would require more loading time, and therefore more labor cost. On the other hand, using only large machines would require more energy to operate and would not offer the flexibility to separate washing loads by category (king sheets, queen sheets, twin sheets, pillowcases, etc).

Using Table 8.1 as an example, if it is decided that the ideal washer setup for this property is three 100-pound and two 50-pound machines, each one using ½-hour washing cycles, the processing of the 5,438 pounds would take about 7 hours. Thus:

$$100 \times 3 = 300; 300 \times 2 = 600$$
$$50 \times 2 = 100 ; 100 \times 2 = 200$$

Theoretically, at full capacity, the five machines can process 800 pounds of linen in one hour. In 7 hours:

$$800 \times 7 = 5,600 \text{ pounds}$$

Dryers

Most commercial dryers are computer programmed so that cycle times and temperatures can be automatically controlled. As with washers, the number of dryers needed to process one par of linen

TABLE 8.1   Linen Poundage Determination

Sheet Poundage

Room Structure	Beds per Room	Total Beds	Total Sheets	Weight per Item (lb)	Total Weight
100 King	1	100	200	2.05	410
200 Queen	2	400	800	1.55	1,240
100 Twin-bedded	2	200	400	1.10	440
400		700	1,400		**2,090**

Pillowcase Poundage

Type of Bed	Type of Pillow	Pillows per Bed	Total Pillows	Weight per Item (lb)	Total Weight
King	Large	4	400	0.40	160
Queen	Large	3	1,200	0.40	480
Twin	Standard	1	200	0.30	60
					700

Towel Poundage

Type of Room	People per Category*	Towels per Person	Weight per Item (lb)	Total Weight
King	200	2 BT; 2 HT; 2 WC	0.70; 0.25; 0.06	404
Queen	800	2 BT; 2 HT; 2 WC	0.70; 0.25; 0.06	1,616
Twin	200	2 BT; 2 HT; 2 WC	0.70; 0.25; 0.06	404
	1,200			**2,424**

Bath Mat Poundage

Number of Rooms	Mats per Room	Total Mats	Weight per Item (lb)	Total Weight
400	1	400	0.56	**224**

Sheets	2,090
Pillowcases	700
Towels	2,424
Bath Mats	224
Poundage	5,438

*2 persons per king and queen bed; 1 person per twin bed.

in a given number of hours depends on the poundage and type of fabrics to be dried. Bed linen that is put through mangles for ironing, for instance, does not need to be passed through dryers. In general, because the drying cycle usually takes double the time of the washing cycle, twice as many dryers of the same capacity are needed to get the job done.

In order to save energy, a battery of dryers should be enclosed on the top and sides so that heat is not lost around the equipment. This contained heat can thus be used as warm intake air. When using gas dryers, the outside air intake for combustion should not be larger than needed so that no extra cold outside air is absorbed into the dryer area. A damper closing the aperture when dryers are not in use can effectively block the outside air from coming into the laundry room. Dryer burners should be cleaned regularly to ensure that lint has not caused the burners to partially clog. The inefficient burning of gas can be identified by a yellowish flame, rather than blue.

Dryer lint must often be removed from the dryer ventilation system and the dryers' adjacent areas. Lint is not only a major fire hazard but may cause allergies and other respiratory ailments in laundry workers.

Mangles

Linen can be ironed by feeding it to rollers or by placing it on presses. When done by hand, ironing linen is a labor-intensive, time-consuming process. Sophisticated tandem units on the market today can dry, iron, and fold linen automatically. These flatwork finishers have a built-in folder assembly that can handle items from pillowcases to king-size sheets that require an ironed look. Most lodging properties use no-iron bed linen to avoid the high labor cost associated with pressing. However, they usually have small or medium-size mangles to iron napkins, tablecloths, and pillowcases to add to the facility's image. In this case, linens go directly from washer to finisher, reducing the amount of energy needed to dry them.

Other Laundry Equipment

Besides washers and dryers, the laundry room must be fitted with additional equipment necessary for linen processing. **Soak sinks** are needed for spot and stain removal using strong chemical formulas. The soak sinks should be placed between the soiled-linen sorting area and the washers. **Folding tables** and **folder stands** should be placed by the dryers and mangles, close to storage shelving. The folding tables are used to fold terry cloth items and the folder stands to fold sheets, blankets, shower curtains, and bed pads. Only one worker is needed to fold items using the folder stand, while two attendants are necessary to fold them by hand. Plastic or vinyl-coated canvas **laundry hampers** can be very useful to transport linen to and from washers and dryers and to hold soiled and clean items while being processed. Stainless steel **mobile racks** are often necessary to hold the clean linen for later transport to the different floor closets on the property. Mobile racks are a must in laundry rooms where shelving space is limited.

 ## LAUNDRY OPERATION

The linen laundering cycle begins with the collection of soiled items from guestrooms and the food and beverage outlets, and ends with the distribution of clean linen to all locations.

Collection of Soiled Linens

Section housekeepers should be trained to sort bed and bathroom linens in order to facilitate the laundry department's work. If at all possible, the room attendants should separate bed from bathroom items, placing them in different containers. Heavily soiled items should be clearly set apart so laundry workers can initiate the necessary pre-treatment as soon as they arrive in the laundry room. The use of hampers to transport linen, rather than plastic bags, provides a better impression to guests, causes no environmental waste, and saves bagging and unbagging time. When the property has **linen chutes**, all sorting is done in the linen room.

Good communication and cooperation is needed between the laundry manager and the food and beverage director to ensure that napery items are sorted and inspected for debris before they are brought to the laundry room. Napery mixed with silverware, pieces of bread, and food scraps should not be accepted by laundry personnel for processing. Items heavily stained with butter, ketchup, wine, or sauces should be delivered separately. Kitchen rags and chef's aprons must never be bundled together with napery items.

Sorting the Linen

Once in the laundry room, linen must be sorted out by category and readied for washing. Because each category requires a different water temperature and chemical formula, linens must be carefully separated before being loaded in the washers. For instance, greasy kitchen aprons require strong washing chemicals while wool needs milder detergents. Colored napery should not be processed with bleach, while white bed linens require bleach to kill bacteria and whiten the fabric. In general, bed linen, terry cloth, napery, blankets, and bedspreads should be washed separate from each other.

Besides sorting the linen by category, each batch should be separated by degree of soiling. Items that are not soiled or very lightly soiled require weaker formulas and less agitation (and therefore less washing time) than heavily soiled items. Because the number of heavily stained items is usually less, having a couple of small-size washers to process small loads will prevent having to use larger machines for partial-load washings. Sorting personnel should be trained to detect unrecoverable items such as torn, burned, or heavily soiled articles, which should be made into cleaning rags.

Pretreatment of Stains

Before loading the linen into the washers, special care must be taken to presoak and pretreat heavily stained items. For example, blood, egg, fruit, and dark beverage stains should be soaked in cold water and spot-cleaned with detergent. Grass, paint, and grease stains should be spot-cleaned before washing. All fabrics, however, should be tested for colorfastness before chemicals are directly applied to them.

Loading

Washers and dryers should be loaded with the maximum amount of linen that their capacity allows; thus, a 35-pound machine should hold about 35 pounds of dry soiled linen. If the soiled linen is damp, as may happen with bath items, fewer pieces will make up the recommended weight. Not using machines to full capacity will increase the operating cost of the laundry as washers and dryers will use the same amounts of water, chemicals, and energy required for full loads. On the other hand, overloading will cause improper results, for the machines will not be able to properly wash or dry items if these cannot be turned and tossed freely.

Washing/Extracting

Most washing machines in the market today are equipped with several washing programs aimed at processing diverse types of fabrics and degrees of soiling. The programs consist of different washing times, water temperatures, levels of agitation, and amounts of chemicals to be used. These programs, used properly, can help conserve energy and lengthen the life of fabrics. For instance, a program for washing lightly soiled linen will be set to use less time, a lower temperature, and fewer chemicals than a program set to process greasy items. The lighter program will cost less to run and prolong the number of washings that the material can stand.

The water temperature needed to wash articles usually varies from 140°F to 160°F. For example, while greasy kitchen items require the hottest temperature, lightly soiled sheets can be washed at 140°F. Some programs, however, are preset to use cold water as some types of stains do not require hot water for removal; on the contrary, warm water might imprint the stain permanently. In addition, no-iron fabrics better retain their wrinkle-free characteristics when washed in cold water. Laundry operators should use cold-water programs whenever possible to save the energy needed to heat the water.

A sufficient level of agitation is necessary for adequate washing action; not enough agitation due to insufficient washing time, improper water levels, or machine overloading will not provide adequate results. Linens washed with the wrong chemicals or with incorrect amounts of chemicals either will not produce good results or will ruin the articles by deteriorating their fabric composition. Using too much chemical can also cause damage to linens as well as waste precious budget dollars.

Each washing program consists of several cycles, similar to those found in a residential machine. The **flush cycle** soaks the linen and dissolves the soils; the **wash cycle** uses soil-breaking products, detergents, and other chemicals to clean the items; the **rinse cycle** removes chemicals from the linen; and the **extract cycle** spins the moisture from the load before it is moved on to the drying or ironing phase.

WATER

Good water quality is necessary for washing linens. Hard water prevents detergents from releasing their sudsy action to remove soils, leaving a grayish shade and an "unclean" odor in finished linens. Often, lodging properties must install water softeners before they can obtain adequate results. Large quantities of water are used in washing linens; some programs may require one flush cycle, one break cycle, one washing cycle, one softener cycle, and three rinse cycles. In locations where water is expensive, special care must be taken to minimize the use of water whenever possible. Partial loads are a waste of water and can cause wear and tear on washing machines. Newer washer-extractors reduce the amount of water necessary to clean linens. Where old machines may use 4 to 5 gallons per pound of wash, newer ones need just two to 2½ gallons per pound.

CHEMICALS

Several factors determine the types of chemicals needed for commercial laundries: these include the water used, the different texture of fabrics to be washed, and the degree of soiling that must be removed. The chemicals commonly used in laundry operations are **alkalies** that help neutralize acids in the washing solution. Alkalies are often necessary because suds in detergents act better on soils and stains if the washing solution is lightly alkaline. **Antichlors** are added to rinses to ensure that chlorine bleach is totally removed from the washed fabrics. **Bleach** is a powerful chemical that is very effective in killing bacteria, whitening linens, and removing stains. Chlorine bleach, however, can destroy some fabrics, particularly certain synthetics. Oxygen bleach is milder and can be used with most washable fabrics, including colored ones, but it is ineffective on heavy stains. **Breaks** are heavy-duty, alkaline compounds designed to break soils in the soak cycle. Breaks are used for heavily soiled loads. The washing agent used in the washing process is the **detergent**. Detergents containing suspending agents and alkaline builders are very effective in removing grease and oils. Some detergents have water-softening ingredients to increase their cleaning action; others contain enzymes that break down and liquify organic stains such as food, blood, urine, and fats. **Softeners** are added in the final wash cycle to eliminate static cling, smooth wrinkles, and make ironing easier. **Sours** are acidic chemicals used to neutralize any alkaline residues left after washing and rinsing linens. A single product that combines a fabric softener and an alkaline neutralizer may also be used. **Starches** are carbohydrate compounds that are added to give linens a stiff appearance. This procedure is commonly used to give a crisp look to cooks' uniforms and toques (chefs' hats).

The use of laundry detergents can be substantially reduced by using ozone in the washing process. Ozone is a gas formed by ozone generators by passing an electric current through the oxygen that exists in the wash water. The gas acts as an oxidizing and bleaching agent, disinfectant, and solvent of soils and oils. The chemical reactions that ozone produces make it possible to clean linens with fewer amounts of detergents and at lower water temperatures. Fabrics washed by the ozone method may last longer than when processed with strong chemicals at higher water temperatures.

Drying

Although drying times vary with different types of fabric, generally it takes twice as long to dry linens as it takes to wash them. Drying temperatures also vary from item to item; for instance, fluffy all-cotton towels require hotter temperatures than thin synthetic fibers. All linens should be loaded into dryers with the minimum moisture possible to reduce drying time. Modern washers are equipped with high-speed spins as a final cycle to remove excess moisture from washed items. Dryers should be loaded to capacity to minimize energy costs. No-iron linens and terry cloth should not be over-dried as they are better folded when very slightly damp.

Ironing

Items that need ironing are best processed when slightly damp; for this reason, they don't need to be dried. Ironing is a labor-intensive process that should be avoided whenever possible. On the other hand, pressed tablecloths, napkins, and pillowcases create a favorable impression for guests, as do cook and serving-personnel uniforms.

Folding

Like ironing, folding is a time-consuming, labor-intensive process, particularly if it is done by hand. Linens should be folded immediately after drying or pressing to avoid wrinkling. Sheet-folding stands can save labor costs, as only one worker is needed to fold the items instead of two employees. Laundry folders should be trained to sort out linen items with imperfections such as tears, fading, stains, and loose seams before they are distributed for usage.

Storing

Once linens are folded, they should be handled as little as possible. Folded linen should be shelved in the linen room, placed on mobile racks for transportation to the floor closets, or placed directly onto the section housekeeper carts for ready use.

Best Results

The ultimate goal of a well-run laundry is to obtain optimum results in terms of appearance, odor, and feel. Regarding appearance, the linen must be snow-white (for white items) and free of wrinkles and spots caused by staining. The odor must be fresh and clean, not stale or musty; the feel should be smooth and velvety, not coarse or rough.

Laundry accounts can benefit from the expertise of nationwide chemical companies to obtain best results; in some cases, these companies guarantee that the quality of linens processed with their products will be optimum. In order to check quality, their service personnel conduct routine tests for water hardness, iron residue in finished linens, and the pH of washed items. Improper results of finished products include discoloration, stains, abraded fabric, lint specks, excessive wrinkling and shrinking, and fabric pilling.

Valet Service

Most first-class lodging properties offer laundry and dry cleaning services to their guests. However, it is common to contract these services with an outside commercial laundry because of the specialization and time-consuming details that valet service entails. Properties that wash and dry-clean employee uniforms and draperies usually process valet service items in-house. In this case, smaller washing and drying machines and dry cleaning equipment need to be installed, as well as additional personnel to tag, process, and bag each guest's articles.

On-premise valet service can greatly encumber housekeeping operations and take up considerable laundry room space. In all cases, good communication between valet attendants and the laundry room must be established, and clear, specific procedures put in place to avoid misunderstandings and complaints. Some of these procedures include setting up times for laundry pick-up and delivery, billing guests promptly after each service, and having a quick response system to compensate guests for lost, misplaced, or damaged articles.

Contracting Out Laundry Services

Small lodging properties may decide to contract out laundering services rather than installing their own on-premise laundry. While the disadvantages are numerous, a few advantages of outside laundry contracts include not having to make a substantial initial investment and having the additional space otherwise taken up by the laundry room. In all cases, contracts must be carefully set up between the lodging property and the commercial laundry company to ensure an efficient, reliable service; for instance, requiring delivery seven days a week on peak occupancy period. The contract should specify details regarding delivery and quality, such as days of the week and time of day, emergency service, appearance of the linen, folding specifications, sorting procedures, billing method, and method of inventory.

Delivery bundles should be clearly marked with the date, time, number of items, and weight. The housekeeping department must check that all items are accounted for before signing the delivery slip.

Laundry Operating Costs

The cost of operating an on-premise laundry is broken down into the categories of labor, linen replacement, energy, chemicals, and other. Of these, the labor cost is the highest. Although expenses can be largely affected by exceptionally high energy or labor costs, depending upon the location of the property, national laundry cost percentages for a typical laundry operation may be averaged thus:

Labor	45%
Linen replacement	20%
Energy	15%
Laundry chemicals	10%
Other	10%

Under normal circumstances, executive housekeepers can work out rough estimates to monitor expenses using these averages as a benchmark. For example, a laundry operation that has had an annual total expense of $50,000 should have spent $22,500 in labor (50,000 × .45), $10,000 in linen replacement (50,000 × .20), $7,500 in energy (50,000 × .15), $5,000 in chemicals (50,000 × .10), and $5,000 in other (50,000 × .10).

 STAFFING THE LAUNDRY ROOM

Laundry operations in large properties are usually coordinated by a **laundry manager** who reports directly to the executive house-keeper. Laundry shifts normally consist of one shift supervisor, several laundry attendants, and one utility helper (houseperson). Because of the different tasks to be carried out in the laundry room, job specifications must be clearly spelled out. For example, the job of wash persons may be to handle the loading and unloading of washers and dryers; the utility helper may presort, count, and shelf linen, others may fold and stack, and so on.

An ideal staffing scenario is to have enough equipment and personnel to process the property's poundage in 8 hours, to avoid overtime. In this case, 6 hours could be spent on washing and drying and 2 hours in other laundry activities. When the property is not 100 percent full, the hours of operation should be reduced or the number of people called to work lowered. If establishments operate with insufficient linen pars, two shifts rather than one may be necessary to turn out enough finished items.

Training laundry workers is of paramount importance, as laundry room operations require the performance of specialized tasks and the handling of sophisticated equipment. Usually the equipment supplier and the company supplying laundry chemicals will provide training assistance. One important training consideration is compliance with OSHA's working standards for laundry workers. Some of these standards specify that all machinery must be equipped with guards to prevent injury to fingers, that steam pipes within employee reach are covered with heat-resistant material, and that power-driven machinery has easily accessible starting and stopping devices. When employing workers who do not read English, safety procedures should be made available in their native language and training workshops should be given by bilingual personnel.

Laundry employees should also be trained in preventive maintenance, energy saving, and expense-reduction procedures. Manufacturers always provide preventive maintenance routines in easy-to-follow manuals. Typically, maintenance personnel make sure that dump valves don't leak or are not stuck in their open positions, that water levels in washers are correctly set, and that lint is regularly removed from dryer traps and ducts. All machines should also be routinely lubricated and calibrated.

KEY TERMS

alkalies	linen poundage
antichlors	mangle
bleach	mobile rack
breaks	rinse cycle
detergent	selection of equipment
equipment layout	soak sinks
extract cycle	softeners
flush cycle	sours
folder stand	specification of equipment
folding table	starch
laundry hamper	tunnel washer
laundry manager	wash cycle
linen chute	washing formula

DISCUSSION AND REVIEW QUESTIONS

1. Give some reasons why having an on-premise laundry can be more advantageous than having the linens processed by an outside commercial company.
2. "Setting up a laundry room requires a detailed analysis of the property's needs." Explain the meaning of this statement.
3. Explain the steps needed to design a laundry room.
4. What are the benefits of installing washers featuring single-pivot tilts?
5. Why are washers with a high G-force preferable to washers with a lower spinning power?
6. Define a property's poundage.
7. What is the purpose of adding softeners to the final washing cycle?
8. How should the training of laundry workers who do not read English be conducted?
9. What are some specifications that should be detailed in a contract for laundering services with an outside commercial company?
10. Based on the national averages given in the "Laundry Operating Costs" of this chapter, what should have been the breakdown for "labor," "linen replacement," "energy," "laundry chemicals," and "other expenses" if the total cost of operating the laundry department had been $47,600?
11. Draw an "ideal" floor plan of a laundry room that has four washers, seven dryers, and one mangle (include soak sinks, folding tables, and one sheet folder stand).
12. What are the advantages and disadvantages of offering valet service to guests in lodging properties?

 MINICASES

Situation 1

Having been hired by a hospitality management company, you have been asked to join the team assigned to open a 500-room hotel in California. Your first task is to work out the "poundage" of the property for bed linen and bathroom linen as a first step to determine the number and capacity of washers to be installed in the laundry room. Do so from the information that follows:

Bed structure:

    200 rooms with one king-size bed in each room
    200 rooms with two queen-size beds in each room
    100 twin-bedded rooms

Bed-linen distribution:

    2 large-size pillows per king-size bed
    2 medium-size pillows per queen-size bed
    1 medium-size pillow per twin bed
    2 sheets for all beds

Bathroom linen distribution:

    king rooms are set with 2 bath towels, 2 hand towels, 2 wash-cloths, and 1 bath mat
    queen rooms are set with 4 bath towels, 4 hand towels, 4 wash-cloths, and 1 bath mat
    twin rooms are set with 2 bath towels, 2 hand towels, 2 wash-cloths, and 1 bath mat

The weight of each piece is as follows:

king sheet:	2.10 pounds
queen sheet:	1.60 pounds
twin sheet:	1.10 pounds
large pillowcase:	0.70 pounds
medium pillowcase:	0.50 pounds
bath towel:	1.25 pounds
hand towel:	0.75 pounds
washcloth:	0.14 pounds
bath mat:	0.70 pounds

Situation 2

After one year in operation, you decide to approximate the laundry costs of the hotel to national average percentages. Your property's costs for the year were:

cost of labor:	$47,700
linen replacement:	15,300
energy:	18,900
laundry chemicals:	5,500
other costs:	4,200

The national average percentages are:

labor:	45%
linen replacement:	20%
energy:	15%
laundry chemicals:	10%
other:	10%

After approximating your costs to national average percentages, list the possible reasons that might have caused the existing discrepancies.

Situation 3

Your company has promoted you to general manager of a resort in Colorado. After analyzing the results for the first 3 months that the property has been under your control, you find that the labor cost in the laundry room of the resort is extremely high. Further investigation points to the fact that the washing capacity of your laundry is very low. For this reason, the laundry has to be operated round the clock, its employees often working overtime.

You decide to lower the labor cost by providing the resort with enough washers to wash one par of linen in 6 hours. The bed linen and terry cloth poundage of the resort is 6,700 pounds. The laundry room is currently equipped with one 50-pound washer to process food and beverage napery and kitchen items. This washer is sufficient to take care of the food and beverage department's needs with one shift, without going into overtime.

The laundry is also equipped with two 100-pound washers to process guestroom linens. Their washing cycles take 27 minutes (roughly one half-hour). How many 100-pound washers do you have to have installed (besides the two that you already have) to finish the 6,700 pounds in 6 hours?

C H A P T E R

9

The Cleaning Function

Hilton Hotel, Instanbul, Turkey.
Courtesy of Hilton Hotels Corporation.

CHAPTER OBJECTIVES

▶ Explain the distribution of work at the beginning of the house-keeping day.

▶ Describe the daily sequence of functions performed by the housekeeping department.

▶ Explain guestroom and bathroom cleaning procedures.

▶ Discuss lost-and-found and guestroom inspection.

▶ Learn about public areas and back-of-the-house cleaning.

▶ Discuss cleaning and maintenance of surfaces.

 OVERVIEW

The primary function of the housekeeping department is to keep its areas of responsibility clean and functional. Every cleaning function must be set in detail in the department's **standard operating procedures (SOPs)**. These procedures describe the routines associated with the daily functions of the department. Specifically, standards are determined to equalize employee workloads, to ensure that employees know what is expected of them, and to maintain high-quality services.

This chapter covers the cleaning of guestrooms, public and employee areas, and surfaces, and describes procedures for inspections, quality assurance, and lost-and-found.

 ## GUESTROOM CLEANING

The essence of the lodging industry is to provide guests with impeccably cleaned rooms and bathrooms. Students of hospitality programs must understand from the beginning that guests do not patronize establishments in which the cleaning function is not conducted effectively.

Sequence of Housekeeping Functions

DISTRIBUTION OF WORK

The housekeeping department is usually opened very early in the morning by an assistant manager or senior supervisor who receives the **front desk report** (Figure 9.1) from the front office department. The front desk report, which is usually prepared by the night clerk or night auditor, consists of a computer printout, or written form if the property is not computerized, specifying the status of each guestroom in the house, the number of rooms occupied the previous night, and the rooms that are expected to check-out and stay-over. This report is an exact copy of the guestroom status found in the front desk computer, or the **room rack** if the property is not computerized. A code beside the numbers of all rooms in the house describes whether the rooms are occupied, vacant, ready, out-of-order, expected to check out today, and so on. The example in Figure 9.1 is for a 400-room property consisting of five floors. Each floor has 80 guestrooms. The night of June 3, 320 rooms were occupied, 83 of which were scheduled to check out on June 4, while 237 rooms were to stay over.

The supervisor receiving the front desk report first verifies whether the number of department employees scheduled yesterday to work today is sufficient to service the number of rooms occupied. If not enough workers were scheduled, the supervisor will have to

Front Desk Report

Date: ____June 3____

Room Occupied: ____320____
Expected Check-outs: ____83____
Expected Stay-overs: ____237____

101:	201:	301:	401:	501:
102:	202:	302:	402:	502:
103:	203:	303:	403:	503:
104:	204:	304:	404:	504:
105:	205:	305:	405:	505:
106:	206:	306:	406:	506:
107:	207:	307:	407:	507:
108:	208:	308:	408:	508:
109:	209:	309:	409:	509:
110:	210:	310:	410:	510:
111:	211:	311:	411:	511:
112:	212:	312:	412:	512:
113:	213:	313:	413:	513:
114:	214:	314:	414:	514:
115:	215:	315:	415:	515:
116:	216:	316:	416:	516:

177:	277:	377:	477:	577:
178:	278:	378:	478:	578:
179:	279:	379:	479:	579:
180:	280:	380:	480:	580:

FIGURE 9.1   Sample Front Desk Report

telephone around to ask people to come to work. On the other hand, if too many workers were scheduled for the occupancy reached, calls will be made to ask some employees to stay away that day, saving them an unnecessary trip to work. Having the right number of workers each day to service the rooms occupied prevents higher than necessary labor costs due to overstaffing or to overtime wages for not having enough employees to do the work in 8 hours.

The information received on the front desk report is then transferred on to the **team supervisor work report** (Figure 9.2)

Team Supervisor Work Report

Date: _____ June 3 _____   Team: _____ One _____

Section 1 HSK Erika	**Section 2** HSK Kate	**Section 3** HSK Melanie	**Section 4** HSK Open	**Section 5** HSK Jennifer
101: OCC	117:	133:	149: OCC	165:
102: C/O	118:	134:	150: OCC	166:
103: OCC	119:	135:	151: VR	167:
104: OCC	120:	136:	152: OCC	168:
105: VR	121:	137:	153: OCC	169:
106: VR	122:	138:	154: C/O	170:
107: OCC	123:	139:	155: OCC	171:
108: C/O	124:	140:	156: OOO	172:
109: OCC	125:	141:	157: VR	173:
110: VR	126:	142:	158: OCC	174:
111: OCC	127:	143:	159: C/O	175:
112: C/O	128:	144:	160: VR	176:
113: OCC	129:	145:	161: OCC	177:
114: VR	130:	146:	162: VR	178:
115: OCC	131:	147:	163: OCC	179:
116: OCC	132:	148:	164: C/O	180:

FIGURE 9.2   Sample Team Supervisor Work Report

to inform all team leaders of the status of all guestrooms in their respective sections. Each team supervisor will then communicate the status of the rooms in each section to the team's section housekeepers using a **section housekeeper work report** (Figure 9.3) which is given to them at the beginning of the shift. When the property is not at 100 percent occupancy, and not all section housekeepers are called to work, the occupied rooms of the sections that are open are assigned to the section housekeepers who are working that day. Figure 9.2 shows that the section housekeeper of section

Team: _____One_____   Section: _____One_____

Date: _____June 3_____   Housekeeper: _____Erika_____

Room	Remarks	Pick-Ups	Remarks
101: OCC		149	E/A
102: C/O		150	
103: OCC	VIP	152	E/A
104: OCC		153	
105: VR			
106: VR			
107: OCC			
108: C/O	L C/O		
109: OCC			
110: VR			
111: OCC			
112: C/O	DEEP CLEAN		
113: OCC			
114: VR			
115: OCC			
116: OCC			

FIGURE 9.3   Sample Section Housekeeper Work Report

4 of team 1 (Maria) has been asked to stay away today. The 11 occupied rooms in section 4 are picked up by the remaining section housekeepers on duty that day—Erika (4) and the remaining 7 by Kate, Melanie, and Jennifer. Figure 9.3 shows Erika's work report with 12 occupied rooms in her section, plus 4 rooms that she will pick up from Maria's open section. The form has a "remarks" column to advise housekeepers of VIP arrivals, early check-ins, late checkouts, deep cleaning, and so forth.

BEGINNING DAILY ACTIVITIES

At the beginning of the working day, housekeeping personnel congregate in the **linen room** where they clock in and receive a briefing on the day's activities. Generally, daily activities in the housekeeping department start at 8:00 A.M., although in some cases this time may be different depending on the type of establishment, day of the week, or special functions taking place at the property. For instance, most of the guests in business hotels do get up early for meeting purposes, to catch an early flight, or attend a convention. On the other hand, on Saturdays and Sundays, guests traditionally get up late and like a late check-out. Also, if the guests of a large convention have been granted permission to check out late in the afternoon, most of the housekeeping work force will be needed to work late to prepare the rooms for that day's arrivals.

The day's work begins with the section housekeepers collecting their fully equipped service cart and work report and signing for the passkey for their respective sections on a key control sheet. In high-rise buildings, all housekeeping personnel should use service elevators only. The work report indicates the status of all rooms in the respective housekeeper sections. Instead of knocking on doors at random, section housekeepers should follow a logical order so that guests are not woken up or disturbed while still in their rooms. Rooms that have already checked out should be serviced first, followed by rooms showing requests for early service, expected check-outs, stay-over rooms, and requests for late service. Last, usually after check-out time, the status of "do-not-disturb" (DND) rooms must be ascertained. It is important to verify what is behind a DND room lest a guest in need of help is unable to use the phone. This situation can occur if the guest is unconscious or in a coma. The first attempt to contact the guest should be done by phone; if the guest answers, the section housekeeper should ask if a cleaning of the room is required. If there is no answer, the section housekeeper should knock at the door and try to enter the room. If there is no answer and the room is double-locked, a manager should enter the room using a master key. In situations when the room is finally opened and the security chain is on, the chain must be cut with a chain-cutter. It is important to remember that in connecting rooms, the guest could have left the DND sign on, double-locked the door, and set the chain in one of the rooms while exiting from the room next door.

Also at the beginning of the working day, hallways, stairwells, vending-machine areas, elevators, and floor closets and vestibules should be inspected by the houseperson of each team. Common problems found early in the morning are leftover room service trays, spills, overflowing wastebaskets, and signs of vandalism. After correcting these flaws, the housepersons proceed to help the section housekeepers in their respective teams by providing them with supplies, moving heavy pieces of furniture, taking soiled linen to the laundry room, and so on. The housepersons usually finish their shift by vacuuming the public areas assigned to each of their teams.

ROOM STATUS VERIFICATION

As the daily work progresses, section housekeepers should notify their team supervisors if any discrepancy is found between the status of rooms as shown in their work report and the real status of the rooms. For example, if the section housekeeper work report shows that room 105 is occupied and there is no sign of guests in the room, the front desk report might have been wrong. In this case, the front office must be immediately notified of the discrepancy.

Some lodging properties require that the housekeeping department file a status report for the accounting department as a cross-reference to the occupancy report submitted by the front office. If the front desk is selling rooms and pocketing the money or if they let employees or friends stay in guestrooms for free, the problem is soon discovered. At about 10 o'clock, the **A.M. room check** is conducted by all teams entering the guestrooms at about the same time. All relevant discrepancies found from the front desk report must be communicated to the front desk as quickly as possible.

As work progresses, the team supervisors coordinate the activities related to the rooms in their sections, such as communicating to the front desk the rooms that are vacant and ready to be sold, notifying section housekeepers of guests changing rooms, communicating the need to clean rooms for early arrivals, VIP treatment, and so forth. In most properties, team supervisors are also in charge of inspecting guestrooms.

GUESTROOM CLEANING PROCEDURES

Section housekeepers should knock at the door with their knuckles, announcing themselves as "housekeeping," at least twice prior to entering the room. The door should remain open, with the service cart blocking the entrance for safety reasons. This way, if someone attempts to pull the cart to enter the room, the section housekeeper would be alerted.

All lodging properties have standard operating procedures for guestroom cleaning; however, these procedures differ from property to property. Usually, section housekeepers are asked to air out the room by opening windows and turn on all lights to make sure that they are in working order. The TV set and the heating/air-conditioning units are then checked, resetting the thermostat to the lowest comfortable setting. The section housekeeper ascertains that no items are missing, broken, or vandalized. If that is the case, the team supervisor should be notified immediately, who in turn will call the front desk so that the guest is charged accordingly. If out-of-order or not working equipment is found, a work order is filled out and sent to the maintenance department. If the guests have checked out of the room, the section housekeeper should ascertain that no personal belongings have been left behind. If they have, the team supervisor is notified as soon as possible, who, in turn, will notify the front desk and security department. If the guests have not checked out, all scattered clothing items, papers, documents or magazines should be placed away neatly, making sure that nothing is thrown away that may be useful to the guest.

The first step in cleaning the bedroom is to empty out the trash in the refuse bag of the service cart, changing the wastebasket liners with new ones and cleaning the ashtrays. The bed is stripped, keeping items off the floor and handling the linen carefully lest guest items have been left there. Special care must be taken with sharps (needles) that may be in the sheets. At this time, the mattress, box spring, blanket, bedspread, pillows, and bed pads are carefully inspected for stains or torn spots and replaced as needed. The soiled bed and bathroom linen is placed in the service cart receptacle for fast delivery to the laundry room for processing as soon as the bag is full. In most properties, the houseperson regularly empties the receptacles into a hamper for transportation.

BASIC BED-MAKING PROCEDURES

The first step in making the bed is to place the bottom sheet smoothly on it, tucking it at the head and sides. The bottom and top sheets and blanket are then mitered at the foot of the bed and tucked along the sides. The bedspread is then placed over the blanket, turned about 15 inches back from the headboard, and the pillow(s) placed over it. Both bedspread and pillow(s) are then rolled back toward the headboard. The bedspread should be smoothed out so no lumps or creases show after the bed has been made. Section housekeepers should be trained to make beds moving around them only once in order to save time and energy.

DUSTING AND WIPING THE BEDROOM

Lamp shades are brushed with a dry cloth or feather duster. All furniture, fixtures, and doors are lightly sprayed with a cleaning solution or furniture polish and damp-wiped with a dust cloth. Air vents, windowsills, light bulbs, telephones, the top of thermostats, and closet shelves are also wiped clean with a damp cloth. Drawers are wiped out and inspected for cleanliness and ease of operation. If the drawers are difficult to open (or close), a work order should be filled out. All recycled items should be meticulously cleaned or replaced. The property or chain literature and phone books must be kept as new, without marks or creases. Missing clothes hangers should be replaced and those not belonging to the property removed. Mirrors and TV screen should be sprayed and wiped with a dry cloth. All drapes, lamp shades, and pictures must be centered and balanced.

The carpet is then vacuumed, including under the bed, starting at the far end of the room and ending at the door. Finally, deodorant spray is applied to curtains and carpet before leaving the room. This procedure is particularly necessary in "smoking rooms."

When the guestroom has a balcony or patio, the floor is swept and the door and furniture dusted. If the room is at floor level, the patio door should be properly secured by setting the security bar in place. Properties offering suites with kitchenettes require considerable labor to service the living, cooking, and dining areas. Dishes must be washed, cooking equipment and utensils scrubbed and polished, and refrigerators, cupboards, and drawers wiped clean.

Some lodging properties have experimented with guestroom team cleaning; that is, having two section housekeepers clean guestrooms at the same time. Although team cleaning may be preferred by housekeeping workers, it usually is not labor-cost effective. In practice, a room that is serviced in 30 minutes by one room attendant cannot be finished by two room attendants in 15 minutes.

BATHROOM CLEANING

Section housekeepers should wear gloves when cleaning the bathroom for chemical and germ protection. After checking all lights, inspecting the faucets for leaks, and dumping the wastebasket, the commode is cleaned inside with bowl cleaner and a toilet brush and outside (including the tank) with a germicidal solution. The bath area should be cleaned by the section housekeeper standing inside the tub on a rubber mat placed at the bottom of the tub to keep from slipping. The bath walls, soap dishes, plumbing fixtures, and shower doors are cleaned with all-purpose cleaner and wiped dry with a cloth. The tub is cleaned, using mild scouring powder/liquid if necessary. The tub stopper should be pulled out, freed from hair, and wiped clean.

The vanity and sink are cleaned with all-purpose cleaner and wiped dry. The sink stopper should also be pulled out and wiped clean. The mirror should be cleaned with a damp cloth or sprayed with a mirror-cleaning solution and wiped dry. The bathroom floor should be wiped with cloth and germicidal, including behind the door. Any lint in the bathroom ventilation vent or fan grill should be removed. All supplies and guest amenities should be replaced as needed. Towels should be neatly folded in racks or hanged properly from towel bars. Toilet and facial tissue should be replaced if less than one-quarter full. A second toilet tissue roll should be left in the bathroom as reserve. It is a good idea to have section housekeepers place a card stating that the room was serviced by them; this increases pride and identifies the worker with the job performed; for example, "Hello, this room has been serviced by Erika. Have a pleasant stay with us."

After the room has been cleaned, the section housekeeper notifies the supervisor that the room is ready for inspection. In some properties, section housekeepers may use codes through the telephone or the television set to inform the housekeeping office that the rooms have been serviced.

LOST-AND-FOUND PROCEDURES

All items found in a lodging property are usually deposited in and controlled by the housekeeping department, given that most articles are left behind by guests in the property's guestrooms. Standard operating procedures for lost-and-found items must be in place and made clear to all employees. In all cases, when articles are found anywhere in the property they must be taken to the housekeeping department (usually to the linen room) and adequately tagged and logged for fast identification. The lost-and-found logbook must include the date on which the item was found, its description, the place where it was found, the person who found it, and the number assigned to the tagged item. At times when the housekeeping department is closed, the article will be securely kept at the front desk and brought to the linen room first thing in the morning. Items containing multiple articles, such as bags, wallets, or purses, should be inventoried and their content described and verified by two employees. All tagged items must be kept under lock and key for security reasons. All inquiries regarding lost-and-found items should be addressed to the housekeeping office. After proper identification, the items are returned to their owners. If the inquiry is made from out of town, the property should send the item free of charge to its owner by mail or UPS package. Valuable articles should be sent by registered mail or insured for their approximate cost. It is customary in the hospitality industry that items not claimed within a reasonable period of time, generally three months, are given to the employee who found them or given away to a charitable organization.

THE P.M. HOUSEKEEPING REPORT

Prior to the end of the morning shift, all section housekeepers conduct a check of all the rooms in the house simultaneously. Each room attendant records on a blank daily work report (Figure 9.3) the status of each guestroom in his or her section. The reports of all section housekeepers are recorded on a blank front desk report (Figure 9.1) and delivered to the front desk. The front desk will then compare the housekeeping room status with the status kept in the front desk's computer, or room rack if the property is not computerized. Any discrepancy between the room status provided by the housekeeping department and the room status at the front desk is quickly investigated and corrected. For example, if the housekeeping room report indicates that room 101 is occupied and the records at the front desk show that the room is vacant, the room is checked as to whether housekeeping or the front desk was in error.

At the end of the morning shift, the housekeepers of every team restock the floor closets assigned to them with clean linen and guest and cleaning supplies, they vacuum hallways, tidy vending areas and stairwells, and dump all trash. If time allows, section housekeepers refit service carts for the following day and store them for the night.

INSPECTION OF GUESTROOMS

The general rule in lodging properties is to have all guestrooms inspected by qualified staff before they are handed over to the front desk for renting them to guests. This control function is important for properties with quality assurance programs, as inspectors are the last employees to catch any errors made during cleaning before guests arrive. Small properties with no or very low turnover may decide to trust their section housekeepers and leave to them the job of inspecting the rooms just after they have been cleaned. Large properties, however, should have a rigorous system of inspecting guestrooms prior to their being rented to guests. Usually, the guestrooms are inspected by the supervisor of each team; some large hotels have designated inspectors whose only job is to check rooms.

In all cases, standards should be set to help section housekeepers and inspectors work toward reaching the same goals of cleanliness and room appearance. Figure 9.4 is a sample **guestroom inspection form** for a suite hotel that can be used in room inspections. Often, inspectors give scores to the section housekeeper responsible for cleaning the room that determine, after a certain period of time, whether the room attendant qualifies for bonuses or rewards attached to superior performance. On the other hand, substandard scores will lead to retraining room attendants or disqualifying them for the job. Inspectors should be trained to do fair and

Date: _____ Room: _____ Housekeeper: _____ Inspector: _____

1. Closet shelf clean	_____	25. Notepad and pen	_____
2. Laundry bag with ticket	_____	26. Ashtrays clean with matches	_____
3. 8 hangers properly placed	_____	27. Wastebaskets empty and clean	_____
4. Microwave and fridge clean	_____	28. Drapes neat and working	_____
5. Shower walls and soap dish clean	_____	29. Window sills/inside windows clean	_____
6. Shower curtain/liner clean/dry	_____	30. Night stands clean/dusted	_____
7. Sink and wet bar clean	_____	31. Telephone books/Bible in drawer	_____
8. Bathtub clean/no mildew	_____	32. Pictures clean and dust free	_____
9. Sink and vanity clean	_____	33. Bed made neatly and properly	_____
10. All chrome cleaned and shined	_____	34. Headboard clean and dusted	_____
11. Stoppers clean and free of hair	_____	35. Carpet edges clean	_____
12. Mirrors clean and spot free	_____	36. All drawers and shelves clean/dusted	_____
13. T.P./Kleenex folded and stocked	_____	37. Vanity mirror clean and spot free	_____
14. Entire toilet clean	_____	38. Light switches clean	_____
15. Bathroom floor clean/no hair	_____	39. Baseboards clean and dusted	_____
16. All linen placed properly folded	_____	40. Thermostat properly set and dusted	_____
17. All amenities in proper place	_____	41. Door frames and doors clean	_____
18. Glasses clean and spot free	_____	42. DND sign clean/in good condition	_____
19. Ice bucket in place/clean/dry	_____	43. Safety lock in good condition	_____
20. TVs and remote clean and in place	_____	44. Entry mat/doorway clean/no cob webs	_____
21. Table and chairs clean/dust free	_____	45. All lights dusted and working	_____
22. Table lamp clean and working	_____	46. Carpet vacuumed and edged	_____
23. All printed collateral placed neatly and properly	_____	47. Clock radio clean/time and station properly set	_____
24. Phones and receivers clean	_____		_____

FIGURE 9.4 Sample Guestroom Inspection Form

accurate inspections. Some properties enter the data collected on a computer to show performance over the long term. The data may show that the performance of a particular team is low in a specific area, for example bathrooms. In this case, additional training in bathroom cleaning should be emphasized to bring the team up to bathroom–cleaning standards. Vacant-and-ready (VR) rooms should be inspected first so they can be turned over to front desk for assignment to early arrivals. The person who inspects rooms must be well trained to detect errors and make sure that everything in the room is in perfect order. Well-trained inspectors can perform this function very quickly and effectively without having to use checklists.

Some inspection programs include the preventive maintenance inspection of guestrooms in order to anticipate mechanical or functional breakdowns before they may occur. Figure 9.5 is a sample **maintenance inspection checklist** used for this purpose. When deficiencies are detected, a **maintenance work order** (Figure 9.6) is filed and sent to the engineering department for immediate attention. Maintenance work orders should be in triplicate—two parts going to engineering and one kept on file until the job is completed. If the deficiency is not corrected after a reasonable amount of time, a **second work order request** should be initiated. The order form for emergency repairs, such as broken guestroom door locks, should be marked "urgent" and delivered to the engineering department in person for immediate action.

THE EVENING SHIFT

The housekeeping evening activities in medium-size properties are usually conducted by a team consisting of a supervisor, a houseperson, a reduced number of section housekeepers, and one or two janitors. In large and very large properties, a greater number of employees is necessary.

The evening team receives the housekeeping P.M. report showing the status of all the guestrooms at the end of the morning shift and continues with the task of cleaning late check-out and day-rate rooms so these can be rented to guests. If the property offers **turndown service**, the evening team will perform the tasks of unfolding the bed, drawing the drapes closed, and refreshing the room by emptying the trash and replacing used towels. The evening section housekeepers also fill guest requests, such as delivering extra pillows or blankets to rooms, providing cribs or roll-a-way beds, or bringing extra towels. The evening teams also wash drinking glasses, restock service carts and **caddies** (portable cleaning-supply containers with a handle), clean public restrooms and, if necessary, process soiled linen in the property's laundry. It is important to provide beepers to members of the evening team so that the front desk or manager-on-duty can effectively communicate with housekeeping personnel.

Date: _____ Room: _____ Housekeeper: _____ Inspector: _____

Bathroom

1. Bathtub safety strips _____
2. Tub and sink stoppers _____
3. Tub and sink plugs _____
4. Shower head clean _____
5. Bath tile/walls _____
6. Toilet drain/flush _____
7. Toilet—no leaks _____
8. Toilet seat, hinges, bumpers _____
9. Toilet seal—no leaks _____
10. Faucets—no leaks _____
11. Chrome fixtures _____
12. Shower rod—secure _____
13. Vanity and tub—no scratches _____
14. Toilet paper holder _____
15. Facial tissue holder _____
16. Soap dish—secure _____
17. Grab bars—secure _____
18. Towel racks—secure _____

Electrical

19. Lamp switches _____
20. Lamp sockets—tight _____
21. Lamp shades—tight _____
22. Plugs and cords _____
23. Light switches _____
24. Wall plates _____

Television/Radio

25. Audio—clear _____
26. Visual—in focus _____
27. Cable connections _____
28. Chassis—secured _____

Telephone

29. Audio—clear _____
30. Bell—ringer _____
32. Message light _____

Doors

33. Handles _____
34. Lock _____
35. Hinges _____
36. Door chain _____
37. Door bumpers _____
38. Door stoppers _____

Furniture

39. Drawer handles _____
40. All surfaces _____
41. Chair/tables _____
42. Headboard—secure _____
43. Nightstand—undamaged _____
44. Pictures—secure _____

Sliding Doors

45. Tracks—clean _____
46. Doorstops _____
47. Latches _____
48. Security bar _____

Windows/Mirrors

49. Window guides _____
50. Window latches _____
51. Window caulk _____
52. Drapery hardware _____
53. Mirrors—secure _____
54. Mirrors—no scratches _____

Room

55. Coat racks—secure _____
56. Baseboards—secure _____
57. Wall coverings _____
58. Ceiling-no cracks _____
59. Smoke detector _____
60. Insulation _____
61. Hot water—120°F _____

FIGURE 9.5 Sample Maintenance Inspection Sheet

Date: _____   Location: _____

Problem: _____

_____

_____

_____

_____

_____

Completed by: _____

Date completed: _____

Remarks: _____

_____

_____

_____

_____

_____

FIGURE 9.6   Sample Maintenance Work Order

The service carts are also stocked in the evening to facilitate operations and avoid confusion the following morning. Each service cart is supplied with bed and bathroom linens, paper supplies, guest amenities, and recycled items. The cleaning supplies commonly placed in caddies are cleaning solutions, brushes, scrubbers, sponges, and cleaning rags. The service cart is equipped with trash and soiled-linen bags. A broom and dustpan and a vacuum cleaner are also placed on the cart. If the property uses keys instead of guestroom entry cards, the cart should also have a locked bolted-on metal box with a slot where the leftover keys are placed. Its purpose is to avoid leaving guestroom keys on top of the cart where they are easily accessible to thieves.

GUESTROOM DEEP CLEANING

Section housekeepers are usually allotted an average of 30 minutes to service a stay-over or check-out room. Periodically, room attendants are given extra time to clean guestrooms in depth, performing tasks such as brushing carpet edges, rotating mattresses, vacuuming drapes, and cleaning under the furniture. In order not to tie up guestrooms for long periods of time, deep cleaning should be combined with maintenance tasks conducted by the engineering department, such as recaulking tubs, changing air conditioning filters, or performing minor repairs. Deep cleaning of guestrooms should be intensified during low-occupancy periods. Generally all rooms in the house should be deep cleaned at least once a year.

 ## PUBLIC AREAS AND BACK-OF-THE-HOUSE CLEANING

The housekeeping department is also in charge of the cleaning and maintenance of offices, public and back-of-the-house areas. Potential guests and visitors have a first-hand opportunity to judge the cleanliness of the property from what they see in the "on-stage" public areas. Public and employee areas are cleaned by janitors, who are scheduled to work regardless of the property's occupancy, because the front- and back-of-the-house areas must be kept clean, whether the property is full or not, 24 hours a day.

The cleaning of public areas is conducted following pre-established area cleaning inventories and frequency schedules (see Figure 3.1). Thus, the janitors will know exactly what and how often all their assigned areas must be cleaned. For instance, while the chandelier in the lobby of the property usually is dusted every two months, the carpet in the same area is vacuumed daily (or twice a day). Besides cleaning, janitors should keep public areas in good order by straightening the furniture, emptying ashtrays, trashcans, and cigarette urns, and taking away empty glasses and used newspapers. The handset of public telephones should be wiped clean with a germicidal solution and the telephone book replaced if it has scribbled lines on it.

Special attention must be given to the foyer and lobby where guests will get a first impression of the property upon entering the establishment. Handprints and smudges on glass doors are common, as well as footprints and traces of mud on the carpet when the weather is inclement. Appropriate matting and runners must be placed strategically to protect the appearance of the lobby's floor. The presence of dust, cobwebs, smudges, dull-looking water fountains, or unpolished wood surfaces in the public areas is unacceptable. Elevators, including service elevators, require frequent attention as bell carts and heavy suitcases do often bump against walls and floor, scratching or marking their finish.

Just as important as public areas is the cleaning of employee areas and other sections at the back of the house. The employee locker room and restrooms are areas where vandalism and graffiti marks frequently occur. The upkeep of these areas, hallways, and the employee cafeteria is a reflection of the care and concern that the company bestows on its employees, which may positively or negatively affect the morale of the property's work force.

RESTROOM CLEANING

Public restrooms require special and dedicated attention, as they are not only used by guests, but also by visitors, restaurant and bar patrons, and people attending meetings or conventions in the property. Public restrooms must be constantly checked, cleaned, and stocked with high-quality sanitary, paper, and soap supplies.

Restrooms should be fitted with automatic air fresheners or other method of odor control. Battery-operated wall cabinets can automatically deliver fragrances using 30-day cartridges. Men's urinals should be equipped with screens and deodorizing blocks containing chelating agents to prevent mineral deposit buildups. Basins and counter tops should be sanitized with a germicidal cleaner. All chrome fixtures should be wiped clean and polished. Toilets should be brushed inside with an effective bowl cleaner and the tank cover (if any) and body of the bowl wiped clean with cleansing solution. Special attention must be given to graffiti and lipstick marks, so common in public spaces. Mops used in restrooms should be sanitized with a strong disinfectant solution added to the water in the bucket/wringer.

SURFACE CLEANING

Surface coverings may be classified into resilient and nonresilient according to their hardness. Cleaning and maintenance of floors and walls depends on the composition of the surface's material. Surfaces must be preserved from deterioration as much as possible by protecting them from wear and tear. Once the surface shows signs of wearing away, it must be redone to bring it back to its original state.

The first step to redo floors is to remove the worn out finish. This process is called **stripping**. Commercial floors are stripped using a stripping solution mixed with water and scrubbing the surface with a rotary floor machine. The resulting mixture is picked up with a wet vacuum or mop and bucket and the floor rinsed with clean water. After the floor dries, porous surfaces are treated with a **sealer** to protect them from wear and tear and liquid spills. The last step is to apply a **finish** to the surface to make it slip resistant and give the floor a glossy, shiny look. Often, sealer and finish are combined into one product. Finished surfaces are maintained by polishing them with rotary floor machines which clean, buff, and burnish the floor using different types of pads.

The most common resilient surfaces found in lodging operations are made of synthetic rubber, vinyl, wood and, of course, carpeting. The most common hard floors (nonresilient) are ceramic, marble/terrazzo, epoxy, and concrete. The composition of the floor determines the kind of care it should receive. For instance, while porous surfaces require sealing, the sealing of nonporous floors is unnecessary.

SYNTHETIC RUBBER FLOORS

Floors covered with synthetic rubber tiles are nonporous and therefore waterproof; however, liquids containing oil, solvent, or grease may cause the material to crack and deteriorate. Rubber floors are easy to maintain, as they just require mopping to keep them clean. The cleaning solution used should be pH neutral, as alkalies and acids would mar these surfaces. These types of floors do not require sealing. Synthetic floors can be kept shiny by buffing them with a water emulsion floor polish. When wax or dirt buildup is embedded in the finish, the floor should be stripped with a mild de-waxer.

VINYL FLOORS

These are nonporous surfaces resistant to most chemical spills. Thick vinyl material is quite durable and can be purchased in a variety of patterns to resemble natural products. If the material is treated with special seals when made, it can be resistant to scratches and abrasions. No-wax vinyl surfaces do not need sealing, stripping, or finishing. Conventional vinyl floors can be treated with solvent-based waxes and buffed to a rich luster. Wax buildup can be removed with a mild de-waxing stripper. Dusting and daily mop-and-rinse will remove most dirt and grime.

Wood Floors

Wood floors are not common in most modern lodging properties, where carpeting, ceramic tile, and synthetic surfaces are the norm, but they may be found in older establishments and in some ski resorts and hunting lodges. Because of its porosity, wooden floors must be well sealed to prevent stains; once stained, the surface needs to be thoroughly sanded to remove the marks. Wood floors can also be damaged by mobile equipment with metal rollers and by moving heavy furniture without first protecting the surface. These surfaces can be treated with a combination sealer/finish made of waterborne polyurethane. When properly sealed and finished, wooden floors just require an occasional buffing to keep them shiny.

Carpets

Preventing staining and wear is more important for carpets than it is for other types of floor coverings. For example, if the lobby of a lodging property is carpeted, the slush, mud, and gritty soil tracked in by guests quickly become embedded in the carpet fabric, causing it to stain and wear very fast. The best prevention for carpet deterioration is adequate protection. Placing walk-off mats in doorways and plastic runners over the most high-traffic sections of the carpet will lengthen its life and save labor hours in cleaning and maintenance.

Scheduled daily vacuuming of carpets is probably the best way to extend their lives. Most of the soil tracked into a building is dry—the kind that can be controlled by vacuuming. The absorption of dust, sand, and grit particles by vacuuming will prevent the erosion of fibers when they are compressed by the weight of traffic from people and carts. Vacuums with top-loading bags are preferable, as they ensure that the vacuum does not lose effectiveness as the bag fills.

Marks and stains can be removed by bonnet cleaning, by which carpet shampoo is sprayed on the surface to be treated and a rotary floor machine equipped with a bonnet is passed over until the stains are removed. When surfaces are heavily soiled, deep cleaning is necessary. Heavy soils can be treated using water extractors that automatically apply the cleaning solution and pick it up with an attached wet vacuum system that recovers water and soil in a holding tank. Carpets should be cleaned with hot water, except for wool fabrics that require cold water. Dry foam and dry powder methods are less effective than water extractors, but it takes less time for the carpet to dry so the area can be used sooner if necessary. Some products applied regularly to carpets are antimicrobial solutions to prevent the growth of bacteria and fungi, antistatic sprays to eliminate static electricity caused by low humidity or high winds, and fluorochemical treatments that resist soiling and prevent spills from becoming hard-to-remove stains.

UPHOLSTERED SURFACES

Upholstered armchairs and couches can be spot-cleaned with most of the same products used on carpets. Machines with special attachments are needed to apply the spot removers to narrow surfaces. Some spotters are fortified with enzymes to treat organic compounds; tougher soils, such as crayon, fresh paint, ink, and gum, require solvent formulas to dissolve the stains.

CERAMIC FLOORS

Because ceramic floors are very resistant to water spills and easy to clean, they are quite common in bathroom and kitchen. Usually, the terracotta that forms the tile is covered with a glossy coat that makes the surface 100 percent waterproof. A disadvantage with this type of floor is that they can be very slippery when wet. These surfaces are cleaned by sweeping and damp mopping. Sealing or finishing of ceramic floors is not necessary, except for the grout between the tiles.

MARBLE/TERRAZZO FLOORS

Marble is a crystalline limestone that is capable of taking a polish. Terrazzo is a floor material of broken stone (marble or granite chips) and cement that can also be easily lustered. Although very hard and durable, these surfaces are very sensitive to oils and acid and alkaline cleaners. A mild detergent is all that is needed to keep them clean. Because of their porosity, marble and terrazzo floors must be sealed, and when stripped, alkaline products should be avoided. The surfaces can be burnished to obtain a mirrorlike finish.

EPOXY FLOORS

Epoxy is a synthetic material that is durable, abrasion-resistant, and easy to maintain. Alkaline compounds diluted in water are used to clean epoxy floors. Epoxy surfaces can be kept shiny with a light finish application. Alkaline products are needed to strip the finish.

CONCRETE FLOORS

Concrete floors, made with a mixture of cement and sand, are usually used as outdoor surfaces, such as driveways, loading docks, and poolside areas. Cleaning is done by sweeping and hosing with water. Concrete is a porous compound that should be sealed to prevent liquid stains from seeping into it. Urethane-fortified products resist water and help protect against graffiti. An alkaline product diluted in water is required to strip the sealer.

WALLS AND CEILINGS

Some wall and ceiling coverings that are different from those normally used on floor surfaces are paint, plastic laminate, fabric, vinyl, and wallpaper. Painted surfaces can be cleaned with mild detergent and water. Dusting and damp-wiping are all that it is required to keep plastic laminate clean, as it is nonporous and will not absorb stains. Fabric materials are very susceptible to mildew and stains. Walls covered with fabric should be spot-cleaned with chemicals rather than with water and detergent to avoid shrinkage. Vinyl covering can be purchased in many decorative motifs. It is durable and easy to clean with mild detergents. On the other hand, most wallpaper coverings cannot be cleaned with water, so they must be replaced if they are marked or stained.

Written procedures for all aspects of daily maintenance of surfaces should be established. In general, grease and dirt are acidic in nature and they are best cleaned with alkaline products. The more grease and dirt on a surface, the more alkalinity is needed in the cleaning compound to treat the area. When light soils are present, particularly on highly polished floors, a neutral product is required (pH range 7 to 8). The higher the pH, the more likely the floor polish will be damaged.

KEY TERMS

A.M. room checks
caddy
finish (floor)
front desk report
guestroom inspection form
linen room
maintenance inspection
   checklist
maintenance work order
P.M. room report

room rack
sealer (floor)
second work order request
section housekeeper work
   report
standard operating procedures
stripper (floor)
turndown service
team supervisor work report

DISCUSSION AND REVIEW QUESTIONS

1. Explain why housekeeping departments in lodging operations must compile standard operating procedures for the operative routines of the department.
2. Explain the purpose of the front desk report.
3. After receiving the front desk report, what must the housekeeping supervisor verify?
4. Which two reports are compiled from the information received on the front desk report?
5. What is the reason section housekeepers should not knock on all guestrooms of their sections early in the morning?
6. What is the difference between the A.M. report and the P.M. report generated in the housekeeping department?
7. Briefly describe cleaning procedures for guestrooms.
8. List the minimum types of chemicals needed to service a bathroom.
9. Why is the lost-and-found function usually administered by the housekeeping department in lodging properties?
10. What is the difference between a maintenance inspection checklist and a maintenance work order?
11. Describe the purpose of stripping, sealing, and finishing floors.
12. What are the advantages and disadvantages of ceramic floors?

MINICASES

Situation 1

As the assistant to the executive housekeeper of the 400-room Royal Hotel, you have been asked to open the department on Monday, June 15. On arriving to work at 5:30 in the morning, you receive the front desk report, which states that the number of occupied rooms the night of Sunday, June 14 had been 385. Checking the adjusted daily schedule posted Sunday afternoon you find that the number of section housekeepers scheduled to work this morning is 21. The workload for section housekeepers at the Royal is 16 rooms to be serviced in 8 hours. What is your reaction to this situation? Would you call around to ask additional section housekeepers to report to work? If so, how many would you call to work? Or would you ask some section housekeepers to stay away because there are not enough occupied rooms for all the housekeepers scheduled to work today? If so, how many would you ask to stay away?

Situation 2

As executive housekeeper of a resort in Boca Raton, Florida, you have been asked to give your professional opinion on the type of floor covering you would recommend for three areas of the property that are going to be remodeled six months from now. The areas in need of new floors are the resort's coffee shop, the main lobby, and the employee locker room. The weather in Boca Raton is subtropical, with warm summers and mild winters. The property has two large swimming pools and the guests practice several water sports at the nearby oceanfront. For this reason, people staying at the resort often go to the front desk and concierge areas dripping water from their wet bathing suits. Sometimes they even go to the coffee shop counter in wet attire.

Present a written report to your supervisor indicating the types of floors that you recommend for the three areas, including the advantages and disadvantages of the new surfaces you advocate.

Situation 3

You have been hired as assistant to the executive housekeeper of a hotel in downtown San Francisco. One of the problems that you have found in the housekeeping department is that some of the team supervisors, fearful of running short of linen in their sections, consistently hoard linen items in their floor closets. This practice causes other teams to run out of linen in the middle of the daily activities, as the laundry room cannot generate enough clean items to go around.

Determined to solve this problem, you want to give specific instruction on how many linen items (maximum) can be stored in each floor closet. Each closet is designed to hold enough linen to service two sections. Each section consists of 16 guestrooms. Each room has two queen-size beds with two sheets and two pillows on each bed. The bathrooms are supplied with four bath towels, four hand towels, four washcloths, and one bath mat. You decide to allow a maximum of 1.5 linen par for each item in all floor closets. What is the maximum number of sheets, pillowcases, towels, and bath mats that the team supervisors can now stock in each floor closet?

PART 4

Human Resources Management

Courtesy of Hilton Hotels Corporation.

Personnel Administration

CHAPTER OBJECTIVES

- ► Understand the need to minimize employee turnover and absenteeism in the housekeeping department in order to maximize departmental income.
- ► Explain the process of selecting, hiring, and evaluating housekeeping employees.
- ► List some considerations to be followed when interviewing employees.
- ► Discuss procedures for testing and inducting workers.
- ► Describe the four major areas involved in housekeeping employee training.
- ► Discuss motivation theories applicable to housekeeping workers.
- ► Describe the concept of employee evaluation and compensation.
- ► Learn how to effect worker satisfaction.
- ► Discuss the necessity of implementing guidelines for disciplining employees.
- ► Acquire awareness of cultural diversity, racial discrimination, and sexual harassment.

OVERVIEW

Employee turnover and absenteeism rates in the lodging industry are very high, substantially increasing the labor cost associated with constant recruiting and employee training. Successful executive housekeepers, however, can minimize turnover by following effective techniques for recruiting, hiring, and training employees. Practicing motivational methods and having in place adequate evaluation and compensation techniques can also create worker satisfaction and reduce turnover. Just as important as creating worker satisfaction is having in place fair, effective guidelines for disciplining those employees who do not perform within company regulations.

As the number of minority workers in lodging companies is very large, this chapter addresses the issue of cultural diversity and provides procedures to avoid racial discrimination and sexual harassment in the workplace.

 THE NEED TO CURB HIGH EMPLOYEE TURNOVER AND ABSENTEEISM

The management of personnel in the lodging industry is complex. The business requires a large number of workers because most of the functions performed must be done by hand. Some years back, the use of robotics was forecast to be a labor-saving panacea for lodging properties but, although some technological advances have been made, particularly in laundries and front desk operations, beds still need to be made, bathrooms still need to be cleaned, and guests still need to be served by employees. The industry is notorious for offering jobs that are quite demanding and for paying workers minimum wage, particularly at entry-level positions. Many people enter the field when they cannot find work elsewhere, perceiving their employment as a last resort rather than a career. This creates a chronic shortage of personnel as employees come and go in great numbers. It is not uncommon for lodging properties to experience employee turnover rates of over 100 percent per year. Today, when unemployment rates are at an all-time low level, the balance of power is shifting from employers to employees, causing a people shortage that is spreading to all sectors of the hospitality industry.

It is therefore critical that executive housekeepers maintain low levels of employee turnover and absenteeism.

There are two basic means to reduce turnover and absenteeism effectively: one is to follow the common technical rules of adequately recruiting, selecting, training, and evaluating personnel; the other consists of practicing effective methods of employee motivation, compensation, and the creation of an environment conducive to employee satisfaction.

RECRUITING, SELECTING, HIRING, AND TRAINING EMPLOYEES

Ideally, a lodging property should employ only cheerful, good-natured people who smile easily and often, particularly when in contact with guests. Conversely, grouchy people, those who cannot keep their tempers, and who feel sorry for themselves should not be hired at all. In all cases, the success of the operation depends on attracting applicants and placing them in the positions most appropriate to their skills and personalities.

Hiring applicants "off the street" may have a very negative outcome. If the wrong person is initially placed in the wrong position, turnover will result, as the person will inevitably leave the company, voluntarily or otherwise. Trial-and-error methods of employment should be avoided; instead, sound recruiting and hiring policies should be adopted.

Recruiting Housekeeping Employees

Housekeeping hires most of the department's employees on an as-needed basis; that is, they are asked to work depending on the daily occupancy of the property. Some employees, who are scheduled regardless of the property's occupancy, are hired **full-time**, such as supervisors, janitors, or linen room attendants. **Part-time** employees agree to work usually less than 30 hours per week, generally receiving no major benefits other than wages. In most cases, part-time workers have an additional source of income, as they may be retirees, homemakers, or college students. Often, because of cost and fear of overstaffing, businesses turn toward staffing companies for **temporary help**. One advantage of hiring temporaries is that it allows the employer to evaluate the temporary employees' qualifications and suitability for the job before offering them a full-time permanent position. Lodging properties should also have a number of people **on-call**, who are asked to report to work when extra help is needed, such as when regular employees are ill or on vacation.

UNIONS

Union contracts, however, may have a significant impact on the composition of the company's work force. For example, a union contract may stipulate that all workers must be guaranteed a 40-hour work week; in this case, no part-time employees can be hired.

In all cases recruiting new employees is a special concern to both organization and newcomer. Management expects good performance and cooperation, while the new employee wants fair compensation, to be understood and recognized and, above all, to be helped during the induction process. In large hotels, the human resources department recruits employees. The order to recruit is initiated in the housekeeping department by filling an **employee requisition form** (Figure 10.1). This form indicates the position that needs to be filled and describes the specification of the job and the required qualifications of the applicant. The **job description** is a detailed statement of the tasks required to get the job done. Figure 10.2 is a job description for section housekeepers. Each job description should include the minimum **employee qualifications** required and desired to ensure that applicants will be capable of doing the job for which they are applying. For example, the job description for laundry attendant may require that the applicant be capable of lifting 50 pounds (weight of laundry detergent pails used in the property) and may state that Spanish-speaking workers are preferred (as are most of the other employees in the laundry).

After receiving the employee requisition, the human resources department advertises the position internally (**internal recruiting**) and externally (**external recruiting**). An organization that develops its personnel exclusively from within may be limiting itself by having to promote employees who may not be qualified for the position. On the other hand, capable employees already working for the company should be given a fair option to advance or change positions, and even departments, if they so desire.

Date: _____ Department: _____

Position Requested: _____

New: _____ Replacement: _____ Number Required: ____

Classification: _____
(Full-time, Part-time, Temporary)

Working Hours: _____

Desired Starting Date: _____

Starting Rate of Pay: _____

Specification (general description of duties):

_____

_____

_____

_____

_____

_____

Special Qualifications (desired or required):

_____

_____

_____

_____

_____

_____

Department Manager: _____

FIGURE 10.1   Sample Employee Requisition Form

Thus, the first step is to inform everyone in the department of the job opening. If no one is interested in applying for the position, employees may have friends or acquaintances who are looking for work. Usually, lodging companies reward workers for their referral of potential employees if these are hired and stay employed for a minimum of 6 months. Friends and relatives are usually well accepted by current employees, who are more likely to help the newcomers adjust to their new jobs. Another advantage of recruitment from within is that it avoids incurring recruitment costs. When

Supervisor: Team supervisor.

Job responsibility: To service guestrooms as specified below. To fulfill any work assignments as requested by management.

Type of job: Full-time but dependent on room occupancy.

Position responsibility:

1. Arrive to the linen room on time and in uniform. Clock in.
2. Pick up guestroom section master key, section housekeeper report, and service cart.
3. Start cleaning section, avoiding waking up or disturbing stay-over guests. Follow the order:
   a. rooms already departed.
   b. rooms showing request for service.
   c. expected check-outs.
   d. stay-over rooms.
   e. requests for late service.
4. Knock on guestroom door twice and announce yourself. Leave door open and place service cart blocking the entrance for security purposes.
5. Prepare room for cleaning by:
   a. open windows.
   b. turn on all lights, radio, and TV to make sure they work.
   c. ascertain condition of the room, reporting any damage to supervisor immediately. Leftover items are turned in to "lost and found."
   d. set thermostat at 70°F.
   e. write a work order for any item in room that needs maintenance.
   f. if guests have not checked out, place away neatly all clothing, papers, documents, or any other belongings.
   g. empty out the trash and change wastebasket liners.
6. Proceed to make the bed:
   a. strip the bed, keeping items off the floor. Inspect mattress, pads, box spring, blanket, bedspread, and pillow for stains or torn spots and replace if needed.
   b. place the bottom sheet and tuck it at the head and sides. Miter bottom and top sheets and blanket at the foot of the bed and tuck them along the side. Place bedspread over the blanket, turn it about 15 inches back from the headboard, and place pillow over it. Roll back spread and pillows over the headboard. Repeat operation on other side of bed. Smooth out lumps and creases after the bed has been made.
7. Proceed to clean the room:
   a. brush lampshades with a dry cloth or feather duster.
   b. spray doors, furniture, and fixtures with cleaning solution or furniture polish and damp-wipe with dust cloth.
   c. wipe air vents, windowsills, light bulbs, telephones, and other surfaces with a damp cloth. Wipe out drawers. Clean or replace all recycled items. Spray mirrors and TV screen and wipe with dry cloth. Center all drapes, lamp shades, and pictures.

FIGURE 10.2 Sample Section Housekeeper Job Description

    d. vacuum carpet, including under the bed.

    e. apply deodorant to curtains and carpet.

    f. If the room has a balcony or patio, dust the furniture and sweep the floor.

  8. Proceed to clean bathroom:

    a. check all lights and inspect faucets for leaks. Dump the wastebasket.

    b. place bowl cleaner in commode and brush it clean. Wipe outside of commode with a germicidal solution.

    c. standing inside of tub, clean bath walls, soap dish, plumbing fixtures, and shower door with all-purpose cleaner. Wipe dry. Clean tub or shower floor, pull out tub stopper and wipe clean.

    d. clean vanity and sink, including the sink stopper.

    e. spray mirror with cleaning solution and wipe dry.

    f. wipe bathroom floor with cloth and germicidal solution, including behind the door.

    g. remove lint from ventilation and fan grills.

    h. replace bathroom supplies and amenities.

  9. Place section housekeeper card on desk or credenza, take a critical final look, and notify team supervisor that the room is ready for inspection.

10. File P.M. report before end of the shift, indicating status of all rooms in the section. Clean up equipment.

11. Restock service cart for following day's operation.

12. Turn in guestroom section master key. Clock out.

Management reserves the right to modify this job description and to assign other tasks to section housekeepers as circumstances require.

Required Job Qualifications:

Able to stand heavy sustained physical activities, including lifting moderate weights, frequent bending, and constant use of arms. Physical agility and dexterity to be able to service 16 guestrooms in 8 working hours is a must.

Preferred qualifications:

Education: able to read and write English.

Experience: over six months previous work experience as section housekeeper.

Personality: pleasant, able to interact with guests and fellow workers.

Appearance: well groomed.

Mental qualifications: able to follow instructions. Self-starter.

FIGURE 10.2 *Continued*

the new opening is for a supervisory position, special efforts should be made to promote from within as a matter of fairness and to provide opportunities for advancement to the employees already with the company. Charts showing the various opportunities for career progression should be displayed for employees to see. In the housekeeping department, the career path for a houseperson could lead from this entry-level position to section housekeeper, team supervisor, assistant to the executive housekeeper, to laundry manager and, possibly, to executive housekeeper.

The most common external recruitment method is newspaper advertising. These ads are particularly successful in attracting the unskilled and young people looking for part-time and temporary employment. The advantage of this is that young, unskilled people can usually be adequately trained to perform the requirements of the job; the disadvantage is that once they have been trained, they may decide to change jobs and leave the department. Radio advertising reaches listeners who do not or cannot read newspapers.

When a supervisory or management position needs to be filled, private employment agencies often provide a valuable source of recruits, but in most cases the property must pay a substantial fee for their services. Public employment agencies may be sources of good employees in some cases. The state employment services are non-fee referral agencies for workers, and so are organizations for the physically impaired. Most physically impaired individuals are very dependable and efficient in the performance of simple, repetitive jobs. In some cases, companies may benefit from tax credits by hiring workers from federally-supported programs.

Schools and colleges are good sources of recruits with special skills. Local community colleges may offer vocational courses in housekeeping or laundry operations. High schools may have work-study cooperative programs. Most hotel/restaurant management programs require students to complete hundreds of hours in pre-graduation employment in the industry. Bulletin board advertising in these schools usually results in applications for employment. Some colleges and universities have summer internship programs that allow undergraduate students to practice in hotels and resorts prior to graduation. The students can be used as supervisors or management assistants or they can be put in charge of special projects, such as taking inventories, developing job descriptions, or getting involved in clerical work.

Selecting Housekeeping Employees

The initial contact with prospective employees begins with their filling out an **application form**. This form is a means of securing standard information about applicants. No person can be denied the opportunity to submit an application for employment; questions to be included in application forms depend on the company but, in all cases, every question asked should serve a purpose. No question should be asked that is not useful for research purposes or for determining the applicant's eligibility for the job. The U.S. Equal Employment Opportunity Commission has been set up to enforce the Civil Rights Act which protects against discrimination on account of race, color, religion, sex, or national origin. Because of increased emphasis by state and federal governments to avoid discrimination in employment, application forms must be carefully worded to avoid requesting any pre-employment information that could be considered discriminatory.

Questions such as those listed in the left column that follows are considered unlawful and should not be part of an application form. Questions in the right column are acceptable.

Unlawful application form questions	*May ask or require*
What race are you?	
Name of your spouse	Names of relatives employed by company
Marital status	
Where does your spouse work?	
Please attach a photograph of yourself.	May be required *after* hiring for identification
Place of birth	
What is your native language?	If job related, what foreign languages do you speak?
Which country do you originate from?	
Of what country are you a citizen?	Are you a U.S. citizen?
Are you a native-born U.S. citizen?	Do you have a permanent immigration visa?
Are your parents naturalized U.S. citizens?	

Unlawful application form questions	*May ask or require*
Which is your religion of preference?	Can you observe regularly the required days and hours of work?
Do you have any disabilities?	Have you any physical, medical, or mental impairments that would restrict your ability to do the work?
Date of birth	Are you between 40 and 70?
	Are you over 18?
Have you ever been treated for AIDS?	
Type of military discharge	Military service: dates, branch of service, job-related education and experience
Do you observe religious holidays?	Can you observe regularly the required days and hours of work?
Have you ever been arrested?	Have you ever been convicted of a crime? (If crime is job-related, hiring may be refused.)
Do you own a car?	Do you have reliable means of getting to work?

PRESCREENING

The property's personnel department usually conducts the **pre-screening interview**. The purpose of this initial interview is to screen out those applicants who do not meet the criteria for the job advertised as specified in the company's job description. For example, a person who is physically incapable of servicing 15 guestrooms in 8 hours will automatically be disqualified. The person in charge of pre-employment screening must be well trained in interviewing techniques, as a high percentage of people applying for jobs tend to exaggerate their skills and abilities, to misrepresent their backgrounds, and to conceal or minimize their weakest qualities. Applicants who are not selected should be notified as soon as possible of the company's decision and their applications kept on file for future reference, mainly for a different job in the company for which they may be qualified.

The personnel department should immediately proceed to check the references of those candidates selected for the interview. Checking references may reveal issues such as extreme absenteeism, irresponsibility, and not giving adequate notice, or may detect a person who always wants to work in a new property and quit as soon as a new establishment opens. References may be checked in writing, although in most cases previous employers will be reluctant to put on paper their honest opinion about the worker; written reference checking is usually limited to a verification-of-employment statement. Telephone conversations can often reveal much more about the applicant, particularly if the person contacted is an industry colleague. Although in most cases it is impractical, the best way to obtain accurate information about applicants is to have a personal meeting with their former boss.

Applicants who are working at the time of the interview may request that their current employers not be contacted for a reference check. This request should be honored, to avoid putting workers in an antagonistic position vis-à-vis their current bosses.

THE INTERVIEW

Those employees who have cleared the reference check are invited to a personal interview. The goal of an interview is to find the best match between the person and the position to be filled. The interview also allows the candidate and the department head to meet face to face to explore the possibility of a mutual agreement for employment. In the housekeeping department, interviews may be conducted by supervisors, laundry managers, manager assistants, or by the executive housekeepers themselves.

Interviewers should evaluate the applicant's technical skills, general temperament, and emotional traits. By asking technical questions related to the job opening, the interviewer should attempt to find out if the applicant is (or will be after training) qualified to perform the job in question. By asking personal questions, the interviewer should try to ascertain the candidate's attitude toward the job and the first impression that the applicant will give in meeting customers and fellow workers. Some of the technical characteristics may be ascertained from factors such as previous work experience and training, knowledge of the job, stamina, and alertness. Some of the personal traits to be sought after are stability, reliability, initiative, and personal appearance. In essence, the interview is a two-way communication effort in which the interviewer states the nature of the job opening and the applicant presents his or her own qualifications to fill the job. Interviews should be conducted in a private, quiet place where the candidate can be made to feel at ease.

Here are some points to be considered in employment interviewing.

1. A checklist can be helpful to avoid overlooking important information. Questions should be prepared from the job description of the position to be filled.
2. The interviewer should allow at least half of the interview time to listen to the applicant's statements about himself or herself. To this effect, questions eliciting "yes" "no" answers should be avoided. Make frequent use of "why?" and "how?".
3. Most housekeeping tasks are tough and require much of the worker's commitment and dedication. Interviewers should not sugarcoat the job to convince the applicant to accept the position, only to find later that the worker finds it unbearable.
4. Interviewers may be swayed in their decision to hire by the neat appearance and smooth talking of candidates (the **halo effect**), only to discover that they are not capable of performing housekeeping work.
5. Avoid hiring someone who is overqualified. These candidates often become frustrated with tasks below their ability level, and eventually quit.

The result of the interview should be communicated to the candidate as soon as possible. If the decision is positive, applicants should know immediately so they can give appropriate notice to their current employers and get ready to start work in the new job. If the decision is negative, applicants should be notified so that they can restart their search for a job in other establishments. In this case, the candidate should also be thanked for the time taken in interviewing with the company.

TESTING

Some lodging companies regularly use tests given to prospective employees as instruments of selection, particularly to those seeking supervisory and managerial positions. However, because tests are only an indirect method of measurement, they are not as valid as the direct measurement of people's abilities. Tests should never be given in lieu of interviews or direct performance observations. Psychological testing, nevertheless, can be a helpful tool to avoid hiring unqualified candidates. **Intelligence tests** used in the industry measure vocabulary and arithmetic skills; some are designed for supervisory and managerial positions and a few for workers at an entry level. Some **aptitude tests** applicable to the industry measure the applicant's hand dexterity; these are suitable for workers involved in manual tasks; others test clerical aptitude and are recommended for bookkeeping, cashier, and secretarial jobs. **Interest tests** provide some measure of an applicant's relative interest for certain fields of work. The lodging industry could use interest tests to examine the candidate's interest in people, as this is a people industry.

When using tests as a method of selecting employees, keep in mind that tests have been found to be inherently discriminatory to anyone who has not had the full advantage of a free exposure to American culture. For instance, the scores achieved by a candidate belonging to a minority group should not be compared with people in general but only to the scores of other members of the same minority group.

Hiring

INDUCTION

After being accepted for employment, workers are usually asked to report to the personnel department for their induction into the company. The purpose of the induction process is to fill the necessary paperwork about the new employee, to answer questions, and to make the newcomer feel welcome. All documentation regarding the new worker should be completed. This procedure includes filling out the W-4 (tax withholding statement), I-9 (proof of residence), and health and welfare insurance forms. At this time newcomers are provided with the **employee handbook**. Properties that hire large numbers of employees should use **employment checklist forms** (Figure 10.3) to ensure that no part of the induction process has been overlooked. The employment checklist includes all prerequisites that need to be completed before employees are sent to their respective departments to begin work.

The induction process continues with the **orientation** of the new employee. The purpose of orientation is to acquaint the

Name: _____ Social Security Number: _____

Address: _____

City: _____ State: _____ Zip: _____

Item	Complete ☑
Application	☐
Resume	☐
Proof of residency (I-9)	☐
Health and welfare documents	☐
W-4 form	☐
Deductions from pay (if any)	☐
Hotel employee handbook issued	☐
Company orientation	☐
Payroll number assigned	☐
Name tag issued	☐

Employee has been turned over to _____ in the
_____ department for training and department orientation.

Personnel supervisor: **Receiving department:**

_____   _____
Signature   Supervisor signature

FIGURE 10.3 Sample Employment Checklist

employee and organization with one another. During orientation, the philosophy of the company is explained, the benefits, pay rate, and deductions are discussed, and the dos and don'ts that the job entails, or general house policies as stated in the employee handbook, are described in detail. The initial orientation session should be followed with a second meeting after the new employee has had a chance to become familiar with the job—anywhere between two and four weeks later. At this time, any questions that the worker may have are answered.

After the orientation process has been completed at the personnel department, the new employee is escorted to housekeeping where a departmental orientation takes place. Here, the hours of work and the necessity for calling in as soon as possible in case of illness or emergency are explained, as well as where to check in and out, uniform procedures, grooming standards, and when breaks and meal periods are scheduled. The employee is then given a tour of the property and is introduced to his or her supervisor who, in turn, introduces the worker to other members of the department. Induction and orientation procedures, if properly conducted, increase substantially the odds of the employee's remaining in the company.

Most new employees in the housekeeping department are hired on a **probationary basis**, usually 90 days, to allow workers enough time to learn and perform their jobs efficiently. After a successful probationary period, usually when employees reach no fault or no errors standards, they become regular workers and are given a raise as an incentive to continue to perform well and stay with the company. If, after the probationary period, reasonable standards of efficiency have not been met, employees are not allowed to continue employment in that particular position.

INDUCTION AND THE PEER GROUP

The peer group is an important part of the new employee's orientation. New employees depend on their coworkers for approval and acceptance. For the newcomer, the pressure to conform is very strong. It is a good idea to involve the most representative members of the peer group in the orientation process. This practice will help the old employees and the new person get to know each other as soon as possible. In fact, the induction process should not be considered as completed until the full acceptance of the new employee by the peer group has been totally accomplished. To end the hiring process, the personnel department should open an individual record file for each employee in which personal information (such as address, telephone number or whom to call in case of emergency) and work data (such as starting wage and title of the position) are recorded. The file is thereafter updated each time a change in status occurs, such as for changes in pay rate, disciplinary actions taken, written warnings, promotions, special recognition, and so on.

Training

The hospitality industry is notorious for attracting large numbers of unskilled workers, especially young workers coming right from high schools and colleges. In addition, members of the hospitality work force tend to change from one job to another, causing a high turnover, and have a relatively low educational background. On the other hand, most hospitality jobs are under the constant scrutiny of the public, hinging on a face-to-face relationship where the inefficiency of one employee may lose a guest forever. A lodging property cannot afford to have an untrained or disinterested worker on the housekeeping payroll.

Training in the housekeeping department should encompass four major areas: **technical skills, employee attitude, personal development,** and **knowledge of the property**. Technical skills training includes teaching workers how to perform the tasks described in their job description without fault or error. In the case of a section housekeeper, for example, it means teaching the person how to service guestrooms, including setup procedures, making beds, vacuuming, dusting, surface cleaning, bathroom cleaning, maintenance of equipment, and security and safety. The employee will have reached regular performance standards when a minimum number of faults are found by the inspector checking the room attendant's section. Technical training contributes to the success of both the organization and the individual.

Attitude training should create awareness of the relationships between the employee and the guest, other employees, and the company. Workers must be courteous, friendly, and approachable, and show keen attention to detail. Sensitivity toward fellow workers must be taught, including toward people of other cultures, races, and religions. This will help develop teamwork within a diversified group, which is always the case in housekeeping. Employees should have a positive attitude toward the company and its management by positively representing the property and mirroring the philosophy of the establishment. Training should also be provided to workers to improve their personal potential and their abilities to make changes in their own lives. This type of training can range from personal grooming sessions to seminars and workshops that will aid in developing their reading and writing skills or to help them increase their perceptions of themselves as functional individuals. Finally, knowledge training should teach employees the layout of the property so that they can give directions to guests and inform them about hours of operation and main features of the different outlets. For example, a houseperson, if asked, should be able to tell a guest how to get to the swimming pool or what type of menu the coffee shop offers.

Lodging properties should have ongoing training programs in place. People in general tend to forget concepts or deviate from standing procedures as time goes by. Clear indications of the need to retrain personnel include an increase of oral and written complaints by guests. For instance, if management keeps getting negative comments about the quality of guestroom linens, employees in the laundry room should be retrained in washing and/or finishing procedures. Another indication of a need for retraining may be a drop in productivity. For example, if in the past section housekeepers have been able to effectively clean 16 rooms in 8 hours and lately some of them incur overtime to finish their job, their room-cleaning methods should be examined to ascertain whether the standing cleaning procedures are adequately followed. These performance analyses should investigate the question "could the task be performed quicker, with the same level of quality?" If the answer is yes, the worker should be retrained to increase his or her productivity performance. There is, however, a difference between **deficiency of knowledge**, in which the employee doesn't know how to do the job better and should be retrained, and **deficiency of execution**, in which the employee knows how to do the task but decides not to perform it correctly for his or her own benefit. In this case, the employee should be called to order and asked to do the job according to established procedures.

The most efficient method of training in the housekeeping department is **on-the-job training**, in which new employees are assigned to watch how the work should be performed, usually observing a supervisor or senior employee. Large lodging operations have designated trainers whose job is to train newcomers or retrain employees who are not performing up to standard. When employees need to be trained to operate new machines or equipment, vendors or representatives of the manufacturing company often conduct **demonstrations** at no cost to the employer; in this case the purchaser of the products. Training of supervisors and middle managers can be enhanced by sending them to conferences and workshops where new industry products are introduced and demonstrated. When employees already in the company are being prepared for advancement, companies should train them in the different operational aspects of the department by following a career ladder or schedule. Thus, committed employees who master each step of the cycle along the way may be promoted to management positions within the property or in other company establishments.

Training programs offer distinct advantages to employers and employees alike. The employer will benefit from an increased learning rate, whereby workers will become efficient sooner rather than learning on their own by trial and error. Workers learn to achieve high levels of productivity and quality performance when their training begins with learning only the best way to accomplish jobs. As training improves performance, employee self-esteem rises, and with it, the willingness to come to work and to increase earning power. Turnover and absenteeism are thus reduced.

The simplest and most efficient way to ascertain the effectiveness of training and retraining programs is by obtaining feedback from guest comment cards. If substantial negative comments are received, training programs must be strengthened. Guest comments should be read at employee meetings. Negative comments should be discussed, without naming the employee who caused the problem, and the entire group should be challenged to find an appropriate solution. The employee who received the adverse comments should be addressed privately.

 ## WORKER MOTIVATION

Employees are vital to the success of the lodging industry. A business that requires face-to-face interaction with people requires a work force that is motivated to deliver excellent service. But the work force usually available to the lodging industry has inherent fundamental problems, such as high turnover, a disinterested attitude, and low productivity. Housekeeping tends to attract individuals with little education who come from lower socioeconomic sources or from minority groups that often do not know how to read and in some cases are unable to speak English. The problem is compounded by the fact that most lodging companies have limited financial resources to increase their employees' compensation beyond inflation rates. On the other hand, employees look to improve their own quality of life by achieving a satisfactory standard of living through job security and adequate compensation. However, adequate compensation, although necessary, is not enough to motivate the work force. People also look for a challenge, recognition, and the opportunity to be part of an organization that is successful in itself. Therefore, to motivate employees the manager must understand what type of environment most effectively utilizes the workers' energy and directs them toward the accomplishment of a common goal.

Maslow's Theory of Motivation

Although first expressed in the 1950s, Abraham Maslow's thoughts on motivation are still quite relevant to employee motivation in the housekeeping department. It can be deduced from Maslow's work that high levels of motivation in employees cannot be achieved unless the employees' basic needs have been met. A worker's **physiological needs** must be satisfied first; that is, if housekeeping employees are working in very poor conditions, such as in a steaming-hot, nonventilated laundry room, all attempts to motivate them will fail. Likewise, if the workers' **security needs** for survival are not granted, motivation will be impossible. This would occur if a housekeeping employee is allowed to work only 28 hours per week and therefore is unable to make enough money to pay for his or her rent. The fulfillment of **social needs** is also necessary prior to motivating people. A Hispanic employee, for instance, would be unhappy working in housekeeping in the midst of an Anglo-Saxon work force that refuses to accept him or her as part of the group. Conversely, an Anglo-Saxon worker working among nonaccepting Hispanic workers will also be hard to motivate. **Self-esteem**, the fourth of Maslow's basic needs applicable to hourly employees, must also be satisfied before workers can be motivated. For example, a houseperson in the housekeeping department hauling trash to the dumpster all day long, whose job is not appreciated by management and coworkers, will be reluctant to be motivated.

Housekeeping managers must always realize that individuals have a scale of needs and that motivating them to be courteous, polite, friendly, or productive does not become pressing to them until their basic needs have been adequately satisfied. Motivation at the departmental level will be easier to achieve if all job descriptions and specifications include both the needs of the organization and the personal needs of the workers.

Herzberg's Ideas on Motivation

Once employees' basic needs have been covered, housekeeping managers must provide their employees with opportunities that are intrinsically satisfying or that embody responsibility. Frederick Herzberg proposes that workers can be motivated by recognition, feelings of achievement, job responsibility, and opportunities for advancement and growth. In other words, if employees feel wanted and are happy in their jobs, they will willingly contribute to the goals of the organization. In a housekeeping department setting, the executive housekeeper can motivate section housekeepers by always assigning them the same section of guestrooms. This individual responsibility will create in them a feeling of ownership and pride. A **career ladder program** to promote people from within can be implemented in the department to establish the possibility of advancement from lower entry-level jobs to supervisory and management positions.

There is a marked difference between motivation and manipulation of employees. Managers who attempt to influence workers to do what they want done seldom succeed. Niccolo Machiavelli, the cynical sixteenth-century writer, observed that because humans are selfish, greedy, ungrateful, and manipulative, they deserve not to be trusted and must be manipulated in turn, a theory hardly conducive to employee motivation. On the contrary, managers who know how to create a climate in which the individual can function to maximum capacity will be successful in motivating employees.

PRACTICAL MOTIVATIONAL TECHNIQUES

Besides understanding the different theoretic approaches to motivation, executive housekeepers can put in place practical programs and plans to motivate housekeeping employees. Removing obstacles that often hinder performance may help workers to accomplish their tasks. Too much paper work, for instance, may be an obstacle to productivity; another could be a badly designed work area that does not take into consideration the human element. Lack of communication may create a feeling of uncertainty about what needs to be done, as people only tend to perform correctly when they understand what is expected of them. The simple act of listening often allows managers to hear useful comments from employees regarding work conditions, suggestions to improve work flow, and the existence of morale problems. The fact that the housekeeping department is often the least appreciated in the property may be the hidden cause of low employee motivation. Housekeeping workers may not gain the same appreciation that the front desk, sales, and accounting people do. It is common for housekeeping to be considered at the bottom of the operational totem pole given that they are paid minimum wage and have little decision-making authority. On the other hand, these workers must perform the backbreaking job of cleaning 16 or 17 guestrooms in an 8-hour shift. In order to motivate the housekeeping work force, employees must be given credit for the work they do and be respected for what they represent.

Some lodging companies have experimented with alternative methods of motivating employees. By paying section housekeepers by number of rooms cleaned rather than by hours worked, some properties have achieved increased productivity and staff retention. Others have established four-day work weeks with 10 hours worked per day. Both methods may help if they are first tried and accepted by management and employees. In general, paying per room cleaned may generate problems of quality, as the section housekeepers will try to service the largest number of rooms in the least possible time. The 10-hour work day may result in workers who are too tired to do a good job.

 EMPLOYEE EVALUATION AND COMPENSATION

Evaluation

The purpose of employee appraisals is twofold: to provide feedback to workers about how they are performing their jobs and to establish a basis for compensation based on the quality level of their performance. The advantages of providing feedback to workers are substantial, as employees who do well need to be recognized for their efforts while those whose work needs improvement must be notified about their specific deficiencies in order for them to be corrected. Using ratings to determine wage payment and promotions helps motivate employees to work hard so they can reap the benefits awarded to those who do a good job. To be effective, evaluation methods must be fair, objective, based on pre-established standards of performance, and accepted by those being evaluated.

To overcome anxiety or hostility, workers should be involved in setting up the standards of performance against which they are to be appraised, provided that their goals are in line with those of the company. **Rating scales** are effective tools for appraisal; they consist of a series of descriptors to which a numerical score is attached to determine the effectiveness of workers in areas such as absenteeism, tardiness, grooming, following instructions, courtesy to guests, and so on. Figure 10.4 is a rating form with a scale of five points, where 1 indicates "superior" performance and 5 indicates "needs improvement." Most companies ask workers to fill out a rating form after a designated period of time, ranging from six months to a year, while the worker's supervisor or manager also fills out a form on the employee being evaluated. At a scheduled meeting, the perceptions of both the worker being appraised and the supervisor are compared and discussed. From that discussion, goals for the next evaluation period are agreed upon. The goals are again evaluated against actual performance after the next appraisal period has elapsed and new goals are set. Where performance is difficult to quantify, as in rating assistant managers or supervisors, the **critical incident method** may be used instead of the rating scale. In this case, the rater may periodically record observations of good or bad performance that are discussed at the time of the rating.

Any appraisal method used in the housekeeping department should be a way of recognizing excellent performance and of identifying areas in which further training is needed, and should be done so that the person being evaluated sees the process as a means of self-improvement. That is, there should be a mutual discussion between superior and subordinate with regard to what conditions must be altered to change or upgrade performance. These changes or efforts to upgrade become the objectives to be accomplished for the next evaluation period.

The first formal appraisal of employees should be conducted at the end of their probationary period. Afterward, evaluation should be done periodically, typically every six months to a year. It is common for lodging companies to have **pay scales** that start with a

Employee being evaluated: _____

Evaluator: _____

Period of Evaluation: From: _____   To: _____

Date of Evaluation: _____

Descriptors	**Rating**				
	Superior				Needs Improvement
Absenteeism	1	2	3	4	5
Tardiness	1	2	3	4	5
Grooming	1	2	3	4	5
Following Instructions	1	2	3	4	5
Courtesy to Guests	1	2	3	4	5
Getting Along with Peers	1	2	3	4	5
Productivity Level	1	2	3	4	5
Accepting Responsibility	1	2	3	4	5

Total Points This Period _____

Goals/Objectives for Next Evaluation Period

1. _____
2. _____
3. _____
4. _____
5. _____

_____   _____
Employee's Signature   Evaluator's Signature

FIGURE 10.4   Sample Employee Evaluation Form

probationary rate and go up in accordance with time on the job. For example, an employee can be started at minimum wage for the first 90 days (probationary period) and then be raised 50 cents to a dollar per year worked to a pre-established maximum hourly rate. Employees who exhibit extraordinary performance are awarded additional increases, regardless of time, based on their positive performance appraisals.

Because performance evaluations are emotionally charged events, reviews should be held in a private, neutral environment, such as in a small conference room. Evaluators should go into the review fully prepared and with an attitude that supports discussion, cooperation, and negotiation. It is better to sit beside the employee rather than across the table from her/him. The meeting should be long enough to clearly delineate the workers' strengths and weaknesses, and show them how and to what degree they must improve their performance.

Compensation

Compensation (pay increases) should be tied to performance. If an employee's productivity is high and the quality excellent, his or her compensation should be greater than that of an employee whose performance is well below standards. When compensation is tied to performance and the evaluation system is fair and unbiased, employees strive to do well at work in order to obtain better wages and benefits. Most employees establish a relationship between the rewards they obtain from their job and the effort they put into it. The ideal **effort : compensation ratio** should be 1:1, meaning that the effort put into one's work should equal the reward obtained from it. If workers see that other employees in similar positions produce less but receive equal or higher wages than they do, they will soon be de-motivated. Managers should regard equity in compensation as a critical part of the motivational process.

 ## CREATING WORKER SATISFACTION

One of the underlying purposes of motivating employees is to reduce turnover. Hovering at about 100 percent for line employees and often costing over $3,000 per hourly employee, turnover represents a substantial loss of income to lodging companies. Thus the challenge is to create worker satisfaction so that employees stay with the company for extended periods of time. Besides using motivational techniques and providing equitable compensation and fringe benefits, what else can the executive housekeeper do to alleviate the problem of high turnover? Conducting **exit interviews** is the first step in attempting to solve high turnover; that is, finding out why employees leave in the first place. Exit interviews help management identify reasons for turnover, paving the way to corrective actions. During the interview, departing employees should be asked to discuss the company's working conditions, pay rates, training, benefits, job security, and so on. If the turnover is severe, current employees should be surveyed periodically regarding wages, benefits, and working conditions. Once the problem is identified, goals and objectives for a turnover-reduction plan should be set. Some of the most common reasons for high turnover are poor hiring techniques, inadequate orientation and training practices, no opportunity for advancement, poor supervision methods, bad department image, and lack of performance standards. Besides correcting these technical slips, executive housekeepers must get employees to feel like valuable members of the total team, boosting their self-esteem by making sure that the department does not have an image problem. The creation of a career path program within the department will make employees feel that there are opportunities for advancement. Encouraging employees to earn professional certification will help them develop the necessary expertise for advancement. Providing literacy classes for those who cannot read empowers workers who then feel more in control of their future. **Incentive programs** are intended to provide employees with such rewards as recognition and appreciation for the good work they perform. Commendation letters, gift certificates, bonuses, plaques, complimentary stays in the property, and designated parking spots in the garage are some of the incentives that may provide substantial employee satisfaction at no great cost.

Wellness programs, designed to prevent illness and enhance the well-being of employees, are effective in reducing absenteeism. These programs include periodic medical examinations, sessions to improve dietary habits, weight control practices, exercise and fitness sessions, free or discounted meals, stress management workshops, and immunizations. **Employee assistance programs** can help retain employees who are substance abusers by helping workers overcome drug and alcohol addiction. Referring affected employees to counseling agencies and supporting them in their rehabilitation will help improve the company's retention of employees. **Transportation assistance** can also be an effective incentive in keeping employees in the workplace. Because a great number of house-keeping employees do not own their own means of transportation, in cities where public transportation systems are reliable and can be used by employees to get to work, the company can provide financial assistance to purchase passes. In localities with poor or no public transportation, employers can provide vans for pickup and delivery of workers to a central location or organize a ride-sharing or carpooling program. With subsidies from state and federal government programs, lodging properties can offer **child** and **prenatal-care assistance** for workers, especially to young single parents. The practice of **participative management** often creates worker satisfaction among employees in that they see themselves as part of the decision-making process. As they contribute to operative decisions, they become committed to the outcome of these decisions and get involved in the successful accomplishment of common tasks.

When everything else has failed, the company may resort to create **retention bonuses** by offering a percentage of a year's pay, spread over a period of several years, to those employees who stay with the company. In sum, any efforts aimed at maintaining high levels of morale, individual attention, and respect for hourly employees will increase service standards and guest satisfaction and reduce employee turnover.

 ## EMPLOYEE DISCIPLINE

The implementation of a standard method of discipline is just as important as motivation for employers and employees alike. Corrective actions for unacceptable or irresponsible behavior must be taken as soon as they occur. Common misconduct cases that take place in the housekeeping department are quarreling, insubordination, intoxication, excessive unexcused tardiness or absences, theft, and unauthorized or unlawful doings. Depending on the severity of the wrongdoing, discipline can range from a simple verbal warning to termination. The most effective method of disciplining employees is the **counseling session**. Counseling sessions should be conducted on a one-to-one basis to ensure confidentiality. In these sessions, the problem or problems should be addressed straightforwardly with the understanding that the only purpose of the meeting is to find a fast, permanent, and equitable solution to the matter in question. Listening to the employee (the other side of the story) is crucial as the worker, not the supervisor, often is in the right. It is important that at the end of the session a mutual agreement is reached and that there is a strong commitment on the part of the employee to positively correct the situation. Needless to say, if the employee persists in his or her wrong behavior, the company always reserves the right to apply punitive measures, as the building of positive discipline requires effective disciplinary actions. Once the violation occurs, disciplinary action follows this sequence: oral warning(s), written warning(s), suspension, and dismissal.

CULTURAL DIVERSITY AND THE HOUSEKEEPING DEPARTMENT

The number of minority hourly employees working in the hospitality industry is very high; in some states, Spanish-speaking people employed in housekeeping are the majority. In some cases, this diversity in the workplace can represent challenging management problems regarding communication, training, and operational performance. In the Southwest, for instance, the entire housekeeping department may be staffed with non–English speaking Hispanic workers. Cultural differences may also be serious obstacles to traditional management practices. Some minorities are deeply individualistic and resist standardization, in contrast to the Anglo-American inclination to follow clearly defined, established rules of behavior. While the North American culture has been built around a strong work ethic, with emphasis on the search for efficiency and aiming at constantly improving the current mechanical and technological frontiers, minorities are often preoccupied with concepts like individualism, family, and leisure. However, language barriers and marked cultural differences do not imply incompetence. There is no valid evidence of differences in most abilities related to the genetics of race or sex.

The vehicle that best promotes understanding is, without doubt, language. Managers and supervisors will be able to bridge the gap between cultures if they are capable of communicating directly with the people they oversee day after day. An elementary knowledge of the language that can be applied to daily housekeeping operations is therefore invaluable, particularly in establishments in urban areas with large concentrations of minorities. Students in hospitality management programs should elect to study a modern language, particularly Spanish, prior to joining the industry after graduation.

On the other hand, dealing with multicultural issues can be a rewarding experience. Using effective communication skills and patience, managers and supervisors can successfully reach, and train, a diverse work force. Listening attentively and speaking slowly and clearly in elementary English are a must. The best method of training minorities with no command of the English language is to follow a "hands on," "learn-by-doing" approach.

One approach to training a multicultural work force is using pictures, rather than written instructions. For instance, videos or photographs can clearly show how to operate equipment and perform routine tasks, like washing laundry or waxing a wooden floor. This approach eliminates the need for translation, as visual aids are universally understood. It is common today to find vendors who provide demonstration videos about their products free of charge.

When dealing with a diverse work force, setups and stocking consistency helps avoid mistakes. For instance, to create a common language among all housekeeping employees, all floor and janitor closets should always be organized and stocked the same way. Service carts should also be organized and stocked the same way to create consistency and eliminate confusion. Using color-coded chemical products and waste receptacles is an excellent way to eliminate safety problems. For instance, the color red is indicative of infectious waste, green means recyclable contents, and so on.

Cultural awareness is another important aspect of managing a diverse work force. Some groups arrive in the United States with a strong respect for authority and will never discuss or dispute a request if it comes from the boss. Others will never volunteer an opinion if they are not specifically asked to do so. Some are socially shy and may wait until they are away from the group to ask an important question. Some lodging companies have English for Vocational Purposes (EVP) classes conducted at their facilities to teach foreign employees how to communicate with supervisors and peers on the job.

RACIAL DISCRIMINATION AND SEXUAL HARASSMENT

Racial problems in the workplace can lead to lack of productivity and costly lawsuits. Productivity can decline if some employees in the housekeeping department harbor resentments; others may decide to leave in search of businesses where racial tension is strongly discouraged. Lodging companies should have procedures in place to reduce friction between employees of different races and know how to respond when a racial incident occurs.

The property must have a written policy that prohibits discrimination based on race, national origin, sex, and physical impairment. It should also forbid discrimination in hiring, promoting, and terminating employees. Racial remarks or jokes should not be tolerated. The written policy must be communicated to all supervisors and employees, who should also be educated about the company's expectations regarding interracial behavior. When a racial incident does occur, action must be taken immediately to make sure that it does not escalate to a legal confrontation.

Sexual harassment is a subtle, hard-to-define form of discrimination. It is not unusual to find that as much as 40 percent of women in the work force have suffered some sort of harassment in the workplace in the form of uninvited pressure for sexual favors, of which cornering, touching, leaning over, or sending provocative notes are the most common. The U.S. Equal Employment Opportunity Commission declared in 1980 that sexual harassment violates title VII of the 1964 Civil Rights Act. In a June 1998 decision by the U.S. Supreme Court, the guilt of all demonstrated acts of sexual harassment in the workplace extends not only to the perpetrator but also to the employer for which he or she works. For this reason, it is important for companies to have anti-harassment plans in place to sensitize employees about sexual harassment by way of training materials, workshops, and speakers. In addition, the company's employee handbook must have clear descriptions of what may constitute sexual harassment, specifically acts such as staring, flirting, suggestive gestures, sexual remarks, touching, sexual propositions, and physical duress.

KEY TERMS

application form

aptitude test

career ladder program

child assistance

counseling session

critical incident evaluation method

deficiency of execution

deficiency of knowledge

effort : compensation ratio

employee assistance program

employee attitude	participative management
employee handbook	part-time employees
employee qualifications	pay scale
employee requisition form	personal development
employment checklist form	physiological needs
exit interview	pre-natal care assistance
external recruiting	prescreening interview
full-time employee	probationary basis hiring
halo effect	rating scales
incentive programs	retention bonuses
intelligence test	security needs (employee)
interests test	self-esteem needs
internal recruiting	social needs
job description	technical skills
knowledge of the property	temporary help
on-call employees	transportation assistance
on-the-job training	vendor demonstration
orientation	wellness programs

DISCUSSION AND REVIEW QUESTIONS

1. What is the difference between a part-time and a temporary worker?
2. What is the purpose of an employee requisition form?
3. Why could a company that develops exclusively from within be limiting itself regarding the composition of its work force?
4. Explain why an interviewer should not ask the question, "Do you own a car?"
5. What is the purpose of the prescreening interview?
6. **(a)** Why should housekeeping managers and supervisors ask prospective employees questions regarding their technical skills?

   (b) List three questions that a supervisor should ask people looking for section housekeeper work to find out if they are technically qualified to perform the job.
7. What is the main reason for housekeeping departments to hire employees on a probationary basis?
8. What four areas must be addressed when training workers in the housekeeping department?

9. What is the difference between deficiency of knowledge and deficiency of execution?
10. What are the advantages of implementing a career ladder program in the housekeeping department?
11. Name and describe four programs or actions that lodging companies may implement to create worker satisfaction.
12. Besides overcoming the language barrier, housekeeping managers must be able to bridge the gap between cultures if they are to reach workers of different cultural backgrounds. Explain why.

MINICASES

Situation 1

After graduating from a hotel and restaurant management program, you have been hired by a nationwide lodging company and sent to work the first year in a resort property in the Southwest. Having successfully completed the training period, the company has promoted you to executive housekeeper of a downtown hotel in a large city in New England. The property is a four-star, 500-room hotel offering meeting facilities, restaurant, bars, and health center. The hotel also has the following problems:

Absenteeism. Prior to your arrival, the housekeeping department consistently reported between 40 and 60 hours of overtime daily for section housekeepers. The previous housekeeping director contended that this was primarily due to transportation problems. He claimed that many of the workers do not have their own form of transportation and must rely on the city's transit system, which is very unreliable. According to one of the housekeeping workers, "If only there was a bus route nearby, my life would be a lot easier. Most of us live 25 minutes from work."

Turnover. The turnover rate of section housekeepers is 150 percent annually. Estimates of replacing a room attendant range from $1,100 to $1,900. The exit interviews conducted by the personnel department have pinpointed some common reasons for the high turnover rate. Some room attendants claim that they can make more money at other hotels in town, which also guarantee a minimum of 35 hours of work per week to most employees.

Guest complaints. The general manager gets a continuous flow of guest complaints about room cleanliness. She contends that the section housekeepers don't know how to clean guestrooms effectively. The inspection system of assigning a numerical value on a 1 to 5 scale doesn't seem to be working.

Productivity. Currently the room attendant workload per day is 13. Workers in most four-star hotels in the area are cleaning 17 rooms per shift. According to the outgoing executive housekeeper, "We would have raised the number of rooms but we didn't want to compromise our standard of cleanliness any further. They are currently making $5.50 an hour and across the street are making $6.00 per hour; this could also be a factor."

From the information given, establish a motivational plan of action including specific ways of applying Maslow's and Herzberg's motivational theories.

Situation 2

The housekeeping department of the Royal Hotel has been going downhill since the property opened 5 years ago. Morale is down, productivity is low, and the department's annual employee turnover rate is over 100 percent. Most housekeeping workers are from Asia and Central America; the majority of them do not speak English and are technically unskilled when first hired. Communications between hourly employees and the English-only speaking supervisors is very poor. Some of the workers are single mothers who live far from the hotel and do not own a car; a few of them may be substance abusers. The company is very concerned about the current state of affairs and decides to create satisfaction among the workers to improve the situation. Funds have been allocated to correct the problem. You have been sent to the Royal for one year, on an on-loan basis, to help management improve the current status.

Present a written proposal to management suggesting actions they should take to address the high turnover problem and lack of employee morale.

Situation 3

Jennifer usually has some excuse for not showing up for work. The excuses during the past three months included four dental appointments, four car breakdowns, and three occasions for which she was unable to find a babysitter. You, as Jennifer's supervisor, find it difficult to schedule your department as a whole because of Jennifer's spur-of-the-moment absences. Mrs. Robinson, another supervisor in your department, has told you in confidence that Jennifer is an unmarried employee who collects government financial aid for her two dependent children. Because the financial aid is conditional upon Jennifer's earnings, Mrs. Robinson thinks that she is trying to keep her work hours low enough to keep qualifying for government aid. What would be your approach to solve this situation?

PART 5

Administrative Controls

Controlling Operations

The Westin St. Francis, San Francisco, California. Courtesy of Westin Hotels & Resorts.

CHAPTER OBJECTIVES

▶ Understand the purpose of operating budgets in the housekeeping department.
▶ Learn the process of compiling operating budgets.
▶ Explain the process of calculating the justification for section housekeeper man-hours.
▶ Explain the structure of the profit and loss statement.
▶ Discuss how to obtain productivity indicators in the housekeeping department.
▶ Learn how to work out the weekly forecast for section-housekeeper work.
▶ Describe how to control payroll.
▶ Learn about automation in the housekeeping department.

 ## OVERVIEW

This chapter discusses the control of resources inherent in the job of executive housekeeper. The control function begins with the compilation of an annual operating budget for the rooms division of the property, of which the housekeeping department is a part. The executive housekeeper must project labor and operating expenses for the upcoming year which, once approved by upper management, become the operational expense parameters.

Because most department expenses are a function of occupancy, their totals must be justified. The justification of man-hours for section housekeepers is based on the number of rooms to be serviced and the workload criteria for room attendants.

As the year progresses, the housekeeping department receives monthly profit and loss statements showing the revenue of the rooms division and expense totals by category. The director of housekeeping uses the information to monitor costs and readjust expense amounts if they are larger than expected. Statistical information can also be used to control costs and productivity in the department by comparing the results obtained with budget indicators. The chapter ends with a discussion of automation applications for housekeeping supplies and personnel control.

HOUSEKEEPING OPERATING BUDGET

An operating budget is essentially a financial plan that allocates funds for expenditures by department for a determined period of time, generally one year. It is also a means of control that provides a measure for performance. Budgeting in large lodging operations requires a full cooperative effort of all department heads and the property's controller, who is usually in charge of preparing the final document before it is presented to the general manager for approval. Budgets are generally compiled for one-year time spans and are divided into 12 months, although some companies divide the year into thirteen 28-day periods to avoid distortion in the comparison of working periods (for not all months have the same working days). Preparation of the operating budget in large lodging properties requires several months of planning and is usually finalized just before the budgeting cycle commences. The budget year can begin on January 1 (calendar year), or at the start of the company's fiscal year. Once top management has established its guidelines and amounts for each department, the respective departmental budgets are distributed down through each level. One of these levels is the housekeeping department.

The housekeeping department budget is part of the rooms division budget, which also includes the front office. The executive housekeeper's participation in determining the amounts allocated to the housekeeping department is essential if she/he is to be made accountable for the departmental control of expenses.

The basic structure of budgets for revenue-generating divisions is: **Revenue** (Sales) – **Costs** (Expenses) = **Departmental Income** (Departmental Profit). The revenue of the rooms division consists of the dollars to be generated by the sale of rooms at a certain unit price (**number of rooms sold × average daily rate**). The costs of the rooms division consist of the expenses incurred by the housekeeping and front office departments. Typically, include **salaries and wages** and **other expenses**. The percent of expenses is obtained by dividing the projected cost of expenses in dollars by the projected revenue. The cost of expenses in dollars is obtained by multiplying the percent by the revenue and dividing by 100.

The first step in the budget process is the compilation of the **consolidated room sales summary** in which the rooms division director, director of sales, and front office manager are directly involved. The summary is a projection of revenues for the 12 months of the upcoming year based on the forecasted percentage of occupancy and average daily rate. The projections are calculated from the room bookings at hand, historical data from previous years, upcoming local events, state of the local economy and, in some cases, the weather prediction for the area. Figure 11.1 is a consolidated room sales summary for a 400-room hotel that includes the predicted percent occupancy, number of rooms, average daily rate, and total revenue. In this example, the average occupancy for the year is 83 percent, the number of rooms to be sold 121,184, the average daily rate (ADR) $85, and the projected revenue $10,371,804. Last year's figures for January through October are real; those for November and December are tentative, as these months had not yet elapsed at the time the budget was prepared.

Once the division's revenue is forecasted, the executive housekeeper and front office manager ascertain the expenses predicted for the year. Typical expense categories of the rooms division are: front office salaries, housekeeping salaries, payroll taxes and employee benefits, travel commissions, outside services, cleaning supplies, linen replacements, guest supplies, telephone, postage, printing and stationery supplies, uniforms, laundry supplies, customer goodwill,

Month	UPCOMING YEAR BUDGET				LAST YEAR'S BUDGET			
	Occupancy %	Rooms	ADR	Revenue	Occupancy %	Rooms	ADR	Revenue
January	65	8,060	75	604,500	65	8,060	71	572,260
February	80	8,960	79	707,840	80	8,960	75	672,000
March	78	9,672	81	783,432	78	9,672	77	744,744
April	80	9,600	84	806,400	80	9,600	80	768,000
May	88	10,912	89	971,168	88	10,912	85	927,520
June	89	10,680	90	961,200	89	10,680	86	918,480
July	95	11,780	92	1,083,760	95	11,780	88	1,036,640
August	93	11,532	91	1,049,412	93	11,532	87	1,003,284
September	90	10,800	89	961,200	90	10,800	85	918,000
October	87	10,788	89	960,132	87	10,788	85	916,980
November	81	9,720	82	797,040	81*	9,720	78	758,160
December	70	8,680	79	685,720	70*	8,680	75	651,000
	83%	121,184	85	10,371,804	83%	121,184	81	9,887,068

*Estimated

FIGURE 11.1   Sample Consolidated Rooms Sales

and auto expense. Of these categories, front office salaries, travel commissions, postage, customer goodwill, and auto expense (airport van) are front office expenses. The categories of payroll taxes and employee benefits, telephone, printing and stationery supplies, and uniforms are shared by the two departments. The remaining categories—housekeeping salaries, outside services, cleaning supplies, linen replacements, guest supplies, and laundry supplies—pertain to housekeeping only. The amounts to be allocated to each expense category are ascertained taking into consideration the percentages from previous years, and factors such as predicted increases in salaries and wages, adding extra employees to the department, upgrading cleaning and/or guest supplies, replacing an unusual amount of uniforms or linens, and so on. The challenge for department heads when requesting expense allocations is to keep the cost percentages as low as possible while maintaining an optimum level of service and quality.

Once the budget has been finalized and approved by management, it becomes the plan of operation for the upcoming year. The director of housekeeping must henceforth operate the department within the budget's limitations so that the percentages of amounts spent in each expense category do not exceed the percentages budgeted. It is important to understand that the cost percentages are a function of the revenue. For example, if the projected cost of guest supplies has been set at 2 percent of a $10,000,000 revenue, the dollar allocation for guest supplies for the year will be $200,000 (10,000,000 × .02). However, if the revenue is less or more than projected, the dollar allocation has to be adjusted accordingly. For instance, if the revenue drops to $9,500,000, the allocation for guest supplies becomes $190,000 (9,500,000 × .02). If the revenue reached $10,500,000, the allocation changes to $210,000 (10,500,000 × .02).

Whenever any substantial deviation from the budget occurs, the executive housekeeper will be asked to explain the variance. If the variance is found to be correctable, a plan of action is usually agreed upon between the director of housekeeping and upper management. Figure 11.2 is a sample budget for the rooms division of the Royal Hotel. The revenue for the upcoming year has been projected 5 percent higher than the current year's to reflect an increase in room rates. The occupancy percentages, however, have been kept the same as in the current year, assuming that a slowdown of the local economy does not allow for a larger occupancy. Salaries and wages have been increased by 0.5 percent from

	UPCOMING YEAR		LAST YEAR	
	Dollars ($)	Percentage (%)	Dollars ($)	Percentage (%)
REVENUE	10,371,804	100.0	9,887,068	100.0
SALARIES & WAGES				
Front Office	549,706	5.3	494,353	5.0
Housekeeping	985,321	9.5	889,836	9.0
Total	1,535,027	14.8	1,384,189	14.0
TAXES & BENEFITS	435,616	4.2	395,483	4.0
TOTAL PAYROLL	1,970,643	19.0	1,779,672	18.0
OTHER EXPENSES				
Travel Commissions	207,436	2.0	197,741	2.0
Outside Services	200	—	200	—
Cleaning Supplies	41,487	.4	39,548	.4
Linen Replacements	103,718	1.0	98,871	1.0
Guest Supplies	228,180	2.2	197,741	2.0
Telephone	20,744	.2	19,774	.2
Postage	10,372	.1	9,887	.1
Printing & Stationery	20,744	.2	19,774	.2
Uniforms	2,000	—	2,000	—
Laundry Supplies	20,744	.2	49,353	.5
Customer Goodwill	20,744	.2	19,774	.2
Auto Expense	20,744	.2	19,774	.2
TOTAL OTHER EXPENSES	697,113	6.7	674,437	6.8
TOTAL EXPENSES	2,667,756	25.7	2,454,109	24.8
DEPARTMENTAL PROFIT	7,704,048	74.3	7,432,959	75.2

FIGURE 11.2 Sample Rooms Division Budget (Summary)

last year's in housekeeping and by 0.3 percent in the front office, anticipating a rise in pay. Payroll taxes and employee benefits will be up 0.2 percent overall as predicted by the hotel's controller. The cost percentages for all categories of "other expenses" have been kept as in 1998, except for "guest supplies" and "laundry supplies." Guest supplies have been increased by two tenths of one percentage point to reflect an upgrade of guest amenities, while the percent cost for laundry supplies has been reduced to 0.2 percent from 0.5 percent following the installation of a computerized chemical feeding system for the laundry washers. The departmental profit (income) projected is obtained by subtracting all expenses from the revenue. In this example, the income has been projected to be 74.3 percent of the revenue, down from 75.2 percent the previous year. A departmental profit of 74.3 cents for every dollar of room sales is a good target for rooms divisions in the lodging industry.

To justify the expenses for the category of salaries and wages, both executive housekeeper and front office manager must submit a statement showing the amounts needed to pay employees in both departments. The allocation to cover salaries is easy to work out as it consists of adding up the yearly pay of salaried employees. To figure out the wages for fixed employees (those who work regardless of the hotel's occupancy), the executive housekeeper must refer to the property's staffing guide to calculate the number of hours that employees will work per shift and multiply the hours by the average wage that workers are paid. For example, if the hotel schedules four janitors daily at an average hourly rate of $6.25 and they all work 8-hour shifts, the annual cost for janitors will be $73,000 (4 $\times$ 8 = 32; 32 $\times$ 365 = 11,680; 11,680 $\times$ 6.25 = 73,000). This calculation would be different if, for instance, the number of janitors was fewer on weekends or if the daily hours worked were also fewer. Besides janitors, the category of fixed employees in the housekeeping department usually includes linen room workers and the evening team.

Section Housekeepers Man-hour Justification

To ascertain the wages of section housekeepers, housepersons, floor supervisors, and laundry workers calculations must be made depending on the room occupancy of the hotel, as these employees report to work based on the number of rooms that need to be serviced daily. Figure 11.3 is a sample man-hour justification for section housekeepers. The purpose of this statement is to warrant the amount that must be obtained for the concept of room attendant wages in the upcoming budget. The form includes the forecasted occupancy broken down into months, the number of 8-hour shifts needed to service the occupied rooms at the rate of 16 per worker, the total number of work-hours (**man-hours**), and dollar amounts for each month. The difference between the amount needed to pay the section housekeepers next year ($369,413) and the amount stated in the budget for the concept of housekeeping salaries and wages ($985,321) will cover the expense for salaries and wages of the department's management team, housekeeping supervisors and housepersons, and fixed personnel, as well as cost for overtime, holiday and vacation pay, and bonuses. These expenses will also have to be justified separately. If the property has an on-premise laundry, the cost of labor, based on the projected room occupancy, is usually worked out in the same manner by the laundry manager.

The calculation of the "taxes and benefits" category is generally done by the property's controller and is based on the cost of employee meals, payroll taxes, insurance, and other benefits. In practice, the controller will apply a percentage to the "total salaries and wages" category based on previous years' costs plus any increment to expenses foreseen for the upcoming year.

The Profit and Loss Statement

Once the year is under way, every hotel division and department receives a monthly status report generated by accounting called the profit and loss statement (P & L). This statement shows the hotel's revenue and expenses for the month and includes a **variance analysis** column which indicates the changes in revenue and expenses from budget by category. The purpose of the analysis of variance is to alert department heads of percentage changes from budget. If the cost percentages are higher than projected, the causes for the difference must be identified and explained to management and a plan to correct them in the future implemented. Figure 11.4 is a sample profit and loss statement for the rooms division for the month of March showing a column with the actual results, a column with the budgeted amounts, and the percentage variance

Month	Occupancy %	Rooms	Shifts	Hours	Average Wage Rate	Expense
January	65	8,060	504	4,032	5.95	23,990**
February	80	8,960	560	4,480	5.95	26,656
March	78	9,672	604	4,832	6.00	28,992
April	80	9,600	600	4,800	6.00	28,800
May	88	10,912	682	5,456	6.10	33,282
June	89	10,680	668	5,344	6.10	32,598
July	95	11,780	736	5,888	6.15	36,211
August	93	11,532	721	5,768	6.15	35,473
September	90	10,800	675	5,400	6.15	33,210
October	87	10,788	674	5,392	6.15	33,161
November	81	9,720	608	4,864	6.20	30,157
December	70	8,680	542	4,336	6.20	26,883
	83%	121,184		60,592		369,413

*The workload for each room attendant is 16 rooms to be serviced in one 8-hour shift.

**$400 \times .65 = 260$; $260 \times 31 = 8,060$; $8,060 \div 16 = 504$; $504 \times 8 = 4,032$; $4,032 \times 5.95 = 23,990$

FIGURE 11.3 Sample Section Housekeeper Wage Justification*

Variance Analysis for the Period March 1 to March 31

	Actual	Percentage (%)	Budgeted	Percentage (%)	Variance
REVENUE	794,200	100.0	783,432	100.0	+.1
SALARIES & WAGES					
Front Office	41,690	5.2	41,522	5.3	–.1
Housekeeping	74,850	9.4	74,426	9.5	–.1
Total	116,540	14.6	115,948	14.8	–.1
TAXES & BENEFITS	30,753	3.9	32,904	4.2	–.3
TOTAL PAYROLL	147,293	18.5	148,852	19.0	–.5
OTHER EXPENSES					
Travel Commissions	16,050	2.0	15,669	2.0	—
Outside Services	1,500	.2	200	—	+.2
Cleaning Supplies	5,150	.6	3,134	.4	+.2
Linen Replacements	6,020	.8	7,834	1.0	–.2
Guest Supplies	17,830	2.2	17,236	2.2	—
Telephone	1,500	.2	1,567	.2	—
Postage	640	.1	783	.1	—
Printing & Stationery	1,654	.2	1,567	.2	—
Uniforms	200	—	150	—	—
Laundry Supplies	1,710	.2	1,567	.2	—
Customer Goodwill	400	—	1,567	.2	–.2
Auto Expense	890	.1	1,567	.2	–.1
TOTAL OTHER EXPENSES	53,544	6.7	52,841	6.7	—
TOTAL EXPENSES	200,837	25.3	201,693	25.7	–.4
DEPARTMENTAL PROFIT	543,363	74.7	581,739	74.3	+.4

FIGURE 11.4 Sample Rooms Division Variance Report

between the two, which can be positive or negative. A positive variance in revenue and profit indicates that the sales have been larger than forecasted and that the departmental profit percentage has been better than predicted. A positive variance in costs indicates that the expense percentages have been larger than planned.

Negative variances indicate the opposite. In Figure 11.4, the results of all categories, as indicated by the respective percentages, are as planned or better, except for "cleaning supplies" and "outside services" where the percentages obtained are positive and therefore overbudget. The executive housekeeper will need to investigate the causes for the increases in cost percentages. For the cleaning supplies, there are several possibilities, such as inflated purchasing prices, inferior quality materials, pilfering, improper mixing of chemicals, or overuse of products. The extra cost of outside services could be due to an oversight in budget planning or to an extraordinary expense caused by an unforeseen event. For instance, a flood in the hotel lobby could have required the services of a carpet cleaning company. The departmental profit line at the bottom of Figure 11.4 also indicates that the overall performance of the housekeeping department for the month of March was better than predicted by four tenths of one percent (74.7 − 74.3 = +.4).

Some important statistical figures can be obtained from the budget. The average revenue generated by one section housekeeper hour worked can be obtained by dividing the estimated revenue by the estimated section housekeeper hours. In this case, $10,371,804 \div 60,592 = \$171.17$. The average number of minutes needed to clean one room can be obtained by dividing the section housekeeper hours by the forecasted rooms and multiplying by 60. In this case, $60,592 \div 121,184 = .50; .50 \times 60 = 30$ minutes.

The **cost per occupied room** is a good determinant of expenses per room sold. The cost can be obtained by dividing each expense category for a certain period of time by the number of rooms sold during that period of time. For example, if during the month of March the cost of guest supplies was $17,830 and the rooms sold were 9,672, the cost of guest supplies per room sold would be $1.84 per room. This figure, compared to that projected in the budget, will provide information about whether or not too much money is being spent on guest supplies. In this particular case, the annual budget was set at $228,180 for guest supplies for 121,184 rooms sold, or $1.88 per room sold. The cost for guest supplies per room sold for March ($1.84) was slightly lower than budgeted ($1.88).

 ## PRODUCTIVITY CONTROL

Productivity is a measure of output compared to input. Examples of output are the number of rooms serviced in a certain period of time or the amount of linen washed in an 8-hour shift. Inputs are the investments made by a business to provide products or services, the materials used to have the job done, and the work of the company's employees. In the lodging industry, the overall result of productivity is measured by the profit, that is, revenue minus expenses. The average departmental profit of the rooms division in the lodging industry is around 75 percent; that is, for every dollar made from selling rooms to guests, 25 cents should be cost and the remaining 75 cents departmental profit.

Indispensable factors to reach good levels of productivity, apart from the influence of department heads, are appropriate investments in the design, machines, and equipment of the facilities. The effects of internal factors, particularly those of supplies and labor, on productivity can be controlled by executive housekeepers. Supplies management is a good example of cost savings through efficient techniques. For instance, every dollar saved by purchasing the right product at the right price is an additional dollar added to the bottom line. Labor management also contributes to increased profits; a worker who has been adequately trained and is motivated to perform effectively can increase the work output by using a minimum amount of time to accomplish the task. Section housekeepers servicing effectively 16 guestrooms in one 8-hour shift instead of servicing 15 will provide better productivity to the company and, therefore, an increase in the company's profit.

Productivity, however, must go hand in hand with quality. It is to no advantage to achieve high productivity if the product is defective. To reach quality control, the housekeeping department must adhere to specifications and inspections. Inspections take up labor hours and are therefore expensive but, if planned carefully to keep costs low, they can be very effective to ensure proper quality levels. A useful ratio to control productivity in the lodging industry is: revenue ÷ hours of work required = dollars per labor hour. Another indicator of productivity is: hours of work used ÷ units produced = mean hour per room serviced.

Weekly Labor Forecast

After the labor expense percentages have been determined in the annual budget, labor cost controls must be in line with the pre-established levels of occupancy and employee workloads. As explained earlier, there are two methods to control the productivity of section housekeepers; one determines the average dollar amount to be generated by one hour of section housekeeper work and the other ascertains the average number of minutes that section housekeepers will need to clean the rooms occupied. The weekly labor forecast (Figure 11.5) projects the section housekeeper hours needed to service the forecasted occupied rooms for a particular week, in this case, one week in March. By dividing the estimated revenue for the week by the section housekeeper hours, the revenue generated per hour worked is obtained. Likewise, by dividing the section housekeeper hours by the forecast rooms occupied and multiplying the result by 60, the average number of minutes to clean one guestroom is also obtained. The results are compared to the amounts stated in the yearly budget for the same concepts. If the amounts are close to the budgeted amounts, the number of section housekeepers scheduled for the week is acceptable. If they aren't, a reduction in the number of scheduled hours will be necessary. It must be kept in mind, however, that the control of productivity using the ratio "estimated revenue/section housekeeper" hours could be easily distorted if the ADR differs markedly from the ADR projected in the budget. In the example shown in Figure 11.5, the ratio revenue/section housekeeper hours equals $170.74 and the ratio section housekeeper hours/occupied rooms is .50 (30 minutes). Compared to the $171.17 and 30 minutes worked out in the budget, the amounts are very close and therefore acceptable. We may conclude that the productivity of the section housekeepers for the scheduled week coincides with the productivity statistics stated in the annual budget.

Date: Monday _____ through Sunday _____

	Monday	Tuesday	Wednesday	Thursday	Friday	Saturday	Sunday
Occupancy %	84	86	86	82	70	70	72
Rooms	336	344	344	328	280	280	288
Shifts	21	22	22	20	17	17	18
Hours	168	176	176	160	136	136	144
ADR	84	98	94	90	72	74	78
Revenue	28,224	33,712	32,336	29,520	20,160	20,720	22,464

Total Section Housekeeper Hours	1,096					
Total Revenue	187,136					
Total Occupied Rooms	2,200				Budget	
Revenue/Hours	$170.74				$171.17	
Hours/Occupied Rooms	.50				.50	

Approved By: _____

FIGURE 11.5   Weekly Section Housekeeper Forecast

PAYROLL CONTROL

Executive housekeepers must develop a formal system of accurate reporting of payroll to the accounting department. The report is a record of hours worked daily by all employees in housekeeping. The system must include a means of control of overtime work. An effective way to control overtime work is to request that all supervisors obtain authorization for all extra time before it occurs. The hours worked by hourly employees are in most cases recorded on **time cards**. Workers are asked to punch a time clock in and out at the beginning and end of their shift. During orientation, these procedures must be explained to employees in detail, such as not clocking in until they are in uniform and ready to work and clocking out at the time they stop working. Some companies allow for one half hour for lunch on company time; others require workers to clock in and out before and after lunch. Breaks of 15 minutes are always on company time. Management should not ask employees to perform any duties off the clock, as this is against labor laws. Punching a time card in or out for another employee should be cause for disciplinary action. Time machines record hours in military time, starting at 00:01 and ending at 24:00. The actual time worked by an employee is determined by subtracting the smaller time from the larger.

At the end of every work week, the summarized hours worked on the time cards are recorded on a **time sheet** from which actual pay is calculated by the payroll office. Besides the hours worked, time sheets should also indicate hours to be paid for vacation time, sick pay, or overtime pay. If workers are asked to perform duties of a different job category, they should be paid at the higher wage rate for that category, as would apply if, for example, a section housekeeper performs the duties of a supervisor for a certain period of time while the supervisor is on vacation.

Computerized Housekeeping Management

More and more lodging companies are using automation to manage operations in housekeeping departments. Executive housekeepers can use technology to perform tasks such as controlling inventory supplies, scheduling operational routines, and tracking departmental man-hours and costs. There are software packages on the market that can perform personnel management tasks such as compiling personnel records, employee absences, training programs, and reports of on-the-job accidents. Other software applications can be supplements to quality assurance programs to evaluate employee performance. Preventive maintenance packages can schedule tasks well in advance, such as stripping floors and cleaning carpets and upholstery. The computer can be programmed to print daily work schedules.

Perhaps the most useful application of automation to housekeeping departments is the tracking of cleaning and guest supplies, equipment, and linen inventories and usage. If housekeeping can control the use of materials, the purchasing function can be improved by buying the right amount of products to eliminate the possibility of over- or under-stocking supplies.

Other applications of computers are word processing and the ability to produce graphs and charts to help directors of housekeeping organize past-performance data and forecast projections to be presented to upper management. Word processing enhances the quality of the correspondence generated in the housekeeping department, including reports, memoranda and letters. Computer programs, however, can be very labor-intensive because of the time needed to input data. On the other hand, the payoffs can be considerable as answers can be obtained by simply striking a key rather than having to perform elaborate calculations.

The first step in selecting a computerized housekeeping management software system is to determine the needs of the department. The second is to select a system that will fulfill the essential requirements to have the job done. Finally, the vendor chosen should be able to provide technical support and employee training. All in all, computerized systems must provide a way to facilitate and improve the management of housekeeping operations in a cost-efficient manner.

KEY TERMS

average daily rate (ADR)
cleaning supplies
consolidated room sales summary
cost per occupied room
departmental costs

departmental income
guest supplies
laundry supplies
linen replacements
number of rooms sold

other expenses
outside services
payroll taxes and benefits
printing and stationery supplies
rooms revenue
salaries and wages

telephone
time cards
time sheet
uniforms
variance analysis

DISCUSSION AND REVIEW QUESTIONS

1. What is the difference between a budget prepared for a calendar year and one prepared for a fiscal year?
2. Which two departments are usually included in the rooms division's operating budget?
3. What is the projected annual departmental income for a resort that plans to sell 130,500 rooms at an ADR of $77.50? The anticipated total expenses for the year are $3,050,600.
4. Classify the following expense categories into (a) front desk only expenses; (b) housekeeping only expenses; (c) shared expenses: front office salaries, housekeeping salaries, payroll taxes and benefits, travel commissions, outside services, cleaning supplies, linen replacements, guest supplies, telephone, postage, printing and stationery supplies, uniforms, laundry supplies, customer goodwill, auto expense.
5. If the projected revenue for the upcoming year is $9,000,500 and the authorized percentage for laundry supplies is 0.6 percent of the revenue, how many dollars should be allocated for this expense category?
6. If the actual rooms revenue for the month of March was $500,400 and the actual expense amount for cleaning supplies was $7,500 for the same period, what was the expense percent of this category?
7. For the same month of March, what would have been the variance percent for the expense category of guest supplies if $19,000 had been budgeted and the actual cost was $21,000?
8. What was the average number of minutes spent per room cleaned for a certain week if the number of rooms serviced was 2,100 and the section housekeeper hours for the week were 989?
9. List possible causes for a negative variance obtained for any given period in the category of guest supplies in the housekeeping department.

10. Explain how you would use the cost per occupied room statistic to help you control expenses when working in the housekeeping department.
11. What is the purpose of time sheets?
12. List possible applications of computers in housekeeping operations.

 MINICASES

Situation 1

The results of last year's operations at the Royal Hotel are:

Net Revenue	$10,100,500
Front Office Salaries	535,000
Housekeeping Salaries	899,000
Taxes and Benefits	394,000
Travel Commissions	202,000
Outside Services	1,500
Cleaning Supplies	35,300
Linen Replacements	64,000
Guest Supplies	240,000
Telephone	18,000
Postage	9,500
Printing and Stationery	21,400
Uniforms	3,500
Laundry Supplies	58,900
Customer Goodwill	21,000
Auto Expense	17,700

Assignment: Calculate the dollar amount and percentage of the Royal Hotel's rooms division departmental profit.

Situation 2

As executive housekeeper of the Royal Hotel, you have been asked to provide preliminary budget information for the upcoming year on the category of "Housekeeping Salaries and Wages." The Royal is a 400-room hotel, the projected occupancy is 78 percent for the year, and the workload for each section housekeeper is an average of 16 rooms per one 8-hour shift. The total housekeeping salaries and wages for personnel other than section housekeepers is $540,000.

Assignment: Calculate the total salaries and wages for your department for the upcoming year.

Situation 3

Compile the weekly section housekeeper labor forecast for the week of July 3 (Monday) through July 9 (Sunday).

The Royal Hotel has 400 guestrooms.

The workload per room attendant is to service 16 rooms in one 8-hour shift.

The occupancy forecast is:

Monday	75%
Tuesday	100%
Wednesday	96%
Thursday	100%
Friday	85%
Saturday	68%
Sunday	85%

The projected ADR for Monday through Thursday is $118 per room per day.

The ADR for Friday and Saturday is $85 and for Sunday $99.

Find: Total section housekeeper hours
Total revenue
Total occupied rooms
Revenue/Hours productivity indicator
Hours/Occupied rooms productivity indicator

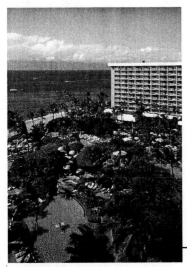

Risk and Environmental Management

CHAPTER OBJECTIVES

▶ Discuss the management of safety in the housekeeping department.

▶ Explain the importance of safety training programs.

▶ Learn about security issues in the housekeeping department, including theft by employees and guests.

▶ Discuss guestroom security.

▶ Learn about environmental issues, including garbage recycling, disposal of hazardous materials, and how to attract environmentally-conscious travelers.

▶ Explain basic ways of fighting microorganisms and improving indoor air quality.

OVERVIEW

Risk management in lodging operations involves the reduction of operational hazards and the minimization of crime. Just as important are the properties' contributions to prevent the continuous decay of the global environment. This chapter deals with the reasons behind the need to involve the housekeeping department in the risk management of lodging properties. Effective ways to control accidents, eliminate safety hazards, and deter theft are to train employees in risk management and to take specific proactive steps to prevent injury in the workplace. Setting up safety committees to coordinate efforts aimed at reducing safety hazards and investigating causes of accidents is of critical importance.

Housekeeping departments are in a privileged position of being able to help recover the sustainability of the planet by implementing recycling programs and by the careful disposal of harmful materials. Source-reduction programs are proactive ways of minimizing waste and pollution by adopting supplies that are recyclable and biodegradable. Lodging properties can also be eco-friendly by asking stay-over guests to request the washing of bed linens and by encouraging them to reuse bathroom linen supplies.

The chapter ends with a discussion of how to fight microorganisms and the need to educate employees on preventing the spread of contagious diseases. The topic of indoor air quality and the prevention of air pollution by toxic cleaning products is also covered.

 ## SAFETY IN THE HOUSEKEEPING DEPARTMENT

There are three important reasons why fire and accident prevention for employees and guests are functions of management. The first is legal: the Occupational Safety and Health Act (OSHA) of 1970 requires employers, by law to keep their places of business free from hazards that may cause harm or injury to employees. The Act assures every working person in the nation safe and healthful working conditions; therefore, housekeeping managers must comply with OSHA regulations to keep workers safe. OSHA inspectors can enter an employer's premises without notice to conduct inspections, review records, and question workers about safety. When serious injury or death is involved, criminal charges can be filed against the property.

Another reason is financial; statistics provided by the National Safety Council indicate that the number of injuries that occur in the service sector is staggering. The average cost of all injuries annually is over $100 billion, with an average loss of almost $1,000 per injury. In addition, thousands of lost workdays cause a huge loss of human productivity and therefore originate a considerable financial burden on organizations. Accidents are the motive for workman's compensation premiums to go up whenever mishaps occur in the workplace. Worker's compensation is insurance required by the states to cover injuries sustained at work. The worker's compensation insurance premium payments are determined by the employer's safety and health records. Besides, courts of law tend to award substantial amounts of money when injured guests and employees file civil lawsuits against businesses for accidents or mishaps.

The third reason is ethical. As employees and guests expect to find a safe place to work and stay, lodging operators must see to it that their properties are free from harm, injury, danger, or risk and that the organizational climate is conducive to the personal well-being of their workers.

The first step toward implementing a safety program is developing **job-safety analyses** for those tasks that might involve any risk of injury and accident. After describing the potential hazards that the task may involve, safety tips about how to perform the job should be provided to workers. Job analyses are particularly necessary for jobs that involve working with industrial machinery, such as laundry washers, dryers, and mangles.

Safety Training Programs

Executive housekeepers should institute **safety-training programs** designed to instruct housekeeping employees in safe work practices. Specific instructions to guard against hazards and dangers unique to their job assignments should also be provided. The National Institute for Occupational Safety and Health (NIOSH), as well as other agencies in most states, provide help, assisting employers in the development of programs on safety standards and practices and providing printed information on regulations and recommendations to maintain health and safety in the workplace. Some of the safety standards that can be adopted by the housekeeping department may include: keeping working areas safe, maintaining adequate sanitation, eliminating accident and fire hazards, providing first aid supplies and equipment, handling hazardous chemicals correctly, keeping stairs and railing stable, adopting safety factors to operate laundry equipment, having proper grounding for electrical outlets, and so forth. Examples of specific proactive steps to prevent injury may include immediately fixing loose handles, missing tiles, and torn carpets; avoiding having wet, slippery walkways at all times; and keeping tub and shower surfaces and room furniture in perfect condition.

When accepting the position of executive housekeeper, it is a good idea to request a site inspection by the company's insurance carrier to determine if the department is complying with standard safety regulations. Implementation of safety programs should start at orientation, when employees should be taught about the safety philosophy of the department (and company), as well as what is expected of them in order to perform their jobs safely.

Programs to improve the department's organizational climate in order to increase the quality of the employees' work life should address the opportunity for personal development, fair compensation, equality, and a comfortable environment. Job enrichment can be achieved by maintaining a productive balance between what the job offers and what the workers seek. Efforts should be made to minimize job routine by providing employees with job variety (for instance, cross-training), responsibility, and challenge.

Housekeeping departments of large lodging establishments often form **safety committees** consisting of three or four employees for the purpose of preventing accidents from happening and investigating accidents after they take place in the workplace. Members of the safety committee regularly inspect all areas in the department, such as the linen room, hallways, service elevators, the laundry room, and employee areas, looking for possible safety and fire hazards. When a potential safety risk is found, the committee requests that the cause be promptly corrected. Examples of potential safety risks are: missing floor tiles, cracked glass panes, inappropriate worker clothing, obstructed fire exits, improperly vented dryers, defective vacuum cleaner cables, wet floors, wrinkled mats or rugs, nonfunctioning fire and smoke detectors, and so on. Another responsibility of the safety committee is investigating the causes of accidents, establishing and keeping records of occupational injuries, and developing strategies to help prevent future mishaps. Employees should also be trained in how to lift loads safely by keeping loads close to the body, bending the knees, and keeping the back straight. Table 12.1 lists some safety tips for housekeeping

TABLE 12.1   Sample List of Safety Tips for Housekeeping Workers

1. Use gloves as often as possible in the workplace.
2. Use goggles when decanting hazardous chemicals.
3. Wipe all spills immediately, particularly on tile floors.
4. Walk; do not run.
5. Report all hallway obstructions.
6. Discard chipped or broken glassware safely.
7. Use pan and brush to sweep up broken glass.
8. Never touch electrical switches with wet hands.
9. Do not use equipment that has frayed electrical cords.
10. Store heavy material on lower shelves and lighter material above.
11. Keep stored material away from sprinkler heads and light bulbs.
12. Do not use chairs or boxes to reach for stored material.
13. Keep loads close to body when lifting.
14. Bend knees and keep a straight back when lifting heavy objects.
15. Never try to give liquids to an unconscious person.
16. Control bleeding by pressing on the wound with a clean towel.
17. Do not use bare hands to push or pull trash in wastebaskets.
18. Handle soiled linen with care to avoid contact with sharps.
19. Always use gloves to handle blood spills or stains.
20. Report any real or potential safety hazard to your supervisor.

workers. By reducing the number of accidents in the department, insurance premiums, lawsuit costs and workers' compensation payments can be effectively contained.

Often, the availability of immediate first aid can save the life of a worker or guest. The housekeeping department should keep a well-supplied first aid kit on hand. In large lodging operations, having a CPR and first aid certified supervisor should be a priority. In all cases, employees should be instructed how to (or how not to) handle injured people and to call a physician immediately.

Fire Prevention

Safety programs must include fire prevention and deterrence. Fires in lodging properties are quite common but so is the fact that most hotels, motels and resorts are equipped with state of the art equipment to suppress fires when they occur. Executive housekeepers can help prevent fires by fireproofing guestroom furnishing. Curtains, carpets, pillows, blankets, and upholstery should be purchased labeled as fire-retardant or flameproof, as cigarette smoking in bed by guests is the typical cause of fires in guestrooms. Foam rubber products are particularly dangerous as they ignite easily and burn rapidly. Excessive accumulation of lint in dryers, painter's supplies, and oily rags can also start fires by **spontaneous combustion**. Kitchen oily cloths should be kept in metal containers and washed or disposed of as soon as possible; painter's products such as linseed oil should be stored in tight containers. Frayed guestroom lamp cables and damaged cords, switches, or plugs may start smoldering fires, as is the case with overcrowded outlets that may overload fuses or circuits.

Safety programs should include fire protection instruction, including fire drills. Fire departments in most localities will participate in employee training by showing films on fire prevention, lecturing on the effects of smoke (generally smoke kills, not the fire itself), and demonstrating the use of fire equipment. Fire safety programs should train employees in combating small, controllable fires, operating fire extinguishers, closing doors to contain large fires, keeping fire exits free of any materials, reporting immediately the smell of burning equipment or the presence of smoke, evacuating the building in an orderly manner if the fire alarm sounds, notifying guests of fire if asked to do so, and so on. All housekeeping workers must be told, at orientation, where the nearest fire alarm, fire extinguisher, and fire exit are located. Above all, employees must be trained not to panic in case of a fire but remain calm in all cases. **Panic emotion** can cause people to feel disoriented, preventing them from acting rationally.

The housekeeping department is also responsible for posting in each guestroom diagrams of evacuation routes and instructions explaining what to do in case of fire.

SECURITY IN THE HOUSEKEEPING DEPARTMENT

One of the greatest concerns of the lodging industry today is the issue of security. Lodging properties in the past boasted one house detective to keep crime in check; today it is not uncommon for large properties to hire a team of officers to maintain security in the establishment. Besides security manpower, lodging properties must provide security training for employees and often are compelled to invest substantial resources in TV surveillance, in-room safes, and impenetrable room-entry systems.

As with safety, there are legal, ethical, and financial reasons to keep guests, employees, and the company's possessions secure. Innkeepers have the legal and moral obligation of providing reasonable care for guests and staff. The costs of property stolen from guests and company, and from lawsuits resulting from criminal activity, can be very high. Security awareness for guests and training of employees must be ongoing concerns of management in order to prevent theft. Examples of guest security awareness are reminding travelers to keep valuables in the property's safe, asking them to use locks and chains, and recommending they look through the peephole before opening the door. The main outcome of any security training program should be ensuring that a property's entire staff understands its security role. Some specific training goals can be to close every guestroom door found open, to notify the security department of suspicious characters loitering in hallways, and to report anything unusual inside guestrooms, for example, weapons of any type, illegal drugs, bloodstains on walls or carpet, etc.

Security-conscious properties should provide printed instructions on table cards for guests explaining how to deter crime and, in some cases, include a direct telephone number at which to contact the security department in case of emergency. Some lodging companies routinely assign single female travelers to rooms that are close to elevators so they don't have to walk down long hallways; others place female guests on their club floor, to which access requires a special key. Some lodging companies instruct switchboard operators not to connect phone calls to rooms without the caller knowing the guest name.

Employee Theft

Estimates of employee theft in the workplace are very high. While accurate statistics are difficult to obtain, it is believed that half of all employees steal from their employers. This is particularly credible for the hospitality industry where wages are low and working conditions leave much to be desired. Housekeeping employees have ample opportunities to steal and pilfer—they can steal from guests, as they have master keys to access the guests' rooms; and they can pilfer company property, particularly guest and cleaning supplies, linens, and tools. Often, employees steal because of sheer need, as their minimum wages are not sufficient for them to make ends meet. Other times disgruntled workers, feeling frustrated by the way they are treated, decide to get even by taking away the company's possessions. In other cases, employees steal simply because security is lax and everybody else is doing it.

Minimizing Theft

Employees who steal use several methods to get supplies out of the property. The most common is using bags, purses, or parcels. An effective way of controlling this type of theft is by implementing a **parcel-pass system** by which employees leaving the property must show security officers a signed authorization to remove any items from the premises. A designated entrance/exit for employees that is controlled by security can be very effective, deterring individuals from exiting the premises through unmonitored doors. However, employees concealing items under their clothing are very difficult to detect and management does have to rely on observation by supervisors or on anonymous tips from loyal workers to pinpoint the culprits. Management should also establish effective controls on linens and supplies, insisting on monthly physical inventories, strict issuance procedures, and on allowing admittance to storerooms and floor closets to authorized employees only.

Another method of stealing is by filling trash bags with linens and supplies and depositing them near the trash dumpster, to be picked up after work or by an outside accomplice. Any trash container left outside the garbage compactor or dumpster should be considered suspicious. Employees should also be asked to park away from the building so that no goods may be easily placed near vehicles.

Properties that use keys rather than cards must establish an effective way of limiting access to guestrooms, floor closets, and storerooms by establishing a **key-control system**. The loss of a floor master key or grandmaster key can be disastrous to the department. Keys must be accounted for at all times by logging them in and out at the beginning and end of shifts. To avoid misplacement, master keys should be attached to a cord or lanyard or placed in large metal rings. Guestroom keys should never be left unattended on the keyhole or on top of service carts. An effective way of avoiding this problem is having a secured locked metal box with a slot on the cart where keys may be safely kept until they are returned to the front desk. Housekeeping staff should be instructed to report any faulty lock on an emergency basis; in no case should a room be handed over to the front desk as ready if its access control device is inoperative.

Theft by employees can also be effectively curtailed by establishing theft-prevention measures in the department. The first step is to make sure that application forms are carefully scrutinized and that references of all employees hired are thoroughly checked. Gaps in employment history, for example, may indicate attempt to hide a job from which the applicant was fired because of theft. References can be effectively checked by establishing an information network by telephone with other executive housekeepers in the area for mutual cooperation. Once employees are hired, it must be clearly stated at orientation and on the employee handbook that theft will be an automatic cause for dismissal.

Usually, the safety committee is also in charge of security matters, such as investigating patterns of theft, conducting security inspections around the property, and maintaining records of crime incidents.

Theft by Guests and Intruders

The proverbial filching of towels by guests is as common today as it has ever been. In some cases, cash-only guests take with them bathroom appliances, coffee makers, blankets, pillows, clock/radios, telephones, TV sets, and, in rare cases, the entire furniture of rooms by parking a van behind the room sliding door/window. Guest theft can be minimized by the establishment's not admitting travelers who don't own a credit card. In any case, section housekeepers should be trained to report immediately any missing item from rooms or when observing a guest's suitcase loaded with linen or other items. The detection of empty suitcases or trunks and the presence of suspicious characters loitering in hallways should also be reported. Section housekeepers should also be instructed to never open a guestroom door to anyone claiming to have forgotten the key in the room; instead, room attendants should kindly request the person to obtain an extra key at the front desk. It is particularly important to train housekeeping employees to spot and report suspicious activities taking place on guest floors, hallways, public areas, and back of the house.

Security in Guestrooms

TV sets and light appliances in guestrooms should be bolted down or secured to the wall, furniture, or electrical socket. Entry doors should close automatically and be fitted with latching bolts that lock the door when it is closed. Besides the latching bolt, guestroom doors should have deadbolts, chains, and peepholes. Sliding glass doors on balconies should be provided with "charley bars" which, when extended down, prevent prying the door open from the outside. Special attention should be given to the connecting doors between rooms. Besides the primary lock on the connecting doors, an additional security chain or deadbolt that can be activated by the guest from within each room should be installed.

Room keys, in use for decades, are not effective to deter crime from occurring; as a matter of fact, lodging properties using traditional guestroom keys are considered to be at a competitive disadvantage. That is the case because it is practically impossible to prevent crooks from keeping room keys if they rent a room, then keeping the key upon check-out, and coming back in the evening to enter the same room when the current guest has gone out. This problem can only be completely corrected by changing the locks each time keys are missing, which requires substantial labor costs and additional manpower. Card entry systems, on the other hand, are designed so that every guest checking into the property receives a card with a combination different from that used the previous night. In fact, the computer terminal issuing cards at the front desk is capable of providing millions of combinations for entrance to the room. Card entry systems can also register around the clock the time and what specific card was used to enter the room. That is to say, printed records can indicate the time guests and staff used the card at any time during the day or night. Besides, if a master card is lost, the entire floor or floors can be reset very quickly.

Some entry card systems are designed to encode two different tracks, enabling the property to control not only the guestrooms, but access to other designated areas such as pools, health clubs, elevators, and in-room safes. Other cellular control systems allow guests to use personal credit cards as room keys. State-of-the-art cellular control systems can be programmed to issue cards that can limit employee access to rooms by name, time, and date. For example, a section housekeeper card can be programmed to access a group of rooms at certain times during the day and on specific days of the week only.

The guest's personal valuables can be effectively protected by providing a small safe in every guestroom. Most in-room thefts take place when guests leave jewelry, travel checks, cameras or cards unattended while they are swimming in the pool or having a meal in the dining room. In-room safes can be operated with keys, cards, or touch-pads, on which guests can punch their own safe-opening codes. While the smallest in-room safes should be able to hold a 35-mm camera or camcorder, business properties need to install briefcase-size or larger units to accommodate portable computers.

The housekeeping department is usually in charge of providing babysitting services to guests traveling with children. The job of babysitting should be offered as a voluntary service to trusted, reliable, long-tenured housekeeping employees. When outside babysitting is used, the executive housekeeper must make sure that the agency has an impeccable record and that it is bonded.

ENVIRONMENTAL MANAGEMENT AND THE HOUSEKEEPING DEPARTMENT

Since the end of World War II, the population of the world has more than doubled and industrialization has become a widespread phenomenon. This out-of-control growth is altering the earth where we live and the air we breathe to the point of threatening our own health and safety and those of thousands of other living species. Some of the current global environmental problems include the accumulation of wastes and the pollution of air and water due to the dumping of toxic by-products. As a result, a substantial reduction (in the order of over 80%) in the generation of pollution per unit of economic output is necessary just to keep the current global unhealthy levels. Most scientists today believe that humans must agree to adopt some strategies to begin recovering the sustainability of planet earth. Executive housekeepers in lodging operations are in a privileged position to help prevent the continuous decay of the global environment.

Recycling Garbage

The amount of trash generated in North America alone stands at 200 million tons per year, with an average waste per person per day of about 3.5 pounds. This enormous amount of trash is deposited in landfills, where rain can wash toxic elements into the soil, and in some cases into the water table. Landfill space to bury waste is becoming scarce. The alternative to burying trash is burning it, but this solution is equally harmful to the environment because of toxic pollutant emissions.

To address the solid waste problem, the Environmental Protection Agency (EPA) has identified some possible solutions, such as reducing waste before it is originated, and recycling by-products as raw materials for making other products. Specifically, executive housekeepers can minimize the cost associated with hauling garbage to be landfilled by strategically placing labeled bins around the property for the disposal of reusable products. This should include guests' areas, as many travelers appreciate the idea of recycling waste even when they are away from home. Common solid by-products that can be recycled are:

aluminum cans

tin cans

glass bottles and jars

newspapers

polyethylene plastic

grass clippings, leaves and twigs

Those that are not recyclable include mirror glass, crystal, light bulbs, and nonpolyethylene plastics.

There are some potential savings from recycling. Corrugated cardboard, for instance, can be sold for over $100 a ton. Local recycling companies will also pay for newspapers and aluminum cans.

Savings can also be realized for every ton deferred from landfills as some close and tipping fees rise for transporting the waste to out-of-state dumps.

In addition, executive housekeepers can cut the costs of cleaning supplies used to maintain the facilities by using source-reduced products. Source reduction can be defined as pre-cycling, as it prevents waste from occurring before it starts. Source reduction involves considering the final destiny of products when making decisions on what to buy: for instance, products that are designed to last longer, and that require efficient dispensing methods and less packaging. The bottom line is to purchase products that minimize waste.

Hazardous Waste Disposal

American throw away over 4 million tons of hazardous waste per year, and part of this toxic waste is discarded by lodging establishments. Prolonged exposure of humans to toxic substances can increase the risk for degenerative diseases such as cancer, severe respiratory illnesses and, in some cases, death. Products labeled as toxic, poisonous, corrosive, or dangerous should be stored carefully and disposed of safely. For instance, toxic products should not be poured into sanitary or storm drains because they can contaminate the water. If placed out with the regular trash, they contaminate the atmosphere if they are disposed of in incinerators. Particularly noxious when burned are synthetic foams and some solvents and cleaning agents whose atoms destroy the ozone layer when they reach the stratosphere. For this reason, hazardous products should be disposed of following manufacturer instructions. Some noxious products commonly found in housekeeping departments are paint and paint strippers, drain cleaners, wood finishes, and antifreeze and motor oil discarded by guests in general trash containers.

Executive housekeepers committed to saving the environment should follow some basic steps to implement a source-reduction program, such as analyzing the purchasing of supplies that are recyclable and that minimize waste while maintaining high performance, controlling product usage where possible, and buying concentrated supplies which usually go farther and cost less than pre-prepared products. Executive housekeepers should also remember that basic cleaning jobs could be performed with green cleaners such as vinegar, vegetable oil-based soaps, borax, and baking soda, although they are not as convenient as using ready-made cleaning products. Pump dispensers with hand triggers are much safer than aerosols whose gas propellants, when released into the air every time the product is used, affect the ozone layer.

Green Lodging Facilities

Some hotel companies are recognizing the fact that environmental improvement in their establishments may lead to economic benefits and competitive opportunities. By establishing programs aimed at minimizing waste and reducing energy consumption, operating costs are lowered; by advertising to guests the actions taken to help keep a clean environment, companies can gain customer loyalty and enhance public image.

The housekeeping department can help regain the sustainability of the planet by implementing recycling programs for employees and guests. Some examples include: reusing as many items as possible, for instance, making cleaning rags out of worn towels, giving partially used soaps to local charities, and using ceramic mugs rather than foam cups; purchasing recyclable and biodegradable products; and composting yard debris, such as twigs, dry leaves and grass clippings.

Some of the waste generated in housekeeping can be hazardous to the environment if discarded inappropriately. Hazardous waste includes substances that are poisonous or toxic, such as insecticides, drain cleaners, flammable liquids, and some cleaning products. In order to keep hazardous products from reaching sensitive environmental sources, their disposal should not be poured into the city sewer, where it could contaminate the city's water-treatment plant, nor into the storm-sewer system, for fear of it seeping into the ground and contaminating the water table. Likewise, toxic waste should not be discarded with the regular trash as it may be incinerated, contaminating the atmosphere. Some common hazardous materials in the housekeeping department are paints, stains, thinners and strippers, wood finishes, and antifreeze and car fluids discarded by guests.

Some lodging companies have introduced the concept of environmentally friendly guestrooms, often called **green rooms**, which appeal to the over 40 million "green travelers" or environment-conscious guests the industry claims exist. These eco-friendly properties stock the rooms with amenities packaged in recycled containers that are themselves recyclable, with recycled paper supplies, and with soaps that are biodegradable; that is, made with vegetable fats and oils without chemical additives. Some hotel chains, focusing on targeting travelers with respiratory ailments, have gone as far as installing special filters in the air-intake ducts in guestrooms and filtering the water in the sink and shower. The usual extra fee to guests for these niceties is $10 per room per night.

Another way to save energy and minimize the generation of waste is to place desktop signs in guestrooms asking travelers to request changing sheets and pillow cases if they are staying over, and giving them the option of reusing the bathroom towels. This reduces drastically the poundage of linen to be processed, with the consequent reduction in water, energy, and chemical product usage. The American Hotel/Motel Association provides on request laminated notices endorsed by the U.S. Environmental Protection Agency for their use in lodging establishments to inform guests of this save-the-environment program (Figure 12.1). Besides helping the environment, lodging properties can save around $2.00 per occupied room per day when they provide their guests with these choices.

Indoor Air Quality Control

Indoor air pollution can have negative health effects on guests and employees. Lodging properties built as tightly sealed buildings, if polluted, can cause workers and guests to suffer headaches, dizziness, allergies and other problems associated with poor air quality. Indoor air pollution may be caused by the presence of dangerous substances, such as chemical cleaning compounds. The problem is accentuated if polluted indoor air is re-circulated. Chemical analyses of air from sick buildings frequently show compounds known to be human irritants. In most cases, toxic levels are quite low and difficult to detect, but when several pollutants are present at the same time, even at below-toxicity levels, they can cause symptoms of irritation and discomfort in humans. Some of the chemicals used in the housekeeping department may be air pollutants; for example, products containing formaldehyde, which is used as wood, linen, and carpet treatment, some cleaning products, and most pesticides and drain openers. Microbial contamination can also result in a

YOU'RE INVITED TO PARTICIPATE!

Good Earthkeeping

Did you know the U.S. Environmental Protection Agency estimates that hotels use more than 180 billion gallons of water each year? That's enough for more than 200 glasses of water – for every person in the world!

In an effort to conserve water and energy, and to minimize the release of detergents into the environment, we participate in the American Hotel & Motel Association's "Good Earthkeeping" campaign.

PLEASE UNDERSTAND...
• As a new guest, your towels are freshly laundered.
• As part of our commitment to the environment, we offer you the option of reusing your towels.

YOU DECIDE...
• A towel on the rack or hook means "I'll reuse."
• A towel NOT on the rack or hook means "Please replace."

Thank you for helping us conserve the Earth's vital resources.

Français, Español, Deutsch, 日本語 ➡

 Laminated to reduce waste.
© 1996 AH&MA

American Hotel & Motel Association

Photo: Bibb Hospitality

FIGURE 12.1   Save the Environment Notice. *Courtesy AHMA*

YOU'RE INVITED TO PARTICIPATE!

Did you know that according to the U.S. Environmental Protection Agency, only 3% of the Earth's water is fresh?

In an effort to conserve water and energy, and to minimize the release of detergents into the environment, we participate in the American Hotel & Motel Association's "Good Earthkeeping" campaign.

PLEASE UNDERSTAND...

- As a new guest, your bed linens are freshly laundered.

- As part of our commitment to the environment, we offer you the option of reusing your bed linens.

- *If you would like to participate, please leave this card on the pillow and we will remake your bed, but not change your bed linens. Otherwise, we will gladly change your linens daily.*

Thank you for helping us conserve the Earth's vital resources.

Français, Español, Deutsch, 日本語 ➡

 Laminated to reduce waste

Good Earthkeeping

American Hotel & Motel Association

UNITED STATES · ENVIRONMENTAL PROTECTION AGENCY

© 1996 AH&MA

FIGURE 12.1 *Continued*

potentially serious health condition known as hypersensitivity pneumonitis. The contamination may be caused by bacteria or mold present in damp carpets, furnishings and ventilation systems, or simply by allergenic microorganisms such as mites suspended in dust. The most effective way to improve air quality is to control the sources of pollution by not using toxic chemicals in the building and by increasing ventilation and cleaning. Housekeeping departments should have a policy in place to open windows whenever possible to circulate in fresh air from outdoors, although this may not always be practical, particularly if the air-conditioning or heating system is in operation at the time. Regular vacuuming of carpets and furnishings can also be effective, as dust mites thrive in areas where moisture and skin scales deposit, such as carpets and sofas. Faulty vacuum bags, however, can spread more allergens than they remove. To prevent air contamination when vacuuming, high-retention vacuum cleaners holding particles larger than 0.1 microns should be used.

 ## FIGHTING THE RISK OF INFECTIOUS DISEASE

In the hospitality industry, great attention is generally accorded to fighting bacteria that can cause food-borne illnesses but not enough consideration is given to the fact that microorganisms are also present in guestrooms and public areas of lodging properties, where they may contaminate guests and employees. Executive housekeepers need to have a basic knowledge of how microorganisms spread and about infection control so that they can be part of employee education programs and provide effective sanitation services. For example, although employees often have serious concerns about contracting a disease while at work, particularly the HIV/AIDS infection, they often don't know that the HIV virus can rarely be contracted by casual contact, from sharing bathrooms or utensils, and even by shaking hands with infected individuals. However, hospital and healthcare workers who have intense exposure by direct contact with patients' body fluids and needles should be instructed about these potential dangers.

There are two kinds of microorganisms that may cause illnesses: **viruses** and **bacteria**. Viruses are infective agents, smaller than common microorganisms, which require living cells for multiplication. Viruses cause poliomyelitis, hepatitis, AIDS, and the common cold if they find their way into the human body, where they may multiply. Most bacteria are the simplest group of vegetable organisms that are involved in fermentation and putrefaction of matter and, unfortunately, the production of disease. Bacteria cause illnesses such as cholera, dysentery, tuberculosis, enteritis, and typhoid. Given the right conditions, bacteria can grow in incredibly large numbers and at a very fast pace. For instance, under ideal conditions, one bacterium can reproduce over two million bacteria in 7 hours.

Luckily, most germs do not cause humans to become sick; as a matter of fact, only some, the **pathogenic germs**, can be deadly. Nevertheless, and just in case, lodging properties must provide employee training and effective cleaning services to prevent the spread of infection. There are three effective methods of reducing the spread of germs in the workplace. The first, **sanitation**, consists of cleaning surfaces, articles, and material to reduce germ count to a safe level according to public health standards and codes. The second, **disinfection**, deals with using cleaning products to selectively kill specific types of germs. **Sterilization** requires steam to eliminate germs in a pressurized container. A variation of sterilization, although not 100 percent effective, consists of washing items at high water temperatures, usually 160–180°F.

Several types of disinfectants are available in the cleaning-supplies market. Most disinfectants belong to the following four categories. **Natural phenolic compounds** are made from carbolic acid and are very effective in destroying germs but are poisonous to humans and corrosive to metal surfaces. **Synthetic phenolic compounds** are milder phenolic products that are effective in killing most germs but without causing corrosive effects. **Halogens**, noxious to human skin and corrosive to surfaces, are composed of the negative elements fluorine, chlorine, iodine, or bromine. **Quaternary ammonium compounds** are safe to use and have very high disinfecting power. Most cleaning jobs can be effectively performed with quaternary disinfectants; however, when cleaning blood stains or any other potentially infectious spills, a stronger disinfectant such as phenolic should be used.

A large number of contaminating agents can be found in public and guestroom trash receptacles. Some examples are needles, razor blades, and body fluids. Every person who handles a trash container should be instructed not to compress the content with the hands and to keep the trash bag away from the body to reduce the risk of being stuck by sharps. The use of gloves when handling trash is necessary.

Housekeeping managers in hospitals must be knowledgeable about how to handle medical infectious waste, which may include cultures and stocks, blood, and sharps. Regulations on how to dispose of infectious waste vary from city to city and state to state. Directions common to all hospital facilities are provided by OSHA's Bloodborne Pathogens Regulation implemented in 1992. Section housekeepers and hospital personnel should be trained to remove soiled linens from beds carefully to avoid sharps and to prevent spreading germs. Soiled linen should be placed directly into a soiled-linen bag rather than first putting it on the carpet or on furniture. To clean up dried blood spills on walls or floors, a worker wearing gloves should spray the area with a strong disinfectant and wipe it with a cloth.

Janitors who clean bathrooms and restrooms should be instructed not just to clean but to disinfect as well. The products needed to disinfect these areas are a bowl cleaner/disinfectant, a glass cleaner, a germicidal all-purpose cleaner, and a cleaner/disinfectant for mopping floor surfaces. Germ cross-contamination can be effectively avoided by not using toilet brushes and cleaning rags used for cleaning toilets and urinals on other bathroom or restroom surfaces. In guestrooms, the tub, shower, sink, and counter top should be disinfected daily.

Germs may also be transmitted by employees. In order to avoid the spread of microorganisms, workers should be instructed to wash their hands with bactericidal soap and hot water after using the bathroom. Gloves and cleaning rags should also be cleaned and disinfected before being reused in a different cleaning job.

KEY TERMS

bacteria

disinfection

green rooms

halogens

job-safety analysis

key-control system

natural phenolic compounds

panic emotion

parcel-pass system

pathogenic germs

quaternary ammonium
   compound

safety committee

sanitation

spontaneous combustion

sterilization

synthetic phenolic compound

virus

DISCUSSION AND REVIEW QUESTIONS

1. Give three reasons why fire and accident prevention are functions of management.
2. How would you describe OSHA?
3. In which jobs are job-safety analyses particularly necessary?
4. What are the main advantages of implementing safety training programs in the workplace?
5. What are the purposes of forming safety committees in the workplace?
6. List four fire hazards common to housekeeping departments.
7. Why should housekeeping employees be trained in security awareness?
8. What are common ways for housekeeping department employees to steal or pilfer company property?
9. Why are guestroom lock-and-key systems considered to be obsolete?
10. Describe two ways to address the nation's solid waste problem as identified by the Environmental Protection Agency (EPA).
11. Explain the advantages of using source-reduced products regarding product waste.
12. Why shouldn't toxic products such as paint thinners be discarded with the general garbage generated in the housekeeping department?
13. What is the difference between disinfection and sterilization?
14. What do you understand green lodging facilities to be?
15. Which chemicals, commonly used in housekeeping departments, may be potential air pollutants?

 MINICASES

Situation 1

You have been hired by a large lodging hotel in downtown Phoenix, Arizona, as executive housekeeper. The general manager has pointed out to you that the property has been suffering from repeated theft in guestrooms and from severe pilfering of guest and cleaning supplies. The director of security has made clear in one of the staff meetings that there is not much that she can do about the situation because of the lack of basic departmental structure regarding security prevention.

Prior to investigating what is going on, prepare a list of possible loopholes that the department may have regarding security.

Situation 2

After solving the security problem by reducing theft and pilfering to very low levels, you decide to turn the housekeeping department you manage into an environmentally friendly operation. Up to now, the hotel has not taken any initiative whatsoever on environmental issues. Draft a plan to be presented to the general manager regarding garbage recycling, hazardous waste disposal, source-reduction, indoor air quality, and guestroom options.

Situation 3

Three years later, you are promoted to rooms division director of a new resort in the foothills of the Catalina Mountains near Tucson, Arizona. Among your many duties, you have been asked by the general manager to draft a plan dealing with the property's risk management that includes safety, security, and the prevention of contagious disease of employees. In addition, management has decided to market the new resort as an eco-friendly property.

Prepare a draft dealing with these issues to be presented to the general manager for her approval.

Index